THE INGERLAND FACTOR
Home Truths from Football

Edited by Mark Perryman

MAINSTREAM
PUBLISHING

EDINBURGH AND LONDON

published in association with

First published in Great Britain in 1999 by
MAINSTREAM PUBLISHING COMPANY (EDINBURGH) LTD
7 Albany Street
Edinburgh EH1 3UG

ISBN 1 84018 211 3

A catalogue record for this book is available from the British Library

Typeset in Garamond
Printed and bound in Great Britain by Creative Print Design Ltd

Contents

The Football Nation: Dreams of Another Country

Acknowledgements

The Ingerland Factor is an exploration of the particular versions of Englishness projected by those of us who follow the national team as fans, home and away. The writers do not simply offer a one-sided story, they investigate, interrogate and intervene from every possible angle, sometimes in agreement with one another, more often than not in quite obvious disagreement. Developing the ideas that helped me to commission, edit and introduce this book, I have been fortunate enough to have been given the opportunity to write about my experiences following England for *When Saturday Comes* and *Total Football*, while Pete Stephens at London's GLR radio station used me as a fan-correspondent on air during the World Cup, an exemplary example of letting the supporters have their say. Any writer needs a group to try out new thinking on, and as an editor you also need to take some time deciding on the questions you would like the contributors to answer. In this I am grateful for the chance to give talks and lectures about Ingerland to the University of Leicester's 'Football 2000' conference, Manchester Metropolitan University's Sport and the Law M.A. Degree course, Birkbeck College's Football, Culture and Society course, and the Hackney Fabian Society. Often unwittingly, the insights and ideas from my fellow participants in the Signs of the Times discussion group have helped me immeasurably as I have tried to think through the often complex mix of identity and nation behind *Ingerland*.

This book is also linked to a practical project to construct an alternative, positive Ingerland. Most, if not all, of these ventures have benefited from the sharp visual and graphically imaginative input of Hugh Tisdale, co-founder with me of Philosophy Football, self-styled 'sporting outfitters of intellectual distinction'. Hugh is a great influence in cooling my wilder ambitions for Ingerland; I'm sure this is a result of all those sad years following Villa. Apart from a natty line in cerebral T-shirts, Philosophy Football has organised two festivals of fan culture, 'Europe United' and 'United Nations of Football'. More than anything else these hugely celebratory initiatives convinced me that Ingerland was something worth bothering with. Thanks then to Sophie Johnson and Gemma Smith of *The Guardian*, Geoff Mason of UNISON, Glyn Ford MEP, Edward Carwardine of UNICEF, Clare Furey, Clare Wharton and John

Gray of the Royal Festival Hall on London's South Bank for the support they gave to these festivals. The festivals would not have been possible without the quite extraordinary commitment of an eclectic bunch of fans with more imagination than perhaps the common sense that would have meant they'd have said no when I suggested this dream was worth working into something like reality. Mel Barker, Konrad Caulkett, John Citizen, Charlie Connelly, Steve Day, Helen de Witt, Julia Havis, Chris How, Stefan Howald, Keir Husband, Ashok Katwala, Sunder Katwala, Mick Kent, Vic Lambrusco, Corinna Merriman, Lennie Thomas, Ben Tranchell, Imogen Tranchell, Nick Walker, Simon Welch, Catherine Welton and David Winner, the drinks are on me, honest.

The place where the Ingerland factor of course really comes alive is at the match, with England playing in front of a packed and passionate support that few other countries can match. In thinking and working through the practicalities of what Ingerland can, and could, mean I have benefited hugely from my involvement with the England Members Club. The FA staff largely responsible for this most ambitious of ventures – developing a fan-led organisation of England supporters – have aided me enormously in the work for this book. Pat Smith, formerly Deputy Chief Executive of the FA, FA Company Secretary Nic Coward, Adrian Bevington of the FA Press Office, Marc Armstrong of the FA Commercial Department, Jill Smith who runs the Members Club office and Ian Murphy of the England Members Club staff together with England Members Club National Consultative Group fan representatives Dave Tomlinson, Kath Bolton and Pete Ryan. They have all broadened my understanding of the potential for England fans themselves to take responsibility for their present and future reputation. The very active support for the 'Raise the Flag' initiative from all these individuals, and others, at Wembley has shown what is possible when fans, the FA and the national team sponsors, Nationwide, work together for Ingerland. This initiative is another example of the efforts to put some of the ideas in *The Ingerland Factor* into practice. Those who have helped on early matchday mornings with Hugh Tisdale barking out his design instructions and me encouraging our squad of flag-layer-outers with a vision of a better Ingerland include James Dawson, Caroline Richards, Nick Aindow, Gareth Burchmore, Tony Mabbot, Tony Dekanski, Fran Davies, Paul Jonson, Ben Jonson, Jacquie Adams, Mike Adams and Deborah Rich. Adam Stebbing of Forrest Press and Maurice the driver complete the roll-call.

Stephen Brasher put his pub-quiz knowledge to good use by helping out with fact checking. Tony Batt has equipped me with the techno-wizardry to at least stand a chance of reading the odd e-mail. Nicky Hickman at Prime Travel got me on more East European airlines than I ever knew existed in the search for an England away win: thankfully there were more than a few of those during the editing of this book. Tony Davis was as brilliant a photographer of a football for the cover as I'd been promised. Stephen Kenny painted the ball in the national colours. Bill Campbell of Mainstream took me to the Groucho Club Bar, for which my street credibility will be eternally grateful, and, for a Scot, didn't take too much convincing that a book about England wasn't such a daft idea after all.

There'd be no point to a book like this though if you can't occasionally just put all the long words, analysis and sociologising to one side, hop on a plane, and shout your heart out for Ingerland. That's my idea of an adventure, and in that I've been hugely fortunate in finding such a lovely, and loving, fellow supporter, Anne Coddington. She's put up with most things on our treks in search of Ingerland, though I suspect one more night under canvas could mean the end of a beautiful relationship. For that, I'll happily burn the tent, but not the bicycles, please.

None of the aforementioned hold any brief for what follows. For that the individual contributors and I are solely responsible. I'd just like all those mentioned – and many more besides – to know that in your many and varied ways you've been an inspiration. Ingerland can be a happy place to be, and wouldn't it be great if alongside spreading some more happiness around we might see the team lifting a trophy or two? Oh go on, just one more time. Then we can start those years of hurt all over again.

Mark Perryman, October 1999

Notes on Contributors

Gary Armstrong has written and edited a series of books concerned with both public order issues associated with football and an anthropology of the game as a global sport. These books include *Football Hooligans: Knowing the Score* and two collections, *Entering the Field: New Perspectives on World Football* and *Football, Cultures and Identities*, both co-edited with Richard Giulianotti. A Sheffield United fan, Gary's book *Blade Runners* is the definitive account of the living history of his club.

Andrew Blake is Professor of Cultural Studies at King Alfred's College, Winchester. Author of *Body Language: The Meaning of Modern Sport*, Andrew's most recent work has been concerned with music culture, including writing *The Land Without Music* and editing the collection *Living through Pop*. He has also edited a special issue of the journal of politics and culture, *Soundings*, on sport in the contemporary political world. A saxophonist as well as a Spurs fan, he can almost remember when they last won the league.

Billy Bragg was only kept from the number one spot in the summer of '91 by Bryan Adams. As a West Ham fan though he's used to life's little disappointments. His first album *Life's a Riot* with Spy Vs Spy was released in May 1983 and included the song that is surely a candidate for any alternative national anthem, 'A New England'.

Ben Carrington has been involved in a number of research projects aimed at uncovering racism in sport, particularly football, rugby and cricket. A lecturer in sociology at the Chelsea School, University of Brighton, Ben was a contributor to the collection *Fanatics! Power, Identity & Fandom in Football* and is the co-editor of a forthcoming book, *Racism in British Sport*. A Liverpool fan, Ben manages to fit his research and writing around scoring more than the occasional goal in semi-professional football.

Philip Cornwall is Sports Development Editor for the internet football magazine *football 365.co.uk*. For seven years he was a writer for *When Saturday*

Comes and remains a contributor to the 'half-decent football magazine'. He is a regular commentator on football news stories for Radio 5 and BBC TV's News 24. Having followed Bulgaria around USA '94 he finally made it to a World Cup finals England game at Marseilles in 1998. A Liverpool fan, he is also a Director of Buckingham Town FC and once bought for the club (Buckingham Town, not Liverpool) a centre forward who scored no goals before going on a free transfer to Saffron Walden FC.

Liz Crolley has contributed to *Perfect Pitch* and is the co-author of *Football, Nationality and the State*. Liz lives in Liverpool while working as a lecturer in Spanish and linguistics at Manchester Metropolitan University but resents any South-of-England-inclined suggestion that Manchester and Liverpool have got anything to do with each other geographically. A Liverpool supporter, she looks forward to what a cosmopolitan defence might do for her club's more than occasional lapses at the back.

Pete Davies wrote one of the books that announced the arrival of the 'new football writing', *All Played Out: The Full Story of Italia '90* – the kind of book that we'd simply never been treated to before. And he didn't stop there: *I Lost My Heart to the Belles* revealed just what men are missing out on when they think of football as a man's game, while *This England* gave an account of the 1997 General Election from the people's point of view. In between supporting Wrexham, Pete has also written two novels, a book about tornadoes and the brand new, sure to be best-selling, *Catching Cold*, the story of the 1918 influenza epidemic.

Dominik Diamond presents the Saturday morning Radio 5 show *Sportscall*, the one with all those quiz questions whose answers are almost permanently on the tips of our tongues. Originally presenter of Channel Four's *Gamesmaster* show, Dominik currently presents the sports magazine programme *110%* for BBC TV Digital and writes a twice-weekly column for the *Daily Star*. A Celtic supporter, he eagerly awaits the opportunity to take his daughter Mollie to a World Cup second round match featuring his beloved Scotland.

Claus Melchior is the co-editor of the German fanzine, *Der Tödliche Pass* (the deadly pass). A supporter of 1860 Munich, he has co-authored a book about the club, *Legenden in Weiss und Blau* (legends in white and blue), and is keen not to be mistaken for a supporter of Munich's 'other' club. Claus owns and runs an English-language bookshop in Munich, 'Words' Worth'.

Kevin Miles co-ordinated the Football Supporters Association's Fans Embassy at France '98. He co-wrote the FSA fans' report on France '98 and is now a National Committee member of the FSA and convenor of the Coalition of Football Supporters. A writer and broadcaster on football matters he has appeared on Radio 5 and written for the *Sunday Telegraph* and *Total Football*.

Kevin is a Newcastle United fan, and former Chairperson of The Independent Newcastle United Supporters Association.

Marcela Mora y Araujo worked for FIFA on their official film of World Cup '98. As a journalist Marcela has written for *FourFourTwo* and *Loaded,* the *Financial Times* and *The Guardian.* She was the Associate Producer of the Argentinian segment of the BBC TV series *Gary Lineker's Golden Boots.* A supporter of Boca Juniors and Argentina, in the summer of 1999 Marcela was the first Argentinian to set foot on the Falkland Islands since the 1982 invasion.

Richie Moran played for the Japanese league club Fujita, season 1989–90, and for Birmingham City, 1990-91. He retired in 1992 as the result of the racism he encountered from his fellow professionals, club coaches, managers and directors. In 1992, Richie wrote of his experiences as a black footballer in *The Observer* and has been involved with anti-racist campaigning around the game ever since. A mental health social worker for Portsmouth City Council, Richie is also a Celtic and Nigeria supporter, not to mention a kick boxing instructor.

John Peel introduced a generation, mostly now in their thirtysomethings, to the joys of late night Radio One from under the bedsheets. His live sessions are legendary, his cool drawl a sound never to put any music lover to sleep. Punk, reggae, dub, rap and thrash metal, plus most aural points between and beyond have all been popularised by John Peel. It's no surprise that his annual appearances at the Glastonbury Festival have become a grand mutual appreciation event for the man and his masses. Now presenting Radio Four's *Home Truths* show too, plus writing a weekly *Radio Times* column, John is as near to a popular institution that you're likely to get. And one whose passion for The Undertones' 'Teenage Kicks' and Liverpool FC remains undimmed.

Mark Perryman is the co-founder of Philosophy Football, the self-styled 'sporting outfitters of intellectual distinction'. When he's not flogging T-shirts he's writing books about football: *Philosophical Football: The Team that Plays with Strength in Depth,* a sort of Feng-Shui meets *Four-Four-Two,* is his new one. A Spurs fan, Mark is also a member of the National Consultative Group of the England Members Club and directed the 1996 'Europe United' and 1998 'United Nations of Football' festivals of fan cultures.

Alison Pilling is the current National Chairperson of the Football Supporters Association, having been the FSA's international officer during France '98. She organised the FSA's Leeds Fans Embassy during Euro '96 and worked on the France '98 Fans Embassy. Alison serves on the government's Football Task Force, is a Leeds United supporter and works in Leeds promoting environmentally-friendly transport policies.

Emma Poulton is a lecturer in sport, health and exercise at the University of Durham. She is currently completing a Ph.D. on the media construction and representation of national identity through sport at Loughborough University. Emma dates her support for Spurs back to growing up in small town Hertfordshire with then Tottenham striker Tony Galvin as near-neighbour and local hero.

Steve Redhead is Professor of Law and Popular Culture at Manchester Metropolitan University. A writer on both clubbing and dance culture as well as football, he managed to combine both interests with his pioneering book *Football With Attitude*, and returned to this mixture in 1997 with the book, *Post-Fandom and the Millennial Blues*, a peculiarly appropriate title for a Manchester City fan. Steve's most recent book is *Repetitive Beat Generation*, published by Rebel Inc., a series of interviews with some of the most influential and compelling young writers who have emerged in the 1990s.

D.J. Taylor has recently completed a book on the life of William Thackeray, *Thackeray*. His novel *The English Settlement* won the hugely prestigious Grinzane Cavour prize for foreign language works translated into Italian. A regular reviewer for the *New Statesman* and *The Guardian*, David is also a Norwich City supporter, and his writing on football has appeared in both *Perfect Pitch* and the collection, *My Favourite Year*, edited by Nick Hornby.

John Williams is Director of the Sir Norman Chester Centre for Football Research at Leicester University. A Liverpool supporter, he is currently editing a book about football and pop music on Merseyside, *Passing Rhythms*. John has helped to pioneer a sociological analysis of football fan culture, co-editing a number of books on the subject including *British Football and Social Change* and *Game Without Frontiers*.

The Ingerland Factor

Mark Perryman

The World Cup, European Championships, these are global and continental platforms on which national reputations, well beyond the score on the pitch, are won and lost. Scotland and Republic of Ireland fans project a happy-smiley face of countries and cultures at ease with their history. A touch of Celtic exotica, touchingly eccentric, harmless fun with a six-pack or two thrown in for good measure. Meanwhile the Nigerians manage to get us to forget their government's frightful human rights record courtesy of the 'Super Eagles' captivating our imagination with a hat-trick at one end and leaking goals like there's no tomorrow at the other. Croatia makes its mark as a new nation in their red and chequer colours and we're left confused and confounded by the deeper meaning of the 'Proud to be a Croat' printed in large letters across the backs of their fans' T-shirts. Are these the good, bad or indifferent guys of the Balkans crisis? Who knows, does anybody care? France lifting the 1998 World Cup is supposed to represent the coming together of a multicultural nation, but institutionalised racism depends on power relationships and inequalities that will take more than a screamer from the six-yard line to shift. And Brazil? How many of us could name their President, principal cities, main industries? But we know all about Ronaldo, Robert, Carlos and that surly sod Dunga, don't we?

International football is a stage on which not just the players perform – the fans have more than just a walk-on part too. For weeks, months, previously the media will be full of anxieties about public disorder, especially if the English are involved. If we are living in a 'risk society' then being around when Ingerland comes to town could be mad, bad and dangerous. Or is it? Tens of thousands of ticketless England fans might descend on a town or city looking for that precious bit of paper that will get them into their field of dreams. But it's a tiny minority who get actively involved in any kicking off with the locals or the other lot's fans. And with drink, hyped-up hysteria and young men abroad, who would seriously expect anything else? Certainly not Ian Jack writing in the *New Statesman* several weeks before the '98 World Cup, confidently predicting: 'The bar-keepers of France should learn the lesson at evening-classes: smile, though your glass is breaking; carry on smiling, even when you are being called a cunt.' Nicholas Farrell in the *Spectator* added his expectation of trouble, speculating on the political effect for bad measure: 'Trouble is likely to occur wherever England fans are gathered together. Any trouble will have political implications. Observers of the already strained diplomatic relations between Britain and France agree that each country's foreign office and sports minister will then blame the other. The 1998 World Cup could turn out to be almost as much a political as a sporting event.'

The vicious recklessness of Ian Jack's self-fulfilling prophecy finds its echo in Nicholas Farrell's barely concealed stirring up of all those anti-Euro emotions. Different motives but they confidently expect the same sordid result. Surely 'It's only a game'. George Orwell, author of *Animal Farm* and *Nineteen Eighty Four*, was one who was never convinced by that particular minimalist maxim. In 1945 he wrote a report on the Moscow Dynamo tour around England and Scotland. The matches were being used to boost British-Soviet relations as the victory celebrations from the War faded away into the grim reality of the division of Europe. George certainly wasn't all that impressed by the contribution that football might make to putting off the onset of the Cold War: 'As soon as strong feelings of rivalry are aroused, the notion of playing the game according to the rules always vanishes. People want to see one side on top and the other side humiliated. Serious sport has nothing to do with fair play. It is bound up with hatred, jealousy, boastfulness, disregard of all rules and sadistic pleasure in witnessing violence: in other words it is war minus the shooting.' In an era of nuclear proliferation, cluster bombs, uranium tipped shells, the scourge of mines and the continuing likelihood that carefully aimed air strikes might miss their intended target, well, football as war without the weaponry has a certain appeal.

We all know what the will to win can do to our critical and emotional faculties. Catharsis anyone? But that headlong rush to the extremes of ecstasy we can get from a 0–0 draw in Rome or McAllister putting his penalty wide, followed by the depths of despair that the penalty shoot-out has become our unique burden to bear, can unleash something quite different from what Orwell haughtily detects in the English crowd. Football is without doubt the premier international language. Everybody's heard the story of how a pistol-toting foreign policeman was calmed down by the magic words 'Bobby Charlton'. The drinks are on us, Señor. And long after 1966 and all that, we have a Premier League stuffed full with French, Italian, Dutch, Scandinavian and plenty of others' talent. Mouth 'Michael Owen' today in some foreign bar and you'll be swapping notes with punters who'll reply with 'Emmanuel Petit', 'Gianfranco Zola' or 'Jaap Staam'. And what price diving Germans when one half of North London will always have a place in its heart for Jürgen Klinsmann? Following England abroad immerses you in this global cultural mix that football has become, to celebrate our differences and feel part of an event that the entire world is watching. To feel as if you're not just reading the news but helping to make it too. Taste the local delicacies, sample the nightlife, even take in a few sights, this is all part of going away to somewhere a touch more exotic than the proverbial wet Wednesday night away trip to Hartlepool. And for immigrant communities long submerged in their host countries – Jamaicans, Turks, Nigerians – following your national team is one of the most potent ways to assert the ties to a nationality few would ever want to forget. With bank upon bank of cameras trained on the crowd in the stands, desperate to pick out a painted face, a funny hat, a kid on someone's shoulders, the fans have their part to play too in the drama that is international football.

The football we share a love for is also being used by governments to boost their standing in the world. When politicians can place such a huge emphasis on what hosting, let alone winning, an international trophy means, is it any wonder that passions have a habit of running amok? Men in suits fall over backwards to snatch that photo-opportunity with ball, goalposts and preferably a player or manager accompanied by a cup, so what hope for the rest of us when it comes to putting the game in perspective? When Iran played the USA during France '98 it seemed for many that this was a contest between two ideologies, not 22 blokes with a football match to settle.

It's not just the politicians and the ideologists who read so much into football either. When France beat Brazil in the World Cup final the loudest whoops were to be heard in the boardrooms of Adidas. They'd put those johnny-come-latelies Nike back in their place, the three stripes down the French shirt's arms licking the swoosh on the Brazilians' chests. Criss-crossing France following your team, it was impossible to miss the campaign as the two sportswear giants battled for our custom. This was Brand Wars on a massive scale, and if you didn't have a ticket you could rest assured the Brand Wars frontline troops, the executive and corporate types, certainly did, courtesy of their expensive sponsorship packages with all the privileges and access these buy. The fans are in mortal danger of becoming just the media backdrop to all of this. What do we have to defend ourselves with? First, the common language that is football. Second, the fan culture that all supporters, wherever they come from, share. Third, the scale and depth of emotion which winning or losing a football match can inspire within us. Football is undoubtedly the poorer culturally without its fans. Our share of the income cake, in terms of ticket sales, might be shrinking. Though even that's doubtful. Who buys the beers, books the hotel rooms, fills up the airplane seats, and takes home the souvenirs that make a World Cup or European Championship a halfway decent economic proposition? But even if sponsorship, advertising and TV deals now do dwarf our economic contribution what on earth would a World Cup that nobody came to be like? It is the fans in the stands and on the terraces that have made football so unique. No other sport matches the culture that football fans have created around their game. A *Fever Pitch* about tennis, athletics or Grand Prix racing? Cricket comes closest, rugby – both codes – a fairly distant third. This is our power as fans – without us football wouldn't be what it is today. And the more sussed of the commercial interests around football realise this. What are these companies after when they pump tens of millions of pounds into football? Associating your product with football delivers. When it comes to shifting fizzy drinks, lager, hi-fi systems, fast food, training shoes and cars, fans are worth piles and piles of dosh– dosh spent on earning our support for these goods. The only difference is we don't get to sign any lucrative endorsement deals with Brylcreem, Reebok or Walker's Crisps. Without the fans football loses its most valuable commodity, authenticity.

Authenticity isn't just something that is of interest to corporations with products to shift either. With increasing frequency Prime Ministers and Presidents take office with grand claims of delivering the birth of a new nation. Tony Blair is the current master of this, and since it's Britain – or more likely middle England – that he's talking to, football has to be fitted in there somewhere. In his final speech to the conference faithful before the 1997 landslide, Blair did his damnedest to milk every footballing emotion in the hall – though one wonders how the ditties went down with the Scottish and Welsh delegates. 'I don't care where you're coming from; it's where your country's going that matters. If you believe in what I believe in, join the team. Labour has come home to you. So come home to us. Labour's coming home. Seventeen years of hurt. Never stopped us dreaming. Labour's coming home. As we did in 1945. I know that was then, but it could be again. Labour's coming home. Labour's coming home and the people are coming home because Britain is their team and they're part of it.' Baddiel and Skinner couldn't have put it better – trouble is they did, six months earlier.

Is it any wonder that football assumes such metaphorical importance when so much of what we had come to think of as 'Made in Britain' has taken such a hammering? As Philip Dodd puts it in *The Battle over Britain*: 'Britain no longer enjoys status as a world power; attempts to halt its economic decline never quite seem to work; postwar immigration has thrown into relief an imperial history that has been repressed; demands for autonomy in Scotland and Wales, not to mention the war in Northern Ireland, have thrown into question the claim that a single Britishness is subscribed to in all these countries; that closer union with Europe threatens to annul Britain's specialness; that the globalisation of the economy has made nations wonder about their long-term survival.' When we've got all this going against us is it any wonder that the historian Eric Hobsbawm's words seem so potent: 'An imagined community of millions seems more real as a team of 11 named people.' And while the imagined community of England remains a nation in search of a state, the team is something solid for us all to hang on to.

With Scotland getting its own Parliament on 1 July 1999 and Wales a National Assembly, there's only one team left that competes in World Cups and European Championships yet lacks any of the obvious trappings of a nation state – England. We make sense as a team right enough, but we're not a country in anything else but name. The think-tank Demos produced a peculiarly ill-timed report in 1997. Just as a new government was due to be elected, committed within months to a Scottish Parliament, Welsh Assembly and surrendering vast amounts of power in Northern Ireland to a combination of self-government and joint government with the Republic of Ireland, the policy wonks at Demos published *Rebranding Britain*. It was a theme that would be embraced by Tony Blair with his support for 'Cool Britannia' and a 'new Britain'. Ill-timed then, but hugely influential all the same. Mark Leonard, author of the report, explains why he feels this 'rebranding' is so important: 'The new institutions and icons of Britishness melded into an extremely robust identity. They crystallised just as Britain rose to success as an imperial and industrial power and they gave British citizens an extraordinary confidence and pride. Today, however, each of the pillars on which that identity rests has been eroded.'

He pinpoints six pillars. First, the institutional heritage: turnouts in elections are at an all-time low; after the death of Diana the monarchy will never be the same; the hereditary peers are on the way out; miscarriages of justice have irrevocably undermined traditional trust in the judiciary and police. Second, empire: with the hand over of Hong Kong completed what have we got left? The shift in power both across the Atlantic and Channel to centres where we are very much equal or even junior partners has been a long, and painful, process with which the English have yet to come to terms. And the Commonwealth – apart from the 'friendly games' and the occasional expensive gathering of Heads of State for no very obvious purpose – what is it for anymore? Third, industry: our consumer patterns indicate that we do anything but 'buy British'. There are no obvious national loyalties when it comes to buying a car, a hi-fi, home furnishings – even fish and chips have been replaced by curry as our national dish. Fourth, language: English is an international language spoken in Australian soaps, Hollywood blockbusters and by most Scandinavians better than plenty of our own. So in what sense does English belong to the English? Fifth, culture and religion: there's no single dominant religion. The Church of England is the choice of a declining minority of the English – and no Scots, Welsh or Northern Irish at all – while the BBC has for a long time failed to monopolise the airwaves – not only the commercial channels but satellite, cable and digital have put paid to that. Sixth, sport: once we taught the world how to play, now they take us to the cleaners, and a pursuit which was once all about team spirit and fair play is currently riddled with drugs, cheats and commerce.

Mark Leonard's six pillars of Britishness, and their corresponding crises, also explain why England is now such an issue, and why football is a key way of understanding the processes through which England may become a nation. With devolution in Scotland, Wales and Northern Ireland an irreversible development, Britain will be a spent force in the not too distant future. A federation of small states whose most realistic option to retain any status will be as a regional power bloc within a grander federal Europe. But only by realising England as a nation can such a process evolve. And where do you see the flag of that nation? In some corner of a foreign playing-field that will be forever Ingerland.

It is no accident that football, the team and the fans, have acquired such a central role in projecting and reflecting what it is to be English. The ages of industry, empire, revolution and extremes have all come and gone. Today we live in an 'Age of Sport' as Martin Jacques put it in *The Observer*. Sport has an incredible power to shape our lives and influence our mood. The clothes we wear are heavily influenced by sport, what would have once only been worn for a sweaty session in the gym is now high fashion. Our media are dominated by sport. TV and radio channels live or die by the securing of hugely expensive broadcasting rights for major events. The broadsheets, and the tabloids, devote huge amounts of space to covering sport on the front pages, in the feature sections, business news and supplements, not forgetting the back pages themselves. Sportsmen and sportswomen are the cultural icons of today. Who hasn't heard of Owen or Beckham – many of us can probably provide details of most of their short lifestory? The best known person in the world today is generally held to be the now retired American basketball player, Michael Jordan. And until recently how were Anglo-German relations played out – Hill versus Schumacher, of course. Women tennis players in particular, Anna Kournikova being the latest, are held up as sex symbols, the picture completed by a racket in the hands and a short skirt. With the media and sponsors in hot pursuit the players match the supermodels and actresses for the glossy spreads devoted to every inch of their bodies. Personal health is a massive issue for many of us, and we're not just talking about women either, men are increasingly obsessed with the flatness of their abdomens as the cover subject and rapidly growing sales of the magazine *Men's Health* testify. And sport isn't just something you play any more, the sagging shelves of works of male confessionals in the wake of *Fever Pitch* have been accompanied by almost every imaginable academic discipline – anthropology, psycho-analysis, business studies, sociology and more – all claiming that they've also got something useful to say on sport, and they insist on saying it too, footnotes and all. But the biggest change of all, of course, is down to the good old-fashioned cash nexus. Sport is big business, it makes or breaks the media magnates. It features on the stock market. It sells everything from crisps to sports cars. Its global events are business bonanzas bordering on a trade fair with a pitch or track attached. Martin Jacques describes the Age of Sport thus: 'Sport has become ubiquitous. It is the metaphor of our times. It has serious competitors: fashion, comedy, music, the internet. But just as rock became the dominant cultural form of the sixties and seventies, so sport has become dominant, invading areas of life where previously it had no presence.' Sport is fashion, it's showbiz. It gives us the body beautiful, either for us to become or to ogle at. Sport is business, a source of value systems; for its champion performers it earns incalculable wealth. We are witnessing the wholesale sportification of our culture, in England, Europe, worldwide. Sport, like almost nothing else, inspires both the intensity of local and national loyalties, while constantly reminding us that the whole world's watching. Sport is both localisation and globalisation, big time.

Following England, especially abroad, is all about finding our nation, but in an international, a continental, a global context. What we English carry with us though – more than any other nation – is our history. Football's in there, of course: Bobby Moore holding the Jules Rimet trophy aloft; throwing away a two-goal lead against the Germans in 1970; Maradona's 1986 'Hand of God' –

and more penalty shoot-outs than we'd care to remember. With Ingerland the memory doesn't go back much further than 1966, unless of course we're turning over the Hungarians in revenge for that 1953 drubbing. But as we drag this great load of national history around with us, the footballing memories in any case quite quickly recede into the background. Think about the teams that made it to France '98: our hosts, the French, well, we stuffed them at Waterloo; the South Africans, Boer War and old colonials; Saudi Arabia, who saved them from Saddam? Denmark, Holland and Belgium – if it wasn't for us they'd be Krauts. Spain, the Armada saw their lot off; Nigeria, lucky enough to have been part of the old empire. Bulgaria, whose side were they on in World War Two? Paraguay, home of old Nazis so same goes for them. Germany, two world wars and one World Cup; United States, avenge the Boston Tea Party! Yugoslavia, Bombs away Slobbo! Iran, mad mullahs aren't they? South Korea, would be North Koreans if it wasn't for us. Mexico, remember the Alamo? Romania, more questions about which side they were on; Colombia, drug-runners; Tunisia, Monty's Desert Rats showed them a thing or two. Argentina, you'll never take the Falklands; Japan, Colonel Bogey. Jamaica, get back to Brixton; Croatia, aren't our Boys doing their bit down there, and which side were the Croats on anyway? The idea is, almost, infectious and certainly very, though not uniquely, English.

It can be, let's be honest, funny too; only the most po-faced could ever live a life never having a laugh at somebody else's expense. But we all know that when it comes to Ingerland it is the connection between the piss-take, and the surly 'what's your problem' about all things foreign that starts the slide towards something humourless and ugly. The image of England abroad, whether or not it's an accurate one hardly matters, is largely negative. We're treated as the perennial party-poopers, and there aren't too many hosts who mind if we fail to take up their invitation. The negative image is a problem for the Football Association – it's not how they want English football thought of – and a problem for sponsors too. Endless TV shots, and tabloid front pages, of a rampaging mob with a great big 'Umbro' and 'Nationwide' logo across their T-shirts is not quite the product placement these companies paid millions of pounds for. And it's not great for the government either, England fans running riot might not have an immediate impact on the balance of payments but it's not the best way to attract inward investment or convince people that law and order is on its way to being sorted or demonstrate that we're at ease with our place in the world, if you please.

The statistical reality is that it is only a tiny minority who get involved in any of the serious trouble-making. And a fair few of these are as much victims as perpetrators. Almost all of the reports that covered the most serious outbreak of trouble involving England at France '98, in Marseilles, talked of some 400 being involved. Yet the self-same reports also stated that some 40,000 England fans were in the city. Four hundred is only one per cent of those present. The fact that 99 per cent of England fans weren't involved isn't a good enough excuse, but surely it's at least worth taking into account. The worry remains though, that amongst the majority of fans there's a more than benevolent attitude towards even the most hardened troublemakers. A benevolence that suggests when the circumstances are 'right' a far, far higher proportion would choose to get involved at worst, cheer on from the sidelines at best. The fear is that the mix of pumped-up patriotism, relishing in the rubbishing of other countries, a siege mentality abroad, all this leads to a permissive majority. Maybe this is the case, who knows? But if a faith in human nature kept the worst extremes of the twentieth century at bay, what's so difficult about sorting out the offending individuals and attitudes that hang around with Ingerland from the rest, who, all things being equal, would rather have nothing to do with their violent, criminal antics?

The solutions that have been proffered though have almost all been about surveillance and intelligence-gathering acting as preventative measures, seeking to isolate known trouble-makers before major championships. A sensible enough strategy in theory, but when the line is blurred between detaining those with a criminal record for violent football-related thuggery and those whom authorities might simply suspect of trouble-making tendencies, where does it stop? Number one crop, tattoos, chanting enthusiastically, can of beer in one hand, St George's flag in the other, yes he will do nicely. Those who will go along with the trouble are an ever-changing group – circumstances change, along with the mood. In all seriousness, how can these measures be expected to work? If it was that easy to identify a well-organised minority bent on violence and mayhem then England's image problem abroad could have been solved years ago. If the identification and isolation is foolproof, then fine, use it. But what if it isn't? Innocent until proven guilty is a much bigger part of Englishness than any tendency to smash up a bar in some foreign town, or at least it damn well should be.

Apart from detaining individuals and groups on the suspicion that they might be 'up for it' the other main drive remains 'No ticket, don't travel'. The Foreign Office even went to the trouble of producing a nice-looking leaflet, distributed via all the top-selling football magazines, with the bold instructions: 'All match tickets have been allocated right up to the final. If you buy a ticket with someone else's name on that ticket becomes invalid. If you do not already have a ticket, you will not be able to get into a match.' Enough to put the fear of Tony Blair into anyone. Not only did it fail to convince most that it was still worth travelling, as tens of thousands in Marseilles, Toulouse, Lens and St Etienne can prove, it was patently untrue. You can only cry wolf once, so even if the glossy and expensive campaign did persuade a few not to bother travelling, it will be even less successful the next time round.

'No ticket, don't travel' flies in the face of football fan culture. This is the World Cup we're talking about not the 'French taxpayers with no Allcomers championships'. It's not much of a party if all the guests are turned away at the door, is it? Shouldn't we have been encouraging the fine citizens of good old Blighty to rub peeling shoulders with their fellow fans from far and wide? Whatever happened to travel broadening the mind?

What possible message were we giving the beleaguered French taxpayers as Jack Straw did his intellectual best to keep every Englishman of a certain age supping his ale at home, a Channel away from all the *vin* and *baguettes* the French were no doubt hoping to sell us. Bars empty, souvenirs left unsold, loads of spare rooms in the hotels, not much *entente cordiale* in any of that. Meanwhile if there was to be any trouble it was as likely to be in the beer tents that the likes of Boddingtons were busy erecting back home. 'Club colours will not be worn' made it obvious that public disorder was very much a football-related issue this side of the Channel too, so what are you supposed to do – blank out the screens and pretend we're living in a World Cup free zone? A bit of perspective wouldn't go amiss. Hundreds of thousands of English pop across to France every summer for their hols, while the French coast hypermarkets are just like the local Sainsbury's for a generation of weekend bargain-hunters. Is France brought to its knees by this invasion? Presumably not or else they wouldn't keep asking us back. So what's so different if football is thrown into the equation. Does a football fan really differ that much from a holidaymaker or shopper, indeed won't quite a few be one and the same person?

Of course, there is something different with football. Nobody gets quite so excited about the cost of Camembert or which direction their tent-flap should be facing as the outcome of a World Cup penalty shoot-out. But is all this new Labour authoritarianism and moralising the answer? A self-fulfilling prophecy emerges. The ticketless fan becomes the latest moral panic, the up-to-date folk devil. No ticket equals heading for trouble, and the more you tell us that, the more the mind-set sinks in. If trouble's all we're good for, we might as well live up to the low expectations people have of us.

Meanwhile the corporate junkets carry on. The seats that should be for fans are sold off as part of each and every sponsorship deal. Football sells itself short when it throws in seats as part of these packages. Why not accept a few tens of thousands of pounds less and cut out most, if not all, the free seats as part of the bargain. Would Coca-Cola, Budweiser, Sony, Adidas and the like really turn their back on their investments if they couldn't get the free seats as clause five, sub-section nine, line three of a multi-million-pound contract? Could they afford not to be involved as sponsors and all the branding that football provides them with ? Just how important are those seats to their executives? We certainly know how important the seats are to us as fans.

Big business has transformed football for ever. It has changed the kick-off day and time to suit the TV schedules. It has ruined many a classic strip with a horrible big sponsor's logo. It has filled stands with executive boxes, and jacked up the cost of the seats to the highest price the chairman and directors think they can get away with. And worst of all, even our grounds are being named in the dubious honour of the corporate investors. From Burnden Park to the Reebok Stadium is a very big journey indeed. What's next, Sega Arsenal? As fans, we know the game is being taken away from us. So when the opportunity comes to behave badly in front of the world's cameras, couldn't part of the explanation be that some of the fans want to spoil the rewriting of the 'people's game' as a leisure industry bonanza with the odd goal thrown in. A couple of hundred lagered-up lads in the centre of Marseilles, smashed up bars, bloodied policemen, screeching sirens and you're front-page headlines, primetime news. How else do you get anybody to take any notice of you? What other ways can you make your voice heard? None of this is an excuse, but it has to be part of the explanation, and an even bigger part of the solution. Politics and politicians are rapidly losing whatever remaining credibility they once had. We are living through a crisis of legitimacy, bigger and more dangerous than we've ever seen before. The French philosopher Jean Baudrillard got the message when he wrote: 'Power is only too happy to make football bear a diabolical responsibility for stupefying the masses.' The public disorder is stupid, certainly, and the outcome invariably ugly, but those behind it aren't necessarily as stupefied as their loftier critics might have thought. A nasty, unsettling conclusion, but one that it would be risky in the extreme to discount wholly. This isn't in any sense a justification or a romanticisation – the Ingerland factor is far too complex for such cosy conclusions. But, at the same time, out-of-hand condemnation shouldn't carry as much weight as it's all too easily given either. When a ten-year ban is seriously proposed as a punishment for those suspected, not convicted, even, of football hooliganism, it's about time some balance was given to this debate.

Fans, all fans, have a well-worn habit of just milling around. Soaking up the atmosphere is a big part of following football. The English, more than most, do have a problem with things foreign. But we're not that different. The Dutch and Germans don't get on too well, the Brazilians have never been all that keen on most of their South American neighbours. And if you thought racist chanting was a thing of the past, you've obviously never sat amongst a crowd of Croats. Because of our insularity and the reputation that goes before us, informing our own 'side' as much as anyone else, we don't pick up on the drowning of the Chilean national anthem by those happy-clappy Brazilians or the monkey chants from the Croatian section every time a black French player touches the ball, or the immense public order preparations underway everytime the Dutch look set to meet the Germans. Again, not an excuse, but a handy dose of perspective. That problem we have with things foreign would be far more effectively dealt with by encouraging a footballing internationalism rather than another authoritarian crackdown. Giving ourselves a chance to feel good about being a part of the human, not just an island, race. An opportunity to discover that the appalling taste of half-time pies and fashion disasters masquerading as away kits are strangely enough the same the whole world over. Fans United, we have nothing to lose but our games.

But there remains something special about Ingerland. We're not easily fooled or impressed, and with all that marketisation going on around football that's no bad thing. Passion, commitment and loyalty are in the mix too. Ironically it was an advertiser, Coca-Cola, that summed up best just how valuable all these qualities are with their slogan, 'If they paid transfer fees for fans how much would you be worth?' Millions, mate. Still when we get too wrapped up in loudly telling everybody we're the real thing and where you can stick your Mexican Waves it can make us seem like right miserable sods too. Rob Newman put it neatly in *Perfect Pitch*:

> Foreign fans have more fun. Apart from England, the only other country not to have a hundred-foot flag or silky banner passed overhead is the USA. This is because Anglo-Saxon capitalism does not encourage collective life; nothing is owned collectively ('Look that's *my* hundred-foot flag, pass it back. Come on please . . .') No collective life is also why England fans are the only ones reduced to singing the fucking National Anthem – of all things – at a game. (France doesn't count because the *'Marseillaise'* is a rebel song named after a town with a large immigrant population. An English equivalent might be the Clash's 'Guns of Brixton'.)

Ah, the national anthem. Is it really more than twenty years since the Queen's Silver Jubilee celebrations were spoiled by the Sex Pistols reaching the top ten with their own very particular version of 'God Save the Queen'? The record had been banned from being played by most, if not all, radio stations but still it reached number two with the angry refrain 'God Save the Queen, She ain't no human being, There is no Future, in England's Dreaming'. Rebellious to the core in the face of most vestiges of authority why, oh why, is the 'Long to reign over us, Happy and glorious' authorised version of 'God Save the Queen' what we're still stuck with as an anthem? A song that celebrates the fact we're subjects – there is something deeply unappealing and humiliating in such a sentiment. 'Happy and glorious' because we're ruled over, how low can our expectations fall? Never mind the fact that there's nothing English about this anthem, she's the Queen of Britain isn't she? Though Irish republicans, Scots and Welsh nationalists might have a word or two to say about that. Andy Crick in the magazine *Prospect* describes the national anthem as 'a miserable dirge with embarrassing words'. He suggests replacing it at sporting occasions featuring English, rather than British, teams at least with 'I Vow to Thee My Country', made famous as Princess Di's favourite hymn. Ironically just like 'God Save the Queen' the tune was composed by a foreigner – 'God Save the Queen' originating as a French national anthem! 'I Vow To Thee' is all about loyalty, sacrifice and faith. It originated as an appeal for peace after the horrors of the First World War. OK, there are the bits about God, but if we think about these as simply a plea for a higher morality, members of all faiths, and none, should have no reason to complain. It's a haunting, hugely evocative and emotional song, and in some quintessential, difficult to define way, deeply suggestive of Englishness.

Cleaning up the National Anthem though is just one part of a much bigger exercise if we are seriously concerned about the plight of what Ingerland has come to represent itself as through football. And it's not all bad news either. Who would have imagined the red half of Manchester would celebrate a League Championship or Cup win, or indeed both at the same time, with a hearty rendition of the *Marseillaise*? Or Chelsea, previously home of the notorious 'Headhunters' and a fair few fascist nutters too, celebrating the management style of first Ruud Gullit, then when he gets the Ken Bates treatment, Gianluca Vialli and his cosmopolitan crew. How many fans nowadays don't yearn for an international being signed; a Scandinavian at least, a Brazilian or Argentinian would do even better. Our local pride has become globalised, provided these fancy-dan foreigners can score of course. It might only be partial, most attitudes are partial until we have the time and space to work them out to any conclusion, but it's another start towards being more at ease with England's place in the world. The local and the global are in a constant state of tension, club versus country is just one aspect of this. Our national team, well that's a relatively simple selection, but when your club team comprises an Australian goalie, a Trinidadian forward, an Irish captain, a Dutchman and a Norwegian in defence, plus your greatest player of recent years is a Frenchman, what are you to do? Why should you adore the plucky English lads in the side any more, or any less? It is maybe not a surprise that when David Beckham found himself taunted by opposition fans throughout the season following his ignominious exit from the game against Argentina that Man. Utd fans shouted in his defence. What was much more telling was what they shouted, 'Argentina!' and 'You can stick your England up your arse'. What price nation, loyalty and pride now?

Not only have our club team line-ups been transformed – not just in the Premiership either, Wigan Athletic's 'Three Amigos' of a few seasons back might have been at first a curiosity; now almost every first, second and third division team has a foreign player, though maybe not a foreign star, on its books. Fan culture has changed too, and the internationalisation of that culture is just one part of it. The fanzines, the independent websites, the mood in the stands, the campaigns of supporters groups, the voice of fans heard on almost nightly phone-ins or captured in print by the exploding football publishing industry. Of course the values that hold this culture together aren't universal but, by and large, most would agree that they represent a good thing, free of the violent hatred that club rivalries have had a nasty habit of spilling over into, yet retaining the wit and the warmth that most of us cherish so much in the solidarity of following our team instead of that other lot down the road. That doesn't mean there's not another culture there, setting up the fights that still take place around many, too many, games, but it's been pushed to the margins, it's not in the mainstream in the way that it once threatened to be. There's an alternative, positive pole of attraction, just as committed, just as genuine, but without the violent overtones.

With Ingerland this alternative, positive pole of attraction lags massively behind the profile it has amongst club fan cultures. Ingerland remains largely a fan culture wasteland in comparison. Is Ingerland then something to be ashamed of, an entirely bad thing that you must turn your back on if you're moral, decent and law-abiding? Charlie Whelan writing in *The Observer* seems to think so. 'I'm not prepared to watch a match surrounded by complete morons. If you bought your tickets from the England Members Club you always end up being next to a sub-human.' And he rounds it all off by looking forward to South Africa winning the bid for the 2006 World Cup. 'The crime rate in South Africa is now the highest in the world – more than 60 murders a day. South Africa would be the perfect place to stage the World Cup. They should give Sheffield, Derby and all their mates the welcome they deserve.' OK, OK, poor Charlie's out of a job as Gordon Brown's spin-doctor and he's trying to make a career for himself as New Labour's answer to David Mellor. But did he think for a moment what he was writing? All England supporters are sub-humans, and if the odd one got murdered, well is that such a big thing? Sorry, run that one past me again Charlie, you're a Labour man are you? But he's just at the extreme end of a band of opinion that has given up on Ingerland and all it stands for. Not just given up, actually. They'd much prefer to lock Ingerland up, and throw away the key, failing that they'll take away the ball so there's no England for us to follow anymore. Another voice from around New Labour, the magazine *New Statesman,* seriously suggested in an editorial in the wake of the trouble in Marseilles that 'football has always been a vehicle for tribal passions and poorly educated young men have always formed gangs'. It denounced football for its 'tiresomely yobbish, foul-mouthed culture that . . . spreads out like an oil slick'. So the solution is delightfully simple, if dramatic. Bring the team home, the *New Statesman* urging 'any match that threatens trouble should be cancelled on public-order grounds, or alternatively, played behind closed doors at a secret location. On that basis, England should not play in the World Cup.'

Now is not the time to give up on Ingerland, and it never will be. This is the politics of despair and they lead to a passivity that permits the most frightening excesses of authoritarianism. A most scary proposition. Ingerland has been allowed to become all about a military history, going to war with other nations, ruling over their land, and the high seas thrown in too, empire and all that. But what about a different iconography of our national past. That poor brave sod Harold with an arrow in his eye, he lost that penalty shoot-out didn't he? And all his troubles started off at the battle of Stamford Bridge, how many times have we heard that before? See, we can laugh at ourselves if we try. Boadicea, she cut those Romans off in their prime. What about Robin Hood, he robbed the rich to help the poor didn't he? So even if we can't give up on a warlike history, maybe there's other ways of commemorating it.

And as for a national monument, what's better than Stonehenge – now there's a tribute to English brickies down the ages, it's stood the test of time better than most extensions to the back room put up in a DIY hurry. Shakespeare, Florence Nightingale, Dickens and Jane Austen, Michael Faraday, George Stephenson, Captain Cook and Scott of the Antarctic; we've not only had the odd good war – a contradiction in terms if ever I've heard of one – but penned plays, cared for the sick, written a few books, come up with inventions that have changed the world, made scientific discoveries and explored uncharted territories too. Of course they're not unproblematic either, why were we at war in the Crimea anyway? But they are emblems and memories of a very different history. And it's not just history that makes us think we know what it is to be English either. The Beatles must surely be in anybody's top ten as an icon of the English the world would all identify with. 'All You Need is Love' would do for me as an anthem of Englishness. One of my most bizarre memories of France '98 was the World Cup Organising Committee choosing this hippy-idealist song to play at every game England played in as our sort of representative song – every nation had one – and it was duly played during the warm-ups. What a different image of Englishness to the one we were all told was the only one to associate with Ingerland away, all mayhem and misery. Do they mean us? And if we accept that music is as much a part of what it means to be English as a history made up of the great and the good, then we can fast-forward all our yesterdays to when black people are as much a part of our past as our present. Ska, soul and reggae, rap and hip-hop, one nation under a groove anyone? That's not to say being English can't be black in a vast variety of ways apart from the stereotype of the DJ, but if we take this as the starting point, not the end-point, of repainting our symbols of Englishness we might just get to where we'd like to end up.

What about English humour? Norman Wisdom, Barbara Windsor and Sid James, Morecambe and Wise, Tony Hancock and Peter Sellers. Or *Fawlty Towers, Only Fools and Horses, Dad's Army, One Foot in the Grave.* Our comedy is as much about how we have learned to laugh at ourselves, and just as popular as Jim Davidson, Bernard Manning and their ilk encouraging us only to laugh at others.

The war, well we're not going to stop mentioning that in a hurry are we? But how about Vera Lynn and 'We'll Meet Again', that was all about the collective spirit that Rob Newman finds so lacking in us today. A sense of hope and belonging, a community facing adversity. It's a different way of paying our dues to moments in our history that simply won't, because they shouldn't, go away. As for the *Great Escape*, it's a minor wonder that no one ever remembers that the ones that got away were an Australian and an indeterminate East European played by Charles Bronson with, and here my memory fades, I think a Scot. The rest were caught. Still, give me the *Great Escape* theme rather than 'Rule Britannia' anytime, however badly played.

Any rebranding of Ingerland will run slap up against what remains a petty-mindedness that is the making of Little Englanderism when it comes to all things foreign. 'Football Comes Home' in 1996 unfortunately said it all, officially, with the FA seal of approval. Reminding the continentals that it was us who taught the world to play, and we'll never let you forget it. There were beautiful giant player portrait banners draped off streetlights to decorate the roads of the eight Euro '96 host cities. Whose bright idea then was it to choose five white players? Didn't anyone stop to think that football is one of the most powerful symbols of our multicultural society? No, another opportunity missed.

Does all this sound like small beer compared to more important matters the FA and other bodies in the game should be sorting out, like England winning a trophy for the first time in thirty-plus years. Obviously, but in an era when TV pictures can be beamed from one continent to another in seconds and you go to an international championship knowing a sizeable portion of the world's population are watching then image is nearly everything. A ruck in Marseilles, beered up troublemakers burning a flag in front of the cameras, a bloodied bystander. The cameras catch the scene in an instant and splash Ingerland all over the story and bulletin. The photographers and cameramen are only partly to blame. They're not there for the match, they're not following any team, they just want a picture and a story to send home. They've got a job to do, and probably prefer cricket anyway. If our fan culture can't generate any other images then is it any surprise that Ingerland is invariably a bad news feature? It is the serious lack of any appealing alternative that has allowed the thuggery to grab more than its fair share of the limelight.

Projecting the positive side of Ingerland must firstly take account, and advantage, of the fact that football at an international level is such a hugely mediated spectacle. Second, any such projection should be built around the passion the English put into being a fan, to seek to dilute this in any way will simply distance the process from those alone who can enact it meaningfully, the fans themselves. Third, the key dividing line that has pushed Ingerland into the realms of the unacceptable is wilful violence. There must be ways found for those who reject violence as a valid part of our fan culture to express that rejection free of any fear of retribution from whatever perpetrators might remain.

How? The icons of an alternative Ingerland might help. A papier-mâché Stonehenge would make a wonderful headdress, which would give all those plastic viking helmets and rasta wigs a run for their money in the playful national stereotype stakes. Harold's arrow stuck on the forehead suggests a nation that can live with the occasional defeat. For terrace anthems, 'Bring Me Sunshine' would do for a country whose reputation for rained-off summers few can match, while 'We'll Meet Again' suggests a quite different way of honouring the war. Comradeship and community spirit rather than Dambusters and 'Two World Wars, One World Cup'. Inflatable fish and chips, Yorkshire and black puddings, wave them in the air to celebrate our national dish, though a giant sachet of curry powder might be more appropriate. The paraphernalia we take with with us to celebrate the fact that Ingerland is coming to town could be joyful and witty, celebratory and affirmative.

Going into a championship with the very clear ambition of coming out at the end of it if not with a trophy, at least a better reputation than the one we went in with, and preferably both, is something only the fans can pull off. But it is a project in all of football's interests. The support of the Football Association, the national team sponsors and the host countries we visit is crucial. If they're not willing to help out with this process then it won't even begin. Take the 'Raise the Flag' initiative at Wembley; 15,000 cards laid out on the seats at the 'home' end, and a further few thousand cards on the seats of the visiting team's supporters. The visiting end's cards are written in the appropriate language, welcoming these fans to Wembley. Without the away fans, after all, what kind of game is it for our fans? And as the respective national anthems are struck up these thousands of cards are held aloft to create giant fans' flags. It's a great sight, but it's more than that. There's no compulsion, the flags happen because the collective, the fans, want it to happen. The opportunity afforded by the fans whose idea it was, the fans who lay them out, the FA who provide the access, the sponsors Nationwide, who in return for a logo placement fund the initiative, and most of all the fans who hold the cards up. It's momentary, but it's an incredibly positive statement of what Ingerland can be about. And with the welcoming cards for the away fans who hold them up to create their own flag we are saying that what we share as fans has as much life in it as the passion we'll be putting into willing our side to victory.

But this all takes place at Wembley. What if such a venture could be taken abroad? Maybe we'd be remembered for something positive. We would have brought something to the party. Icons, songs, symbols and thousands of cards that turn into colourful flags. It's all ephemeral but these sorts of initiatives depend on active support, co-operation and can catch the eye of a TV camera crew or photographer. Small beginnings, but part of a vital process.

English fan culture is undoubtedly respected the whole world over. Not as the 'home' of football. As a new millennium dawns, where is that? The shanty towns of Argentina, the beaches of Brazil, a bunch of college girls in the USA playing what is rapidly becoming their national female team sport, a dusty pitch in the midst of an African village, or downtown Tokyo kitted out head to toe in English Premiership counterfeit replica kits? It's all these places, and more. We have our place in this rich panorama of football as a global culture, it's a special place, but then every one of these places is special in its own way. The key is understanding, and projecting, what makes our way special. Wit and humour, commitment, getting through the wind and the rain, the game's roots in the industrial working-class strongholds of cities and heavy industrial areas, a past that is embedded in the game's history everywhere, the depth and the breadth of our passion, it's all of this. Isn't this something which we should want to carry with us as ambassadors of Englishness. Yet our Fan Embassies, essential and pioneering as they are, focus on coping with problems rather than providing the images and language that would explain what it is about English football that means Ingerland is coming to town. A touring exhibition, a foreign language fanzine from the England fans, a range of souvenirs to give away to the friendly waiters, the shop assistants, the coppers, the turnstile operators, the stewards we come across on our travels. Something for them to remember us by, it could give a whole new meaning to away fans leaving their calling cards. Simple, low cost steps, requiring the minimum of infrastructure yet capable of effecting widespread one-to-one change.

And the thugs? Well they're not going to join in any of this are they? It will marginalise them more quickly, and more effectively than a vast panoply of bans, statutes and surveillance. The essential point is that all this activity, provided it is fan led, will offer a positive pole for the great majority to identify with at least, and quite possibly actively support. Non-violence must therefore become a core value of being a fan, in the same way that it is a core value for a vast range of protest movements. Who would doubt the eco-protestor's distrust of authority? Their ability to resist authority, their capacity to effect change. Yet they do all this with non-violent direct action. By rejecting violence we don't lose any of our authenticity as fans, yet we establish a dividing line between us, and those who are willing to engage in such wanton acts of thuggery. To glory in it, to wear it as their ill-fitting armoury of fabled courage. Our rejection must be public too, and collective. Individual rejection is lonely and ineffectual. 'Football Yes, Violence No', a badge to be worn with pride alongside our enamel St George's Cross and three lions on a shirt. It will become our message to the footballing world; who'd have thought it, eh? Well it won't happen by accident, but work at it, give the fans the opportunity at least to embrace the message before we're clobbered with another set of restrictions and intelligence-gathering operations that infringe any thinking Englishperson's most cherished civil liberties.

Image, impact and values, together these suggest another country, a different Ingerland to the one we're used to. Yet loyal to our traditions, passion and culture. The two processes working together in tandem to the same end. There remain, however, some simple structural changes that could help too. Much of the disorder around drinking is linked to the dangerous weapons easily at hand, namely glasses and bottles. Chuck a plastic beaker and you're not going to hurt anyone. A full can, well there's no accounting for taste is there? Leaving it to those who prefer fighting with their bare hands will further reduce the ranks of those who can too easily slip from flag-waving to bar-smashing mode. It must surely be in the interests of all those beer and lager companies who pump billions of pounds into the sponsorship of football to fund and organise such a campaign to remove glass objects from bars and shops in cities where England are playing. And a clearing-up crew after we've left, provided by the fans themselves, wouldn't go amiss either. What a different memory of Ingerland that would leave behind.

Some part of the solution should also be concerned with public order preparations that England fans have traditionally borne the brunt of, but have affected fans of all nations. Sure there was trouble at France '98, and some – though by no means all of it – involved England's travelling support. James Brown, formerly editor of *GQ* and *Loaded,* neatly put this into some sort of context, writing in *The Guardian*: 'Put a million priests from around the country together for a month in France and ask them to hand over their hard-earned cash to watch their own personal saviours, and then sit back and expect no problems. It just wouldn't, doesn't happen.' The trouble that did occur was almost exclusively well away from the actual stadia. This is all the more important to think about as with the huge sale of touted tickets to England fans there was no segregation of any significance in the stands. There's not going to be any immediate change but maybe, just maybe, if you treat two nations' sets of supporters as two mutually exclusive tribes it's not such a surprise that they end up misbehaving like they do. Sitting almost side by side, sharing in the atmosphere, enjoying the banter and the wind-up imposes certain natural limits on behaviour that most of us are quite happy to abide by without any supervision. Likewise the now traditional locking-in of England fans for anything up to several hours after the game has finished. Left to our own devices with all that pent-up emotion while everyone else is streaming away to the bars, the hotels, the beaches; in what state of mind is that likely to leave our collective psyche? Not safe to be let out with the rest of 'em, what have we got left but to live up to the reputation?

Following Ingerland we carry our ancient, and our recent, history before us. It goes with the luggage. It can also give us an identity to play with, nothing about it is fixed, certainly not now on the edge of a new century. Not only should we be at ease setting about our own fan culture, but we could be a lot more sensitive to the changes that mean there'll never be an all-white England team, like those heroes of '66, ever again. And that when we cheer our side on it isn't a blokes' thing anymore either. If we can't get our eyes fixed on the present and future what hope is there of putting the past into some kind of perspective. Misty-eyed memories of '66 are all well and good but when they become a fog that obscures everything that followed, we're getting locked into an identity crisis that's more about the years of hurt and defeat rather than that one wonderful Wembley Saturday more than thirty years ago.

Ingerland can be about feeling good about England, England in Europe and a fair chunk of Europe in England too. A country cheering on their team, but keeping an eye out for how club heroes playing for another country are doing too. A nation at ease with its Scots, Irish, Jamaican, Turkish and a panorama of other immigrant communities willing their team to victory as well. The Ingerland factor treating us all to the spectacle of a popular internationalism. Romantic, fanciful even, but what the hell, it's worth a go, isn't it?

The Ingerland Factor Playlist:
Can You Hear the English Sing?

John Peel

A list of music you might like to hear played in a stadium overseas that would make you feel specifically English. I have – well, we have, because I involved my family in this and even sought help from Radio One listeners – tried to avoid triumphalism. Living in a world in which every other person seems to have become a Man. Utd supporter overnight, I know all about triumphalism. I try telling them they are merely supporting a global financial conspiracy which happens to be based in Manchester, but they don't listen. The fools, the fools. Anyway, let the music speak for itself.

1. The Fall – 'Kicker Conspiracy'

I have to admit that I have never fully understood what this is about. This is true of many Fall tracks. But there is a venom in it which seems to capture nicely some of the feelings you have about football even when you know it is inappropriate to have them. A fair example of this would be my feelings when Zoë Ball tripped into my studio one evening – I'd never met her before – and started crowing about Man. Utd. I suspect her commitment to the team is fairly recent, the depth of her interest pretty shallow, but I was outraged. We have a friend who lives in Manchester, always has done and is a life-long United supporter – you thought no such persons existed – and he was cross when his girlfriend, now his wife, taunted me over some United success or other. 'You don't understand how these things feel,' he told her. He was right, of course. 'Kicker Conspiracy', probably the best football record ever, apart from Pepe Kalle's 'Roger Milla'.

2. Barmy Army – 'Sharp As A Needle'

Produced by Adrian Sherwood, it doesn't really get much better than this classic Barmy Army track. Years after its release, I still can't hear it without a lump in my throat. Incongruously, there is a West Ham reference – Sherwood is a Hammers fan – but the music relates otherwise to Kenny Dalglish, with a sideways nod to Ian Rush, a striker who actually scored goals rather than a striker who was famous for being a striker but omitted to score off the dancefloor. We adored Kenny in our house – still do really – and any appearance by the great man on television still brings us running to hear what he has to say. Although I've not had any contact with him for years, I've always felt that the grim, monosyllabic Dalglish of popular myth wasn't the real Kenny at all. '. . . And Dalglish has scored. Kenny Dalglish – sharp as a needle.' I'm even getting tearful just thinking about it. I think the moment he scored the winning goal against Bruges at Wembley in the 1978 European Cup final was the best moment of my life so far. His greatest strength was the uncanny manner in which he seemed to know where every other player on the pitch was and where they were going. Actually, we think he's underrated. We love you Kenny. If I heard this in a stadium overseas I would cry uncontrollably.

3. The Kop – 'You'll Never Walk Alone'

Nobody seems to sing anymore. Perhaps it's uncool. No recording of the Kop will ever really capture Anfield at its Shankly-era best but the song and the sentiments are simply astonishing.

4. Georg Friedrich Händel – 'Zadok The Priest'

The hymn that is best remembered as being sung at our royal coronations. I'm not a royalist, not even a patriot, more of a European I suppose. But then Händel was a German and this piece of music, and the way it builds and builds until it finally explodes in joy is pretty much unstoppable. Obviously the sheer complexity of the work and the necessity for orchestral accompaniment would put it beyond the range of most groups of supporters, and yet, why not? Perhaps one day we'll hear Ipswich Town's North Stand giving it a go. Ipswich is only 12 miles away from our home and we can get to it easily enough. Although if it was a question of an Ipswich versus Liverpool match we'd all go red of course. Our son William who, prior to going to University – Liverpool, naturally – had no interest in football whatsoever, is now obsessive. He's endlessly surfing the internet for gossip, rumour, wild surmise. He occasionally managed to scrounge a few Ipswich tickets when he was a student but alas, we can't get even in there nowadays. Never mind, we do still love Ipswich all the same.

5. The Members – 'Sounds of the Suburbs'

The updated version by The Samurai Seven is a tempting alternative choice for the number five spot. Much of punk and post-punk has not dated well. A lot of the big tunes of the era now sound like empty posturing. Perhaps part of the reason is the subsequent behaviour of assorted members of the Sex Pistols and The Clash. But this track still sounds funny, sharp and surprisingly relevant. I've never lived in a suburb – more of a country boy, me – but this captures something of the England I like, as much as other records by artists praised for their Englishness – XTC or The Kinks.

6. The Kinks – 'Waterloo Sunset'

I've never lived in Waterloo either but this was the record most mentioned by listeners who responded to my plea for e-mailed assistance with this play-list. I am, as a man born just three days before the outbreak of World War Two, naturally fearful of nationalism. But I appreciate music, football, and much else that can convey those subtle shadings of feeling that should be the sum of your commitment to the place of your birth. Somehow, 'Waterloo Sunset' does this rather well.

7. Billy Bragg – 'A New England'

This selection has nothing to do with the obviously apposite title, but everything to do with Billy. A genuinely decent man in an often loathsome business. Unless he has deceived me – and many thousands of others – there's something about Billy that is immensely reassuring. As a pretty much unreconstructed old Labour type myself – what a pity Tony Benn or the Beast of Bolsover never made a terrace anthem – I admire Billy's politics too. Politics that are prone to ridicule these days although they rest essentially on the proviso that you do as you would be done by. Something I try to stick to myself and which I have only heard reflected by football fans on the terraces of FC St Pauli, Hamburg. Not that they actually sing that, you understand, either in German or English, but there is that feeling, especially when they explain where they stand on beer distribution. I've seldom been as pissed as I was during the St Pauli match against Leverkusen, and happily pissed too, where confrontation seemed to be in no one's mind. Hamburg is a great city, second only to Glasgow. And Liverpool. Oh alright then, third.

8. Rod Stewart – 'Maggie May'

The Faces, with Rod Stewart, I loved them live. Best gigs ever, just about. With their concert in Sunderland – the night Sunderland had beaten Arsenal at Hillsborough in the FA Cup semi-final, 1973, the year they went on to beat Leeds in the final – the best ever. A football band for a football crowd equals pure ecstasy. The Faces had sometimes let me kick footballs out into the crowd from the stage, as have Teenage Fan Club. I hope everybody noticed that I routinely got balls further out into the concert hall than anyone else. Just thought I'd mention it. Muriel Gray once told me I had footballers legs. I've venerated her ever since.

9. Blur – 'Song 2'

A band often accused of epitomising Englishness. That always seems so limiting somehow. Nevertheless, a modern classic that would serve to remind you of home if you heard it pumping out of a public address system just about anywhere.

10. Robert Wyatt – 'Shipbuilding'

There has to be a slower and more reflective tune in here somewhere. And I've plumped for Robert Wyatt's recording of 'Shipbuilding' by Elvis Costello. For a start Robert is just one of the funniest, most thoughtful and thought-provoking people I know and hearing this would make me think of him, and Alfie his wife. Plus his voice has this almost unbearable melancholy to it. I'd really like to hear Robert do more cover-versions, you know 'Try A Little Tenderness' or 'My Funny Valentine', even 'Crying in the Chapel'. As for 'Shipbuilding', the song reminds us of the dangers of mob emotions, mob politics, mob rule. And hopefully reminds us too that these emotions are in the opposing stands as well. My friend Charlie, my Man. Utd supporter friend, understood this alright as he gently chided his girlfriend over the Eric Cantona toy she sent me after United had beaten Liverpool at Wembley in the 1996 FA Cup final. But United did play that benefit for the victims of the Omagh bomb, and in Omagh too. You have to love them for that. Hard for me to write, but true all the same.

Two World Wars and One World Cup

Billy Bragg

The Southern *Altiplano* of Bolivia is a desolate and dusty place, a high plateau almost 12,000 feet above sea level, between the western and eastern ranges of the Andes. The houses are made the old way, dust held together with water and straw. The staple diet of the inhabitants is sweet potato and llama meat, that is if the dust hasn't ground their teeth away to stumps. In the town of Corque, they have a midsummer festival that gives them the excuse to wet their dust-dry throats.

I once attended the Fiesta de San Juan de Corque in the interests of public service broadcasting. The festivities began on a Friday afternoon when numerous brass bands converged on the town, arriving in open-top trucks, their instruments glinting in the fierce Andean sunlight. As the bands formed up and marched through the town, each was accompanied by a troupe of dancers who preceded them, three abreast, through the broad streets, performing a sort of marching line-dance, some in garish costumes, others dressed as if attending a wedding. The women were distinctive in their *chola* dress: a large skirt, a woolly jumper and a shawl over their shoulders, all topped off with a bowler hat. The one thing that the dancers had in common was that they each carried an open bottle of brown ale, which was in a constant state of overflow, due to their dipping and whirling gyrations.

There were dozens of these bands and their dancers winding around the unmade streets of the town, all converging on the main square, where the dancing and playing and drinking took on a somewhat competitive air. Some of the bands looked and sounded professional, wearing uniforms representing a local mine or factory. Others were less well turned out, but no less passionate in their playing. As the Plaza Mayor filled up, it seemed the bigger the brass, the better. Lines of trombones, french horns and tubas are quite imposing at close quarters, but nothing is as intimidating as a phalanx of sousaphones – those great big horns that coil around the upper torso before opening up like a huge golden sunflower above your head.

The overall effect would have been cacophony, were it not for the fact that all the bands were playing the same tune, over and over again. I can still hear it in my head now – it was unsettlingly close to the theme music from Spike

Milligan's *Q* series of surreal comedy shows from the late '70s. After sunset, more crates of brown ale appeared and each band set up in one part of the square, blaring away like competing sound systems, and, like a bunch of luv'd up clubbers in an Ibiza disco, the locals danced the night away to the same song over and over again. They were still drinking and dancing to Spike Milligan when I turned in for the night. The tune lulled me to sleep. And woke me up in the morning. They had not stopped once. Playing this same tune. Two minutes in duration. All day and all night long. The only thing that was missing was the appearance of a victorious Corque Utd in an open-top bus.

I was reminded of the Fiesta de San Juan de Corque recently whilst watching a documentary on The Sheffield Wednesday Kop Band and their adventures playing for England during France '98. There seemed to be certain similarities: the brass band, the dancing with a beer in your hand. Granted, there were no *chola* women to dip and twirl in their bowler hats, but the followers of the Kop Band have their strict dress code too – the compromise of colours that is the England strip.

The white shirt evokes the image of the bare-chested Englishman at home during the sunless football season. The away shirt is reminiscent of the same half-naked man 'away' on his summer holidays – a painfully sunburned red. But hang on. What about those blue shorts? Like a bowler hat on the Bolivian *Altiplano*, the colouring of those shorts appears somewhat out of place. The flag of St George is a red cross on a white background and therefore England's colours are red and white, not red, white and blue.

What subliminal message are we sending out with those blue shorts? That the Union Jack belongs to us? Look at footage of England fans during the '66 World Cup Final and you'd think so. The Scots have as much right to it as we do but you don't see them sporting red shorts with their blue shirts. Neither the Scots nor the Welsh associate the Union Jack with their sense of national identity and nor should the English – it is the flag of the British state, not of England, the country that we live in. The day may come when the United Kingdom is forced to enter a team in international competitions but until then, it's much easier to paint the English flag on your mate's face.

The thing that most reminded me of Saturday night on the *Altiplano*, however, was the fact that the Kop Band played the same annoying tune over and over again. Not the music from Spike Milligan's comedy series but the theme from *The Great Escape*. How has a snippet from Elmer Bernstein's rousing soundtrack to this 1963 movie come to represent our nation? Yes, I know all about the draw in Rome, but why has this particular one minute wonder risen above such classics as 'Here We Go' and 'Vin-da-loo' to become the most popular tune at England games?

What is it that has drawn English football fans to appropriate the mantle of this particular film? Surely it's not the acting? On the face of it, all the English actors in the movie are stereotypical officer types: rash Dickie Attenborough, obviously a rugger man; twitchy Donald Pleasance, obviously a pederast; straight-backed Nigel Stock, obviously a stuck-up bastard, and so forth. I suppose Steve McQueen offers a role model for the modern fan, although he is of course an American, which may explain why, when everyone else is in uniform, his clothes seem to come from the local Gap.

McQueen's performance as the laconic 'Cooler King' makes him the undoubted focus of attention but, if I remember rightly, it's not keepy-uppy that gets him through those frequent spells of solitary, it's baseball. No, it's neither the acting nor the plot nor the footie content that has them chanting in the stadiums, it's the context – World War Two.

For our Scottish and Welsh neighbours, the long struggle against the English oppressor is central to their sense of identity. It offers them a cultural framework within which to exact symbolic revenge for centuries of injustice. Rangers and Celtic fans will stand together when it comes to taking on the Auld Enemy. Conversely, for the English, it is their shared experience of the Second World War that binds them together in the face of opposition.

This tendency can be detected in the community singing sheets that the *Daily Express* used to print and give away during home internationals. In April 1965, when England took on Scotland at what was even then still referred to as the Empire Stadium, the Band of the Coldstream Guards played 'I Belong to Glasgow', 'Loch Lomond' and 'I Love a Lassie' for the benefit of the visiting fans. The English were happy to express themselves by singing such wartime favourites as 'It's a Long Way to Tipperary', 'Pack up Your Troubles in Your Old Kit Bag' and 'Keep Right on to the End of the Road'. Even after the watershed of the 1966 World Cup, little changed. At the same home international fixture in 1969, the contents of the *Daily Express* song sheet remained almost unchanged. Just one brief nod was given to modernity – 'Pack up Your Troubles' having been replaced by the Beatles 'Yellow Submarine'.

Did the Band of the Scots Guards play similarly suitable songs of national reference for the England fans when they travelled to Scotland? I put this question to Richard Williams, curator of the Scottish Football Museum at Hampden Park. He was kind enough to spend a couple of weeks searching through his archives looking at music mentioned in programmes from matches played against England in the '60s. A Scots band played 'Colonel Bogey' in 1960 but other than that there was no sign of 'I Belong to Glasgow' being reciprocated by 'Maybe It's Because I'm a Londoner'. They did have their own stab at modernity, though, when, in 1969, the Band of the 1st Battalion Black Watch played 'Those Magnificent Men in Their Flying Machines'.

If your grandad fought in the war and your dad stood in the Empire Stadium and sang about packing up his troubles in his old kit bag, then adopting the tune to *The Great Escape* does seem to offer a comforting sense of continuity. So many generations have passed since we last felt a genuine threat of rampaging Scots or Welsh invaders that, when faced with an external threat, our only point of reference is the Second World War. And whilst our neighbours have done so much to renounce their British birthright, it has been left to the English to find inspiration in the speeches of Winston Churchill. When it comes to post-war expressions of English national identity, all paths lead back to our 'Finest Hour'.

Maybe this is not so surprising given that any study of the history of Europe over the past hundred years gives the impression that every significant event during the first half of the century was converging towards 1940 and that everything since has been shaped by it. After the Fall of France in the June of that year, when, of all the nations that had declared war on Germany, only Britain remained unconquered, Mass Observation volunteers recorded this comment, overheard on a London bus, perhaps the earliest and most pure expression of what we now refer to as the Dunkirk Spirit: 'Well, at least we're in the final – and it's going to be played on our home ground.'

Growing up in East London in the 1960s, a fair number of my relatives still had bits of the Second World War at the bottom of their gardens, low lying objects of indeterminate shape and size, half hidden in the undergrowth, covered in tarpaulin and smelling strongly of stagnant rainwater. I get a dank whiff of it in my nostrils whenever I hear someone mention the Dunkirk Spirit.

Of all the things that our people faced and overcame in 1940-41 – the Battle of Britain, the Defence of London, the destruction of the ports and manufacturing centres – I have never understood why it should be that the evacuation of the beleaguered British Expeditionary Force became central to our received notions of national identity. That it was an incredible feat of bravery I do not dispute. What puzzles me is that, post war, we return again and again to that disaster as if it were the defining moment in our island story. In other ages, great victories were evoked when the nation was in difficulty. Yet we feel the need to constantly remind ourselves of a time when we were so ill-prepared that we were forced to abandon our friends and run back home to safety.

The humiliation of Dunkirk has been presented to successive generations as a triumph in the face of adversity. In truth, and perhaps this fact was not lost on those who accompanied England to that make or break match against Italy in Rome, what happened on those beaches still gnaws at our national psyche: a moment of glory was snatched in the face of *self-inflicted* adversity. For, beneath the shabby tarpaulin cover of the Dunkirk Spirit there lies an unanswered question: who put the safety of those 338,000 men, indeed the nation, in such mortal danger? The lessons of the summer of 1940 resonate around our football stadia to this day: it is unwise to pin our hopes on the performance of others.

During the eighteenth century, the Scots, the Welsh and the English redefined themselves as the British, a mercantile people whose society was founded on the need to increase and sustain the power of their state by constant competition with hostile rival nations. Since it is no longer vital to maintain this stance in order that our society might prosper, is it any longer necessary to keep up the pretence of being British? The growth of trans-national corporations has had the effect of reducing the nation state to little more than a geographically defined market based on local tastes. However, replacing age old traditions with consumer trends is not simply a matter of market forces.

Our High Streets are beginning to show signs of a flourishing European café culture that 50 years ago hadn't yet crossed the Channel. Until recently, however, such establishments would have been staffed by people who were only offered the lowly status of immigrant. Now, they are run by dynamic young locals serving similar fare to that found in pavement cafés in Paris, Amsterdam, Rome and Berlin. If you can judge a nation by its buying habits – and, frankly, that's as good a measure as any – we are now a casually cosmopolitan society. Despite this, it is clear that we have yet to dispense with that element of our national character that was defined by years of hostility towards rival nations.

The old bulldog bellicosity manifests itself in different ways. In its most malevolent form, it is the racism that soils the streets of our cities and the xenophobia that infects our political discourse. A milder expression can be seen in the playing out of old enmities on the football pitch. Perhaps the most benign manifestation can be found in our deep-seated and genuinely felt yearning for some form of meaningful collective endeavour. Searching for a context for such feelings, it is perhaps inevitable that, after years of watching movies like *The Great Escape*, we should draw upon the language and folk-memory of the Second World War.

In the latter half of this century, post-industrial society has tended to disperse people: emptying the factories, undermining the communities, elevating the individual. By contrast, struggle unites: war, football, the camaraderie of the Blitz, the mass emotions of the stadium. Such events allow us to submerge our individual identity, to achieve a certainty of purpose which is seldom experienced with such clarity these days.

There is a beautiful simplicity in supporting one team pitted against another. Once a week, home and away, we are able to feel and, more importantly, express emotions that most of us keep in check. We shout, sing, stand together in awestruck silence, men hug other men – practices that would mark us out for ridicule elsewhere – all done in the presence of thousands of strangers. Amongst our fellow supporters, we can see clearly what is happening before us, we know from the reactions of the crowd exactly how we feel about it and even when we are three–nil down, we feel psychologically at ease because we know that what we want as an individual is completely at one with the desires of those around us. A football match allows us to do this because it presents an event on to which a one dimensional world view can comfortably be projected free of any ambiguities.

So where does this mindset come from, that your club is superior to every other club, no matter how much evidence you may have witnessed to the contrary? Maybe you remember happier times when your team won the Cup or topped the League. Maybe someone handed those events down to you as a memory. Chances are that the way you feel about your club stems from things you learned during childhood, that the unshakeable belief that you have in them was forged then and that you are fond of disparaging the current players compared to those you recall as a child. Every team has its trophy cabinet to remind supporters of their finest hour and a half.

In order for this sense of belonging to manifest itself at international matches, local rivalries are suspended and what emerges is a beast which gets its traditions not from the trophy room but from the classroom. The history that we learned as schoolchildren provides us with our sense of superiority and offers us a glorious backdrop against which to parade our sentimental attachment to days gone by. In this form, national identity can sometimes be reduced to little more than a security blanket which insulates us from an ever-changing society, that encourages us to revisit the certainties of childhood and relive the collection of ripping yarns that we think of as history.

The way we felt about our country as a child, the pride and prejudices we learnt at school, stay deep within us and, like the players who first inspired us to support our team, these feelings take on a legendary status – we yearn for a simpler world, an innocence lost. If only we could get back to those days when we felt secure, before everything got complicated, before all these others came in and changed the rules and spoiled things for us. The way that we teach our imperial history leaves an indelible stain on our modern society. Having been brought up to believe that we should rule the world, some of our citizens have great difficulty coming to terms with the reality of Britain's post-war status.

The British have been members, in one form or another, of the European Union for a generation now, but, increasingly, it is the English alone who seem content to revel in the isolation of the nation state. In Scotland and Wales, the pro-independence parties are also pro-Europe.

However, the most successful independence party in England, the UK Independence Party, is fanatically euro-sceptic. When the possibility of a European single currency is floated, the electorate cry: 'We don't understand! Educate us.' This may shed some light on why an embarrassing 75 per cent voted Don't Know in the 1999 European elections by staying at home on polling day. Yet, no matter how much it may serve our national interest, whilst we continue to glorify the empire that used to belong to the British, it won't be easy for the English to become good Europeans. Our natural propensity for self-inflicted adversity will see to that.

Following the poor turnout at the European elections, it is becoming increasingly clear that Britain's entry into the Single European Currency will not be able to be slipped through on a wink and a nod. The government will be forced to make a positive case for the Euro if they are to convince the British people to give up sterling. A committed moderniser like Tony Blair should have no difficulty in setting out the rational arguments for joining. However, as soon as he begins to campaign, those chaps with the little golden pound signs on their lapels are going to start wrapping themselves in the Union Jack and all rational argument will go out of the window.

Right-wing columnists from the *Daily Telegraph* to *The Sun* have relied for years on a deep reservoir of popular jingoism within our society which they feel able to tap into at any time and, as a rule, politicians run scared of confronting it. They are certain of jingoism's existence and its awesome power: once unleashed, logic evaporates before it. However, events in the wake of the death of Diana, Princess of Wales, confused commentators by suggesting that the public are capable of breaking with the strict social mores of their parents' generation and rejecting tradition in favour of something closer to their own experiences. Might this be evidence of a nation willing to leave jingoism in the past? Already the bulk of the hereditary peers have been removed without a murmur of opposition from the electorate and the whole edifice of the House of Lords looks set to follow them.

In his efforts to convince a majority of us of the benefits of the single currency, Tony Blair will be forced by the Conservative press to go beyond mere euro-pragmatism. Rational economic argument alone will not overcome the emotional attachments of the 30 per cent of members of the Institute of Directors – hard-headed, no-nonsense businessmen all – who responded 'Never!' to being asked when they thought Britain should join the Single Currency. To take these people on, Blair will have to take on the folk-memory of this past century, which hinges on 1940.

If Blair has the vision and ability to inspire in the rest of us a progressive view of our common European inheritance, then we may yet witness the emergence of a new English sensibility, similar to that which has sprung up in Scotland over the past few years. North of the Border, a new type of nationalism has been inspired that appears to have replaced insularity with a sense of independence that is both inclusive and internationalist. This change has come about over the past 25 years during which the Scots felt themselves to have a different set of values to those of the British – distant rulers whose embodiment they saw in Margaret Thatcher. When the chance came to vote on whether or not they wanted their own parliament in Edinburgh, they saw the opportunity to identify themselves with something new and different. A vote for Scotland was a vote against the British.

This didn't mean abandoning their past, merely reclaiming it from the unitary state called the United Kingdom. In this way, they gave themselves a sense of belonging to a new country called Scotland. They summoned up years of history and tradition in order to give themselves the courage to vote yes. And when, by an overwhelming majority, they did, the result was a rejection of the imperial urge to be in constant competition with rival nations. Consequently, they are a people at ease with the idea of European integration.

I accept that England is a different case, but it shows what can be achieved when a society feels secure enough to put the past into perspective. And we may yet have our chance. Blair's promise of a referendum on joining the Euro will give the people of England the chance to vote for or against the British state and all that it stands for. The pound, the flag, the monarchy, the imperial legacy itself, all will be dragged into the debate by those who favour the status quo. A vote against them will give a clear sign that, whilst we respect the past, we are no longer in thrall to it.

Bewildered by the pace of reform of the House of Lords, William Hague has complained that if we follow Labour's policies, we shall wake up one day in a completely different country. Wouldn't it be good if he were proved right – and that new country was called England.

Kicking Off with the Wannabe Warriors

Gary Armstrong

> The nation – an agglomeration of people, that is, who believe themselves to share origins, loyalties and values – is the political extension of the family, itself the strongest of all social units. It is an organic, instinctive association. That it develops its own myths down the centuries does no harm. On the contrary, national myths help to evolve the collective confidence that is essential to public happiness – public tolerance, too. Patriotism is not only the last resort of scoundrels; it can also be the comfort of kind and decent people, and the best foundation of greater unities.
>
> Jan Morris, *The Observer*, 1 February 1998

The French novelist Gustav Flaubert said it better than anyone: 'Our ignorance of history makes us slander our own times. Things have always been like this.' Thus when England fans at the 1998 World Cup fought running battles in the streets of Marseilles with local French youths, North African immigrants and riot police, there was nothing particularly novel about such scenarios. The English had fought the French periodically since the 11th century and had fought on the shores of the Mediterranean against those of Islamic backgrounds since the Crusades. The football warriors of June '98 carried on one side the paraphernalia of Islam whilst their opponents gathered around garments displaying the red cross of Christianity on a white background. The big difference to bygone days was that the casualties this time around were minimal, and of the 36 England fans arrested only nine were actually charged with any offence. The English combatants numbering around four hundred over those five days in Marseilles lived to fight another day. To many English commentators, however, such men by their actions had shamed the nation in the eyes of the world.

The stock responses to similar disturbances over the previous 20 years hadn't been much in evidence after the last major public disorder outbreak associated with England fans, the 1995 disorders in Dublin. Many members of the opinionate were telling us how football hooliganism in England was finished. The new audience of top-level football – family oriented and feminised – was supposed to mean that 'the lads' and their antics were a distant memory. Then came Marseilles. The ostensible umpires for this England away fixture, the CRS French riot police tended to favour the home side; and so the alienated North African immigrant youths found a unique situation wherein they fought alongside the states' representatives, who had been responsible for the death of three of them in the preceding months. That's football really, the most unlikely loyalties can be forged in some circumstances. And so the battles raged, who knows who started it and really, who cares? Images were and remain more important than truths. The world saw cars overturned – one contained a TV camera crew who had provoked the anger of the combatants – people ran in all directions. It was noisy and messy and the senior police officer seconded from England to prevent this behaviour told the world's media that hundreds of young men were behaving like 'Category C' hooligans but the police database had no idea who they were.

The response to all of this was predictable but slightly different to previous incidents. Predictable was the sound-bite hysteria combined with hyperbole and cliché. As such it mirrored the politics of our time. Sports Minister Tony Banks described the fans as: 'A bunch of drunken, brain-dead idiots who seem determined to disgrace our country.' Following him came Home Secretary Jack Straw who explained: 'We've given the French every support they need in cracking down on the English hooligans.'

Personally, I thought the job of government was to seek to protect its citizens when abroad, not invite attacks from forces with a reputation for violence. What was totally new to previous incidents was Prime Minister Tony Blair urging English employers to sack any of those arrested and convicted if they were employees. What was also new was an alternative vision of events, which was offered by the recently deceased maverick Tory MP and historian Alan Clark and the Dowager of Reading, both of whom reflected on the English fighting with the locals and police as a compliment to an English warrior spirit. This interpretation of history was howled down in parliament and the press.

It had seemingly all gone so well until Marseilles. The pre-tournament opportunities and opportunism had given the police and the Home Secretary a lot of longed-for publicity. The latter on Christmas Day had released a story of what he was going to do to potential hooligans should they misbehave in June. Thus when the entire population sat around their screens on Boxing Day the lead story of every bulletin was an unseasonal message of threat and retribution. The same man two months later hosted an international conference in his electoral constituency attended by 100 delegates from 26 countries which informed them of English expertise in policing football hooliganism, a claim which, like the conference itself, struck me as terribly arrogant seeing as the World Cup was to be played in a neighbouring country. A month before the first game kicked off the Home Office released visual warnings to England fans thinking of attending the tournament. This extraordinary series of short but stylish adverts shown on TV during and around televised football matches cost the taxpayer £1m and in a roundabout way told fans not to travel unless they had a ticket otherwise they would be arrested and deported.

The police seized their moments as would be expected. The specialist Football Intelligence Unit and other senior officers seconded to the event told of their intelligence databases and their sophisticated system of classification of individuals in order of dangerousness (A–B–C). We learned that some individuals they knew about would not be allowed on French soil. That up to two dozen of their expert intelligence officers would be working alongside their equivalents in France and that the police in England were recognised the world over for their expertise in policing hooligans. The theatrical pre-tournament 'dawn raid' on suspected hooligans duly took place and we learned of a core of 600 leaders who were going to France to orchestrate the thousands of gullible but willing footsoldiers. Inevitably the hooligan formations were quasi-military and were of course more sinister than ever before. Closer to the first match of the tournament in a quite extraordinary move, the police gave mugshots and profiles of 24 men with previous convictions for hooliganism to the *Sunday Mirror*, which printed a centre-spread telling readers that these men were going to be the leaders of the English following and would seek to wreck the tournament. When events in Marseilles were underway the media found the 'leader' – a father of three in his early 30s, who whilst not known to police as a hooligan, had what the media required – a balding pate, a naked torso and a St George's cross tattoo. He also had handcuffs and two French policemen either side of him. He became 'The Pig of Marseilles' for the tabloids and a much repeated image for the next three weeks.

Media involvement in the build-up to an event is crucial. In England, where they are now firmly established as an extension of police public relations, the media sources unquestioningly printed what the police wanted the public to know. Given footage in April of a 'dawn raid' the media broadcast pictures of police officers in armour using a sophisticated battering ram to knock out the front door of suspected hooligans. At one level this dramatic function was understandable. It was linked to an incident in March when a 24-year-old Fulham supporter had died in an after-match tussle with rival Gillingham fans. Taking a punch he fell, banged his head on a concrete kerb and died. It was a one in a million chance and it came at a time of apprehension around the impending tournament. In practical terms however, the dawn raid was ludicrous. Why are these theatricals used? Unless the police thought suspects would abscond to a country without a mutual extradition treaty why did they not ring the suspects up and ask them to visit the station? As a result of their efforts, one man was charged with manslaughter and jailed for three years. Another ten who were arrested were only charged with minor misdemeanours yet were fined and barred from football grounds for offences ranging from swearing to gesticulating. Since when has swearing ever merited an armoured dawn entry into the suspect's home by six police officers? Other journalists got in on the act without relying on the police and followed the lead of a man who was Young Journalist of the Year in 1990 – Jocelyn Targett. Shortly before the

World Cup of Italia '90 he visited Sardinia where England were seeded to play their preliminary matches and where thousands of England fans would stay. He wrote a Sunday broadsheet story telling of the local boys awaiting the English and provided for the visitors a glossary of insults in both Italian and English, presumably for them to use. For France a similar enterprising journalist visited Marseilles months before the tournament and wrote in a Sunday broadsheet of how he discussed with local Arab youths what they were going to do with the English. A Sunday middlebrow tabloid meanwhile gave the location of a French shop where flick-knives could be bought for £7. It was sabre-rattling stuff. The same papers were inevitably 'appalled' when fighting broke out months later.

The England team did their bit at the tournament. In the face of exaggerated optimism, they lost two games and won two and so were knocked out. The tie with Argentina was the best game of the whole four weeks. Over 23 million people watched the game on TV and all bar one miscreant who got sent off were spoken of in heroic terms, but in the figure of David Beckham we had manifest the now procedural search for a scapegoat for a sporting defeat. The team had lost but they had displayed all that made an English team – guts, passion, and heart. They could not be faulted in what was a very English response – that which valued effort and style over ability and success. The England following came home with them and for some reason Marseilles was played down in the post-mortem. Maybe a week is a long time in a world of hysteria. The 40,000 followers had represented their country in the way they knew best – they drank copious amounts of alcohol in groups, sang a variety of historical and nationalist songs and faced up to and fought whoever came their way.

Our nation gave football to the world and, if one wants to follow an illogical line of argument, one could argue we thus gave the world football hooliganism. But the disorder manifest around the game the world over is not an English export; it was always there. Disorders associated with football across the globe have separate evolutions, local socio-historical antagonisms and at times specific local class and cultural antecedents. If some participants borrow English words for their gatherings or use English paraphernalia in their support, the task of analysis is not to see this as simple copying but to ask how and why local conditions were so receptive to such ideas and how they have translated them into their own fan cultures. The meanings need unpicking when in Poland, China, Yugoslavia, Morocco or Brazil. The issue as to whether our hooligans are worse than anyone else's is a non-starter. The question raises the complex problem of cross-cultural comparison. It requires a knowledge of local dynamics and it raises the question of what constitutes a 'hooligan problem' in various nations? And with it the unasked question in all of this debate: to whom exactly are the hooligans a problem?

Of course when the whole world's eyes are on the World Cup these questions gain a huge currency. The very idea of a World Cup is a celebration of nationalism which, whilst offering the chance for nations to watch each other, also encourages stereotypes and national myths. Gung-ho nationalism is even encouraged – the new tactic of intrusive cameras filming the players in pre-match formation, ensures they are somewhat forced to give their utmost in the national anthem singing. Following the English national team is an exercise in nationalism. But there are a multitude of nationalisms being played out at such tournaments. Some fans play for sympathy very well, for example, the Scots Tartan Army have, via a sophisticated and deliberate attempt to re-brand their national masculinity, become the world's footballing nice guys – yet recorded domestic crime rates show a higher level of violent assault than in England – the Danes get drunk but are never as menacing as they look. However you can usually count on the English and Germans to recreate images of militarism. Unlike fans from many countries, the English don't seem to worry themselves with being popular or enacting a kitsch version of national identity. The massed ranks of the media that await national stereotypes at these events have as their ideal the young muscular male England fan complete with bottle of beer and surrounded by similar peers. This becomes the icon of 'Englishness' to the watching world. Considered insular and hostile to locals, these followers' ignorance is presumed complete when located outside the token English pub in any city they gather. This comes overladen with ideas of taste and class but in what way does their patronising of English patterns of behaviour, albeit that of working class men, differ in principle from the English 'colonies' of the Dordogne and Tuscany? If the fans on holiday want a full English breakfast and a pint then so be it. Who's to say that this is wrong in an age of tourism apartheid, when so many organised tour groups stay safely within their own culture?

The 11 players become, at such tournaments the proxy warriors for the rest of us. And those following the team as supporters are considered to have some kind of responsibility for the national image. For those who seek to associate the game and its followers with the state of the nation, try this quick exercise. Take a look at the 32 nations who qualified for the World Cup – most of which England had either conquered, ruled or fought over the previous 400 years. Index the following categories: racial violence/discrimination, military government, wide-scale torture, lack of human rights; throw in crime rates, murder rates, the absence of democratic rights, indiscriminate shootings and bombings and even civil war. Having done this, tick the countries that can say they have in the past 30 years avoided most of these. Few countries at France '98 had a prouder record of liberty and political checks and balances than England. The Brazilians might samba for the TV cameras but at home death squads shoot their street children and the middle-class live on segregated, walled estates. The Japanese fans might be quaint and polite but the South Korean migrants' life in Japan is none too good and criminal syndicates control the government. Most countries would readily trade their social problems for the boorish England football followers.

Due to an increasing media self-interest in promoting football, the response to incidents around the game is increasingly hysterical. The English media's reporting of stories of team performances are peppered with ideas of 'battle' and 'victory' and when the opponents are Germans the journalists too go metaphorically over the top. The media set the agenda and the politicians, who need enemies to justify their existence, speak out and get their words reported knowing their condemnation of 'the hooligan' will never be challenged. There is both political and commercial gain to be made from attacking this symbol.

The problem for me is that football is given too much emphasis in the debate around national identity and national life. The significance of the game and its followers is taken out of proportion. Consider the following two incidents: the first occurs when Eric Cantona of Man Utd attempted a flying-kick on a young man who had abused him as he walked to the dressing-room having been sent off for stamping on a rival player at Crystal Palace in 1995. For this most trivial of all assaults the Metropolitan Police treated the incident like a murder inquiry. At one time ten officers were working *full time* on the case and took a total of 70 witness statements. The outcome of all this was the abuser receiving a fine of £500 and a banning from London football grounds and Cantona receiving a suspended sentence. Was there ever, in British policing history, a more detailed inquiry for common assault? Four years later, on a day people waited 24 hours in hospital casualty or died unattended on trolleys in corridors and the level of mortgage repossession rose, Tony Blair was live on the *Richard and Judy* morning TV show not to discuss these issues, but to give his comments on the utterances of the England team manager, Glenn Hoddle. The latter's reflection on re-incarnation and karma and physical and mental handicap earned him the condemnation of the Prime Minister and, shortly after, the sack. What is truth was not the issue, what is palatable was. It gets dafter. Days after the heroic victory of Man Utd over Bayern Munich in the 1999 European Cup final, one columnist, Rupert Cornwell in *The Independent*, saw the victory as giving the Prime Minister a sense of certainty in the NATO campaign in Kosovo. The result apparently being a glorious way of preparing for war!

The previous decade has seen football and politics mix metaphors and moral imperatives seemingly at will. The re-branding of football has gone hand in hand with the re-branding of the Labour party. New Labour wants a party safe for control freaks and a football audience to suit, where no one stands, shouts, smokes or sneaks in drinks. In this, New Labour are at one with a corporate culture that now dominates the World Cup. The tournament organisers and TV companies want nationalist passion at the same time as they want fans to be telegenic, sensuous, or perhaps just mildly eccentric. They don't like it when footage broadcasts the English taunting the riot police with chants of 'If it wasn't for the English you'd be Krauts'. But history won't go away. England had a good war, collaboration was barely an issue, few nations in Europe can celebrate such virtue even if it is over fifty years old. The same fans frequently chant reminders of Empire and military conquest – 'Rule Britannia', 'Land of Hope and Glory', 'God Save the Queen' and 'No Surrender to the IRA'. People might not like this but we might ask what else can the followers of an England team sing to celebrate their nation? This nation has been involved in wars every decade for the last two centuries. We don't have a single national song that is free of our past. Having an empire that the sun never set on obviously produced over the generations myths and ideas that celebrated conquering, which may explain why, during 1999, three of the top five best selling non-fiction books in Britain were about military campaigns. Many English rejoice in their willingness to fight the good fight. A standing army for 800 years which has not been at peace since 1945 must have had some impact on the national psyche. That said, there was always a binary opposite of the Englishman abroad. On one side the ideology of the English gentlemen always encompassed within it ideas of trust, incorruptibility, duty and fair play but alongside it came periodic rioting from the accompanying military, 'the poor bloody infantry' and the 'brutal licentious soldiers'.

This harking back to the past, and the glory of militarism is quintessentially English. Why do millions visit our shores? Because of their fascination with our men in obsolete military uniforms marching to battle anthems around Whitehall and Buckingham Palace. Such activities symbolise the English in the eye of these millions of tourists. From their social democracies and republics they flood to watch in awe and clap this most evident manifestation of hierarchy, obedience and militarism in Europe. Some may feign a lack of interest and favour the 'higher' culture that London offers. However, when visiting the plethora of museums that the metropolis offers, they had better not inquire too deeply how so many artefacts were obtained. The answer in most instances is the state sanctioned piracy of the high seas – imperial plunder.

Today in the absence of any political alternative it is the football team that takes on the mantle of the most obvious expression of Englishness. In recent years only the death of a princess has brought the nation together more forcefully than the English national football team. Consequently, events around football get taken out of all proportion. When England footballers are found to be drunks abroad and our fans are not aesthetically pleasing, too many people are quick to give the game and its followers the role of being the epitome of national decline. A decline that is measured against the myth that is 'Englishness' but which at the same time is ludicrous. Consider the FA official video for Euro '96; this gave visions of England drawn from a 1960s biscuit tin – thatched cottage and pubs by the river – omitting to mention that most of us live in cities and it is the late twentieth century. But even those given the task of governing us are equally ridiculous. The last General Election was preceded by John Major's now infamous vision of England which was of warm beer, cricket on village greens and old maids cycling to communion. This evocation of the early 1950s was considered good enough to inspire votes. Today the 'Cool Britannia' of Tony Blair is proving to be just as vacuous, once the hype and spin have melted away.

As the search for national meaning trundles on, football has come to represent more and more of what England should and should not be. To be a football fan is now the epitome of social form. Football is now almost impossible to avoid; the TV channels are full of live matches, there are endless documentaries and chat shows about the game, what had once been a private devotion has became a matter for celebrity status. Politicians from the Prime

Minister downwards are desperate to be associated with the game by declaring themselves 'life-long fans'. By the 1990s it was almost ill-mannered for middle-class males and females not to have something to say about the game and its players. Successive World Cup tournaments had combined the culture of the offside with that of the opera. Various books giving accounts of self-deprecating 'laddishness' permitted the articulation of those who were ashamed to be football fans in the 1980s or wished to recall their hooligan near-misses. Thanks to all of this the 'Hooligan' took on a greater demonology than ever as the game became a tool in the late twentieth century 're-branding' of English identity and consequently part of the electoral campaign of New Labour with Tony Blair photographed with Kevin Keegan and Alex Ferguson and borrowed the 'Football's Coming Home' cry replacing it with 'Labour's . . .'

Of course what exactly the football hooligan represents depends entirely on the diagnosis offered for the hooligan 'disease'. He is as functional to our society as dragons, sorcerers and Communists were to other times and cultures. Who really knows a hooligan? More important is that we think we know him. The hooligan is synonymously linked with other pejorative groups, such as 'yobs', 'thugs' and 'lager louts', and is considered as an outward manifestation in an inner decay. A crucial part of the demonising process is the presumed absence in the observers of any of the attitudes they abhor among those under scrutiny, even though they share the same country and are at times part of the same culture. For these observers, however, the young male working-class football fan is an icon of horror for which all right-thinking people feel revulsion. Described and explained away by the mainly middle-class authorities of media, police, politicians and the predictable, media-loving academics, 'hooligans' – often synonymous with all young male working-class fans – do not walk, they 'swagger', whilst some appal those observers by various vulgarities; shouting in public; drinking alcohol from cans! Sometimes, in warmer climes, they will look neither chic nor elegant as they expose pale and flabby skin and that symbol that stigmatises the lower orders – the tattoo. They have, apparently, according to academic experts, missed the 'Civilising Process' evidenced otherwise throughout the rest of the world, strange really when one considers this is the century of Total War. Revulsion in such circumstances at times is as much aesthetic as it is socio-political.

But these young men are clad in clothes of Europe and North American designer houses, they drink European-brewed beers, smoke North African hash, and were intermittently dancing to a tune released for the World Cup in celebration of England's new national dish – an Indian sub-continent speciality by the name of vindaloo. Are such lads really the personification of Little Englanders? To some they are but herein lies a deeper issue. Contemporary England may be pursuing internationalist credentials but still the football hooligan instils fear into many middle-class observers as the icon of a white working class. Their behaviour and presence demonstrates the frailty of social control. From what they realise is a highly precarious social position these onlookers need targets of abomination. Their unreasoned fear of the activity of the 'mob', another very English trait, as a dangerous collective, is a result of the increasing isolation and atomisation of the middle class. Increasing insecurity caused through cultural uncertainty, rising unemployment, loss of faith in church and state, the privatisation of welfare services that were to protect from cradle to grave, and other political processes have all helped to generate unfounded concerns about victimisation that have little objective reality.

English society was never free of either the revelries or the incivilities of young men. In the past we transported the recalcitrant or had an empire and army to put them out of harm's way. We had the turmoil of 'Merrie England', the Apprentice Riots, Town and Gown disorders and industrial disorder on a massive scale. We might have an occasionally green and pleasant land, but riot and disorder is also part of the social history of England. The problem has been to keep such contradictory forces in perspective. Between 1945 and the late 1960s we were living in a 'Tradition-bound society', normalised by local residence and marriage patterns, occupational inheritance and family networks that were constraining of individualism. However, these social patterns changed because of increased social and geographical mobility, new employment patterns, increasing unemployment, new technologies and trans-national media influences. In the past male identity was largely derived from the work situation, but this has lost its gender specificity as many former 'macho' industries and occupations have declined or died. Male socialisation norms via occupational life patterns have consequently declined and unemployment has meant an absence of the disciplines of labour. Today, the ethos of work status is less important and has given way to the individualistic criterion of status being related simply to the amount of money earned. To millions of others, tradition has been replaced by the vagaries of economic survival.

Outside of the workplace is where many seek alternative excitements to fill the gap; such leisure time permits challenges and creativity. Beyond our worktime activities many of us share in cultures of risk. How this risk-taking and ordeal construction is chosen is often dependent on economic resources, or what is locally or socially available. Some climb mountains, some take white-water canoe holidays, some go off-piste skiing, or holiday in war-zones; others walk along roads in pursuit of rival football fans: their equivalents in age, appearance and attitude. What such gatherings provoke and provide is the pursuit of the indefinable 'crack', 'buzz'; basically, enjoyment and uncertainty, as the individual confronts the drama. We enjoy the danger yet we know the excursion is usually to a known edge and are aware of the return route. Fun is no longer confined to relaxation or amusement, but is evident in any search for identity – and can vary from banal amusement to cults, poses and bizarre dramas. Taken to extremes, the risk in football hooligan dramas contains elements of the sublime in that it can be terror-producing. Such activities allow an individual to explore personal, social, cultural and physical limits, and just as importantly allow for innovation. For in the pursuit of such movement, various selves can be gathered, gain credit or, in turn, be discredited. Such events cannot be harnessed into 'good causes' – regulated they then lose their appeal. They defy structure and are not quasi-military or conducive to orchestration and leadership, rather such gatherings, like the nation, are organic and instinctive associations.

In such activities people can pursue *collective* activities they would probably consider repugnant if practised alone, and participants can enjoy the journey or voyage from superficiality into fantasy. To be a hooligan-participant is inherited, narrated, interpreted and enacted differently at the everyday level by constantly changing participants. And the social dramas they enact renew the desired values and norms the participants hold or aspire to. Such dramas achieve a communion between disparate individuals as they pursue achievement and selfhood. The company of the like-minded therefore provides emotional ties of shared ordeals, the pursuit of reputation in a contest underpinned by ideas of honour and shame enacted in the course of seeking a masculine reputation. These values are seen and enacted daily throughout England and indeed the world over, there is nothing particularly 'English' or indeed 'football' about them. Millions however, cannot understand this and so prefer to attribute disorder down to fascist orchestration or prefer to label the participants as morons.

Football support generally *and* football hooliganism both contain elements of rebellious carnival. This carnival combines elements of excess, laughter, degradation and offensiveness as well as risk to produce a world lying outside and beyond that preferred by officialdom. Carnival is disrespectful, it opposes the powerful and ridicules the self-important guardians of propriety; this is its appeal. Its English origins lie in the histories of non-conformism, riot and disorder and self-deprecatory humour. In recent decades carnival is evident around excessive consumption of alcohol and illicit drugs. Never before in English history are the under-40s so informed about alcohol and drugs yet millions 'abuse' the former and half a million take the latter every week. Such people are not stupid, they know what they are doing even if they cannot explain why. The same applies to England's football followers – they might not be telegenic but most are not fooled by the corporate-fest that is both the World Cup and international club football. Not for them the feigned eccentricity of the 'Mexican Wave'.

The level of suspicion and ability to resist orchestration manifested by England followers is in part a result of living in a society governed by a range of regulations far beyond those necessary for an orderly existence. We have a contemporary obsession with safety. Enslaved by ideas of rationality, technology and economic systems we suffer a loss of creativity and experience disenchantment; our emotions become repressed. Epics of struggle and heroism are excluded from daily life and from the social construction of self-identity. However, repression inevitably seeks release in alternative outlets, and that which is denied becomes the most hotly pursued. With modern-day consumer lifestyles increasingly lacking any sense of danger or ordeal, the issue becomes one of transcending monotony. Consequently, many urban dwellers seek to escape drudgery by creative self-expression in spontaneous group association or partisan spectating. Such activities when manifested around football create a comradeship of fellow fans, but is double-headed; for in-group friendship is linked to hostility to others. Who gets drawn into this association or the circumstances under which they meet – like the precise role of 'enemy' – can vary considerably. In this process, fan/hooligan gatherings became free from convention and cliché, and as in 'Carnival', such activities – although liberating and progressive – could go beyond 'meaning' and drift into excess.

The appearance of football hooliganism as we have known it in the past 30 years coincided with the end of National Service and was thus part of an era of change, when horizons for young men altered dramatically. From 1961, young men were no longer conscripted into the military, and the state no longer planned their lives for two years; or controlled their bodies to the extent that it had the right to send them off to die. With the ending of empire and the 'civilising process' of imperialism, there was no way now to legitimise and applaud state-controlled violence. Meanwhile, young men continue to do what generations of their peers have done, and get involved in disorder – albeit in new and different arenas. In the circumstances, it becomes almost ironic to reflect that compared to the way their forefathers conquered by pursuing mayhem, the acts of the hooligan pale into insignificance. This is so often forgotten in debates about national and masculine identity.

The political Left are traditionally perturbed by patriotism, but like racism it is a cross-class phenomenon. They therefore dislike English football followers because they are the most obvious manifestation of patriotism. Whilst fringes of the far-right do attend national team games and some do make *Sieg Heil* gestures, what we see manifested by the majority is a form of contextual opposition which is not embodied in any deep-rooted philosophy. Some observers seek causation for all this in gender and find the characteristics associated with elements of masculinity excessive and inappropriate. The 'yob' and the football fan – the terms become interchangeable – become a metaphor and symbol of most of the ills of English society. Yet extremes of male behaviour are still at work in the City, in the police, in the media and in most other professions. The discredited male however becomes the fall-guy at the end of an era of what is somewhat myopically identified as a period of progress and reason; for, as the dissenting voice of feminist Rosalind Coward points out, the icon of the yob: '. . . is carrying the weight of masculinity which, for a variety of reasons, middle-class society finds increasingly unacceptable, and rhetorically dumps on to the men of the lower class. He is the classic scapegoat; lugging around the sins of our culture while the rest of us look sanctimoniously on.' In a society which has never before been so uncertain, many male characteristics have become an unwelcome reminder of a past which, following the social changes that swept the western world from the 1960s, now hold little kudos. In this situation, Coward's 'men of the lower class' can be narrowed down to the 'football hooligan', who is perhaps the most significant symbol that epitomises, for many English, disorganised society, a symbol that is reaffirmed, ritualistically, by condemnation and legislation. Society might do well not to condemn out of hand those young men who like to fight, and who prefer action as a substitute for thought. For the ability to be introspective is a luxury not available to everyone, and leaves us with a group who, in the past, have often been prepared to fight at great risk against what others define as evil, who are then suddenly 'our brave lads' come the Falklands, the Gulf War and now the Kosovo crisis. Then again, with the growth in private security, those same sections of society who use the terms 'thug' and 'yob' so liberally might do well to realise it is often those young men with these same personal and physical proclivities in their role of security guards who allow them to sleep so well at nights.

We should be wary of the consequences of the law-and-order society that has developed since 1979. The overt growth in police public-order tactics from the 1980s are an example of 'Empire coming home', so that the colonial tradition of policing is now part of domestic tactics. The tactics normally associated with despised totalitarian regimes have become commonplace around football matches – mass surveillance, body searches, random photography, restriction of movement, undercover plain-clothes officers listening to conversations they define as conspiratorial, and show trials presented and accepted by an un-questioning media. What was traditionally a policing task aimed at preserving tranquillity now aims to identify those involved with a view to retrospective arrest and prosecution. The eye of the police camera lens objectifies and masters, it maintains a distance but is unforgiving. The police and policy makers can now operate within the philosopher Heidegger's definition of technology: a way of arranging the world so that one does not have to experience it. Such surveillance reflects the way police now seek to combine motivation with observable behaviour and to this end formulate predictive behaviour sequences in training seminars. As surveillance expands so do the aims of policing units. As a consequence the net that defines 'hooliganism' is ever widening. Those who are considered perpetrators are 'known' to police by their database dossiers. Some have no convictions but are recorded because they have the *potential* in police eyes to commit criminal acts and legislation is now being drafted to enforce preventative custody of people without a criminal record but considered hooligans according to police intelligence. This is the home of Tomlaine and John Stuart Mill. But who sees the irony of the full power of the state dedicated to containing those who are the most patriotic and who sing the National Anthem with a gusto not evidenced anywhere else in contemporary England?

Most societies tend to operate by forming competing moralities. The problem is to decide if the one that claims to have right on its side has any legitimacy. Such a claim depends on a recognised bounded community that is accepted as the norm; and this creates difficulties of identification. Where does this norm lie today? In the light of a drift towards social plurality, it is difficult to suggest there is a consensus – and even if this could be claimed, can we determine exactly where its moral and social boundaries lie? The split in moralities is enormous and is growing, and if politicians fail to provide moral leadership then moral strictures will emerge as an alternative. While our Home Secretary shows his toughness by jailing children or placing curfews on them, or by threatening single mothers and inevitably football hooligans, he might seek to address a target population whose behaviour is extremely destructive towards ideas of citizenship and consensus – the very rich. There is now a small élite who have the ability to manipulate information in pursuit of loyalties that exist for them at a global rather than a local or even national level. We have seen a moneyed élite eschew the public services through privileged access to private education, private health care and private pension schemes. Their successful acquisition of wealth has made their residences and their social habitats increasingly fortified, watched over and separated from the majority. As trans-nationalism and communications technology has seemingly reduced the size of the world, so their attachments to any national or local framework of obligations or to those who might have less, have weakened. Theirs is a disruptive form of citizenship encompassed in an attitude that helps nobody but themselves. Maybe this is why football has suddenly become so popular amongst the wealthy and social aspirants. In an era of rampant individualism football promises images of 'community' and offer those without a culture a fiction of collective life.

Like morality, Englishness defies definitions. Being English is enshrined in various identities based on history, family, region and class. If a national characteristic of the English is sought then 'pragmatism' will do as well as most. In contemporary politics we combine pragmatism with intellectual ideas. Thus, faced with a directionless youth and the contemporary crisis over what works in the judicial system, both the political Left and Right seem to have joined hands in punitive solutions to 'disorder'. As social disintegration moves on apace, we look at who to blame, whilst appealing to 'decency'. And in the absence of an agreed norm consensus, we hear the Right and Left parading their slogans, both of which are attempts to find something cohesive in a changing world. From the Tories we heard of 'Back to Basics' – a cry not much different from the Left's vision of a cure for society's ills founded in some half-formulated idea of communitarianism, which ignores the reality of a fragmented Britain and atomised population. When only nostalgia remains, there is seemingly no effective solution to the basic problem of what can keep us all together. The collective confidence essential to public happiness does not seem to be evident in contemporary England.

A new Labour government meanwhile introduces a curriculum so that citizenship can be taught to all children attending school in England with the stated aim of reinforcing pride in our cultural traditions and heritage. One of the aims of such a curriculum is to challenge anti-social behaviour and racial discrimination. Should this intellectual idea not work well, the government is also building 22 more prisons whilst we already house the highest number of prisoners in our history and the most per capita in the whole of Europe. The curriculum will inevitably speak of peace and ethics, but almost certainly won't question the role this nation plays in the international arms trade. When ethics compete with trade the latter usually wins. This is pragmatic but presents an intellectual problem: to find the men who really shame the name of England, attend an international arms bazaar. There you will see men who, free from the trappings of police surveillance or condemnation from the government, export weapons of mass destruction to today's friends, who invariably and ironically turn out to be tomorrow's foes.

In an era lacking in grand narratives, dominated by powerful corporations, riddled with irreconcilable forces of culture and materialism, appeals to patriotism and displays of disorder such as 'kicking off' around football will continue. At the same time, we have to accept that if men manifest violence in one arena, namely football, it is not necessarily a defining characteristic that permeates their life, neither is it especially English. We have also to realise that patriots and brawlers can also manifest kindness and decency – the hooligan is always the boy you don't know, never the one you do. And history teaches us that the arenas and personnel that provide for violent disorder, patriotic or not, change but the loyalties and values they encompass remain. Whilst the self-appointed forces of good will continue to claim to have 'cured' those they consider the scoundrels of Perfidious Albion, there always remains the land called 'abroad' to host occasions that celebrate shared origins, loyalties and values which many young Englishmen take comfort in. The public mood, however, is not tolerant but we need ask those who pontificate and rage what precisely is your world vision, and what kind of England do you wish to live in?

The author is extremely grateful for comments made on a draft of this chapter by Mark Perryman, Dr Rosemary Harris and Dr Roger MacNally.

Lads Will Be Lads

Liz Crolley

More women are being lured into football than ever before. Is this a welcome development and has it affected the atmosphere inside grounds? Is the presence of women eroding the values of football culture as we know it? Have women cleansed football of its hooligan image? What role, if any, does 'laddism' play in influencing football culture? To what extent do patterns of support following England mirror those occurring within the domestic game? A glance at the pages of the national press, or articles in the football magazines, fanzines and books tells us of the range of issues surrounding the game currently debated. With the football business booming across the continent, so we see football encroach into the financial sections of the Sunday broadsheets and onto the front halves as well as the back halves of the national press. Yet, the question of gender remains a relatively silent topic within football. Where attempts have been made to draw attention to the relevance of gender issues in football, it has usually been within the context of examining notions of masculinity and football, and sometimes with reference to masculinity and notions of nationalism. The sister issue of sexism in football has been much less debated. Refreshing exceptions of the likes of Anne Coddington's *One of the Lads* and Sue Lopez's *Women on the Ball* and occasional features such as those in publications like *When Saturday Comes* have been sporadic but have helped raise awareness of the issues. Most of the post-Hornby boom in football writing based on fans' experiences relies on a notion of football as a masculine sport, dominated by masculine values, and in particular those which draw on concepts of nationalism.

As football settles into a revolutionised post-Hillsborough culture with so-called 'traditional fans' – white, working-class male locals – disillusioned with their largely unsuccessful attempts to resist change and the emergence of 'New Fans' who've been latching onto football, especially since Euro '96, attracted by the new image of football – the relative comfort of seats, improved facilities at grounds, wearing colours, the welcoming of families – the whole relationship between football and society is being re-evaluated. While old-style fans bemoan the loss of the more positive values involved in terrace culture – the collectiveness, the spirit of camaraderie, the spontaneous wit – others look more positively at the changes and observe that football is no longer a hotbed of nationalism, racism, violence, closed-minded parochialism and machismo. Or is it? To what extent has football really become 'feminised'? Has 'laddism' set back any potential trends?

There are highly complex, occasionally contrasting trends in process as far as football and the gender order is concerned. First, it seems that patterns which emerge in domestic football are not necessarily reflected in following the national team, England, where the added ingredient of nationalism has ramifications which affect the gender issue. Second, concentrating on developments taking place in the 1990s, there are two apparently contradictory movements. While English football grounds can generally appear more female-friendly than in the previous decade, there is at the same time an increasing resentment of female fans by a vocal minority.

Traditional gender roles are often reinforced by football. Some of the qualities admired most in players and fans alike are the competitiveness, the solidarity, the aggression and the stamina typically considered as masculine and highly valued in a patriarchal society. Unwritten rules of masculinity have dictated the behaviour of football fans – and players – for a long time. Eric Dunning, Pat Murphy and John Williams in *The Roots of Football Hooliganism* provide a detailed exploration of the links between football fans and theories of working-class male aggression. The fact that men are more aggressive than women, it is argued, is part of the male socialisation process. This link between maleness and aggression becomes a key ingredient in the construction of the English national image.

It has been socially acceptable for people to behave in a certain way at a football match, a manner in which they would not usually behave elsewhere. As football fans we have been able to indulge in extremely aggressive, violent, racist and sexist behaviour and language without threat of retribution. Tempers are more easily frayed at football and hence there has always been a certain sympathy with people 'just getting a bit carried away' at a football match. Men who felt uncomfortable in this environment were often put off from going to football matches. When I was at school if a lad wasn't totally obsessed with football he had to pretend he was if he wanted to avoid the stigma of being labelled as either effeminate or just a bit weird. For a girl to enjoy football or even to condone the behaviour was seen as 'unfeminine' to say the least and was incomprehensible to many.

There are pressures on females not to behave in a masculine way. Equally there are pressures on male football fans to behave in an overtly masculine way. Homophobia creeps in as an extension of the pressures to assert masculinity. On the terraces – and in the stands – the ultimate insult is to question masculinity. Sabo and Messner in *Whose Body is This?* refer to how 'homophobia serves to enforce the traditional gender roles, thereby reinforcing male hegemony'. To call a footballer 'a tart' or 'a woman', or worse still, to question his heterosexuality, is a huge insult.

Despite progress in the women's game, football is still largely perceived as being a sport played by men, for men, and masculine, heterosexual values prevail. But it doesn't have to be. Despite the fact that we hear 'It's a man's game' reverberate around football grounds every weekend, there is nothing intrinsically masculine about football. Indeed, in the US it is viewed as something of a namby-pamby, non-contact, non-physical, 'girlie' sport. Its strength and popularity among girls and women in the US was demonstrated when the US won the Women's World Cup held there in July 1999, regularly attracting crowds of 70,000 to 90,000, benefiting from sponsorship deals and enjoying considerable media hype. Yet in England we are culturally conditioned to believe that football is not for women. The fact that football is viewed as a 'man's game' is down to the socialisation process, based on unfounded yet commonly held beliefs about gender-appropriate sports.

So has football become more female-friendly? Has it become 'feminised'? To what extent has football evolved in recent years in terms of the gender balance? On the one hand, approval of football in the eyes of the 'New Man' of the 1990s has become apparent. Football is no longer sneered at from above as being a working-class sport as it has been embraced by the middle classes and become 'gentrified'. Football is fashionable across social groups and isn't perceived as being simply the working-class man's game. On the other hand, however, we sense a rejection of these changes by some of the more traditional fans, a backlash to the infiltration of 'New Fans' into our precious sanctuary.

It is undeniable that things are changing within the English game. It has become less of an oddity to see female fans, either in the presence of male family or friends, or in female groups. There are fewer overt signs of hostility towards us. There are fewer taunts when the tea ladies go past. Even irritating cheerleaders often get away with nothing more than a few wolf whistles. Female stewards only get a reaction at away games. The establishment of all-seater grounds has made the policing and control of individual behaviour in large crowds much easier. Whereas pre-Hillsborough anyone could shout racist chants, grope the odd young girl, even throw a few punches, safe in the knowledge that they could make their escape in the crowd if necessary – rarely was such behaviour given social acceptability – today this is much more difficult. The physical presence of seats makes such conduct harder to accomplish, and individuals are more easily identifiable. Hence it is not surprising that some of the raw edges of terrace culture have worn away. But has there been a helping hand?

There has been much talk of the feminisation of football. The term 'feminisation' really came into use in the post-Heysel period of the late 1980s when the promotion of football among women was seen as a step to eradicate violence from the football terraces. Women were being exploited for the moral well-being of football. Later, in the build-up to Euro '96, football was promoted through women's magazines in a deliberate attempt to attract female support. The more cynical might suggest that since half the population is female, it is in the interests of football clubs to attract female support. Clubs could potentially double the demand for their product if they managed to woo the women –

without, that is, losing too many men in the process. They could then sell more merchandise and raise prices even higher knowing there was increased demand.

Most clubs actively encourage family support, as do England – sponsors are keen to promote football in the women's magazines and every issue of every women's magazine in the period surrounding Euro '96 and France '98 carried articles on football. This gradual encroachment into the territory of the traditional fans, began with families segregated from 'traditional' areas. It is now developing into a more integrated approach in which all fans can sit anywhere. This is cause for concern for the likes of best-selling author Dougie Brimson who complains: 'As a bloke I want to watch the game with other blokes not with loads of wives, girlfriends, mums and kids. That's one of the reasons why I love going to football, to get away from all that and now there will be no escape . . . These people are coming into my environment, an environment I have grown up with, and therefore they should respect my wishes, not the other way around.' His verbal attacks on women are scathing and the foreword to his book, *The Geezer's Guide to Football*, reads: 'If it's political correctness you want, or if you're the type of person who thinks females have as much right to walk into a football ground and stand on the home end as any male, you can piss off right now. This book is not for you. I make no apologies for saying that it's sexist, abusive, ageist and élitist.' I very nearly threw the book down in disgust, but since I reckoned that that was probably precisely what he would want me to do, I read on. Quite disturbingly I discovered I related to quite a few of the points he made concerning the domestic game – the dismissive attitude towards armchair 'supporters', glory hunters and 'New Fans'; replica shirt-spotting while out shopping – every time I'm in town I check Liverpool shirts outnumber Everton by at least five to one; tales of pre- and post-match pub routines and away travel on football specials and, post-Heysel, by coach.

It is easy to understand the accusation that female fans are 'feminising' football, diluting and eroding its unique atmosphere with our 'refined' ways. Female fans are usually lumped together and perceived as fickle glory-hunters, part-time supporters or worse, as slags or girlies who just go to look at the footballers' legs – although I'm not sure there are many men who actually believe this. In fact, there is diversity among the female fans who go to football just as there is among male fans. There is far more to feminisation than an increase in the number of female fans at football.

As football in the 1990s became more attractive and fashionable to the more affluent sectors of society it underwent a process of gentrification, and along the way it has lost some of those characteristics which identified football as a 'man's game'. Football has been marketed in such a way that it has attracted different types of fans, including some from social backgrounds not formerly associated with producing keen football fans. These are the fans who are sometimes termed 'New Fans'. Football has at the same time undergone a minor revolution which has changed forever the nature of football supporting. The effect has involved a change in the ambience of grounds to a less overtly masculine atmosphere within both the domestic game and on a national level at home games.

'Feminisation' is often quoted as the source of the change and women are usually blamed for it, which is hardly surprising given the nature of the assertion. It is also unfair. It shouldn't be surprising if a greater proportion of females at football dilute the atmosphere of masculinity, but surely the extent to which this happens depends on the types of women attracted to football, and also the type of men. Admittedly there exist some females who are casual supporters – just as there are male casual supporters – and there are also those who object to overtly masculine behaviour such as violent and abusive language, but there are also those who 'enter into the spirit' and can be just as 'macho' as the men. It is also over-simplistic to assume all men are the same highly committed die-hards who turn aggressive as soon as things stop going their way. Not all are like this. There has also been a change in the type of male fan at football. Many nowadays, especially those who were brought up in the 'violent era' of the early '80s, have either outgrown such behaviour or reserve it for very special occasions and specific grudges only. Others are committed pacifists anyway and hardly raise their voices at the referee never mind turn aggressive towards fellow football fans. Others, sadly, and perhaps this is the real source of regret, simply don't care enough to get worked up. Perhaps it is the men who have become feminised and this is the real disappointment to those traditionalists who lament the feminisation of football. It is quite possible for men to lack those qualities which defined masculinity in the traditional sense, and also for men to display qualities which have traditionally been considered to be feminine qualities. It is these changes to the nature of support which traditionalists – male and female alike – begrudge. While some football fans might consider a display of verbal, even physical, aggression as a pleasurable indulgence and view it as an essential ingredient of the football experience, others simply want to go and watch football, passively. I must admit this is something of a mystery to me, how or why any fan can go to football and sit silently for the whole game. Why don't they just watch it on television? They want to savour the atmosphere without contributing to it. Little wonder that they are resented.

It is the presence of so many new types of supporters at football matches which has led to a backlash. 'Traditional' fans feel threatened by the presence of these 'New Fans'. I believe that although female fans are often resented, it is the 'New Fan' who is the real enemy of traditional fans. So who are these 'New Fans'? No one really knows. Not surprising, since no one actually admits to being one. Of course, the majority of 'New Fans' are probably male, but the most *visible* group is female. The traditional fans feel the game as they once knew it slipping away from them and becoming something else, no longer representing what it did before, no longer being a refuge where they could let off steam and bond with (usually male) friends. A way of attempting to claw back some of this loss is by ridiculing and belittling the newcomers, but all of them – male or female – do not share the same notions of masculinity as traditional 'lads' and are largely responsible for the feminisation, or rather the de-masculinisation, of football.

At the same time as this process is taking place, it has become fashionable to air deliberately provocative, 'politically incorrect' views regarding women and football. It is part of the trend sometimes referred to as 'laddism'. Laddism is an artificial concept, an attempt to label a phenomenon which is as difficult to define and elusive as its predecessor the 'New Man'. It involves a societal trend or fashion which promotes an image of males who deliberately aspire to being as 'politically incorrect' as possible. Laddism is often espoused by middle-class men who are conscious of their decision to be outrageously, provocatively, and supposedly ironically, sexist and racist. The 'New Lad' is a reaction against the 'New Man' of the late 1980s, the supposedly feminised, caring, 'New Man' who was prepared to undertake roles traditionally considered as female such as housework or childcare. According to Ben Carrington, 'The New Lad was a partial reversion back to the traditional "laddish" masculinity of old, although the new lad was now supposed to have accepted the basic claims of feminism and so any ironic behaviour, gestures or actions that appeared to be sexist were now deliberately ironic and not meant to be taken literally.'

Dougie Brimson's portrait of a 'geezer' owes much to laddism. Among other attributes a 'geezer' is unequivocally and proudly sexist. This particular bastion of manhood appeals to those men who find it difficult to cope with women as equals and recoil into the safety of their male world. 'A geezer is, to put it simply, a male of the species who has managed, through fair means or foul, to resist the oppressive influences of the female race. Confident and proud to the point of arrogance, a geezer will, above all, remain loyal to his sex, his mates and his chosen football club.'

Laddism is epitomised by television programmes such as Skinner and Baddiel's *Fantasy Football* and Nick Hancock's *They Think It's All Over* in which risqué comments, often with overtly sexual overtones, are turned into jokes and the viewer is left unsure as to whether or not the jokes are made tongue-in-cheek. In a sense it represents a certain nostalgia for an era before the gender roles merged, before women encroached into another bastion of patriarchal society. Unfortunately the irony and tongue-in-cheek nuances supposedly encapsulated in the 'New Lad' are often lost and the fact that some high-profile presenters make blatantly sexist remarks creates a fashion in which others legitimise a more simplistic and blatant sexism that so often takes place in football grounds. I don't believe that the sexism within football grounds has its roots in laddism, although the phenomenon has probably contributed to the perpetuation of sexist taunts and behaviour. Laddism has served merely to legitimise and increase the social acceptability of such behaviour among males.

So bearing in mind parallel trends of the gentrification of football and 'laddism', has football really become more female-friendly? There is no doubt that clubs have publicised their attempts to rid the game of some of its worst characteristics, in particular racism and violence. Fans, clubs and players have joined forces to some extent to combat racism in football, via, for example, the 'Let's Kick Racism Out of Football' and 'Kick It Out' campaigns. Les Back, Tim Crabbe and John Solomons have demonstrated through their research that although far from being eradicated from football institutions, anti-racism has progressed much further than the anti-sexism. Prior to these campaigns in the mid-1980s clubs were forced to tackle violence and enjoyed some success in expelling violence from football grounds. Nowadays violence is no longer an essential ingredient of masculinity. The new generation of football fans from all backgrounds are not as interested in hooliganism.

Women are now involved at every level of the game as administrators, players, fans and journalists. Anne Coddington's recent contribution to football writing *One of the Lads* details the presence of women at every level, in all aspects of the sport but despite strides taken by individual women, and despite an increased presence of women in grounds, ultimately, the image of football as being a male sport remains undiminished.

Attempts to make football more female-friendly have been sporadic and poorly targeted. Research seems to suggest that women who like football but don't go to football matches are put off by high prices and the fact that they still carry the burden of family responsibilities which occupies their time. Women do not tend to be discouraged by abusive or aggressive language, though they are intimidated by the threat of violence. Neither do they relish being singled out for being different from the rest of fans. Few clubs address all these issues and although significant changes have been experienced over the last decade in particular, football is lagging behind other aspects of society in terms of equality of opportunity and acceptance of females into the environment.

Whereas we can at least witness an evolution taking place in the make-up of football on a domestic level, and certainly some changes in the atmosphere within English football grounds, we cannot find evidence of such widespread changes when it comes to following the national team abroad. There is a notable difference between England's support at home and away. Where the national team is concerned, the atmosphere of nationalistic fervour that can prevail has not necessarily been diluted by 'feminisation'. Partly a legacy of old imperialist values of supremacy and domination, and partly rooted in nostalgic glorification of the military successes of the English male, whatever the source, there is a close link between nationalism and masculinity. Images of England fans abroad transmitted via the pages of newspapers or in post-France '98 diary accounts are consistently images of men. We hear of 'lads' everywhere. Whenever there is trouble, groups drinking or singing, whether they are 'our lads', that is, English, or 'local lads', they are always 'lads'.

The image of following England, especially abroad, has changed slower than that of the domestic game, if indeed it has changed at all. It is not unusual for trends at the national level to differ fairly radically from those that exist on a local level. There exists a mythical notion of Englishness which it seems you are forced to assume when following England. This English image is one of a patriotism bordering on xenophobia; of male lager louts who believe themselves to be a superior race, prepared to fight to maintain their image. Although there is some resentment of this image, and in particular of the media's one-sided coverage of any incidents involving England fans abroad, travelling away with

England does generate a certain solidarity and spirit of 'comrades against all odds'.

The English press chooses to perpetuate this myth and those back home often believe what they read. The image of England's support presented by the media perpetuates a one-dimensional notion of national identity which depicts the England fan abroad as being a violent thug, an image which is decidedly unappealing to 'New Fans'.

However, this image is a simplistic vision of reality. While it is undeniable that the make-up of England fans abroad differs widely from those watching games played at Wembley, to anyone who has travelled to see England play away in recent times, it is obvious that the fans do not constitute a homogeneous group. They are not all lager-swilling drunks with tattoos, beer bellies and shaven heads. They do not all strut arrogantly assuming a superiority complex over 'foreigners' and insulting or belittling anything foreign. They do not all travel in large groups of young males. There is a mixture of social types. Some travel alone or in twos. Some go unnoticed and quietly sit in bars in side streets supping a glass of beer, or even a coffee, blending in with the locals. It is, however, still relatively rare to see family groups, rare to see women at all, and practically unheard of to see women-only groups. So although not all England fans can be boxed off as being the same type, there does appear to be more in common among England supporters than is the case in the domestic game and the role of masculinity remains strong. There are several factors which contribute to this feature of England's support.

The fact that the press report on England fans' experiences abroad in such a negative manner, exaggerating the violence, ignoring any positive features and reinforcing the stereotype of the English hooligan, discourages 'New Fans' from travelling. The consequence of this is that of those who do travel abroad there is a higher concentration of people who don't mind the possibility of trouble. The image of England fans is then in danger of becoming a self-perpetuating myth.

In order to follow any football team abroad a higher level of commitment is required than that necessary to stimulate home support. This is as true with England as it is with any other club. In the case of England, as away games are always abroad, and therefore more expensive and time-consuming, only a small proportion of England fans will be tempted to travel. In addition, for many football fans, their commitment lies at club level rather than with the national team. Some who might be prepared to make sacrifices for their clubs will not do so for their country. Even for many England fans for whom a trip to Wembley is a welcome day out, the time, the expense and additional hassle involved in trying to get hold of tickets for an away game is simply not worth it. Hence, the highly committed will form the bulk of the England support abroad. This sounds logical enough, but it is extremely significant in that dedicated England fans differ from fans with close links with their local team in that they feel a strong sense of patriotism or nationalism. They usually feel something for the rather vague notion of nationhood associated with being English. So when they are abroad they feel they are representing their country, a country in which many feel great pride.

These often latent feelings of patriotism can be exaggerated when abroad, on foreign soil, mixing with others of a similar disposition. The concentration of nationalistic fervour is often a short step away from a belief in the supremacy of the English as a race, and intolerance of other races. One key way in which this is demonstrated is by proving masculinity via physical, quasi-military prowess. Eddy Brimson explains it in *Tear Gas and Ticket Touts* as: 'What most people, coppers and politicians don't get is that when you're away with England you're on duty. Every day, every minute . . . we didn't let our country down. We proved to the world again just who the top dogs are. England turned up and did a job. Not like the Germans, the Dutch or the Italians who shit out, and that's how you show the rest who's top.' The temptation to gloat over off-the-pitch battles is therefore irresistible. The notion that the English are 'hard', 'courageous' and 'don't bottle out' of a 'good fight' pervades accounts of England supporters abroad. There is a pride in claiming: 'I'll never forget the faces when the England lads came together . . . England had come to town and we just took the place over. A little bit of England, won with English bottle.' Other nationalities can run scared, but not the English.

There's particular pride in 'victories' when they take place on foreign soil. There's no doubt either that 'the lads' are 'doing it for their country'. Their behaviour abroad as reported by the media and via football writing suggests that masculine attributes such as aggression, heavy drinking, gambling, group solidarity and more extreme demonstrations of nationalism are highly valued by many England fans, and England's following abroad shares much of the image of English fans more generally over a decade ago. Justification of violence relies on a nationalism which overlaps with xenophobia and which harks back to times when the English formed part of a powerful colonial force. Again, Eddy Brimson has something to say on this matter. 'I am sick and tired of the rest of the world treating us like dirt. The people that run our country should be ashamed of themselves for giving away so much of what our fathers fought for. They have forgotten what we as a country did for the world.' This represents a desperate clinging to a long-gone era of military supremacy. As England is no longer respected world-wide as a major military power in its own right, a sense of insecurity stimulates an attempt to compensate for this decline by proving military expertise and physical power via other means – and football provides a useful vehicle.

Many England fans today, and in particular 'New Fans', do not share this vision of national identity so closely associated with England fans abroad, and unfortunately for them the strongest image of England fans is a negative one associated with violence, hooliganism and intolerance. These images reflect only a partial reality and portray an image which few England fans wish to embrace. In many ways other Europeans have a more rounded picture of English fans. Their newspaper columns, although still relishing and exaggerating any incidents of violence involving the English, do at least present other dimensions.

Coverage of the World Cup '98 in France, Spain and Italy, for example, offered a far more comprehensive and fairer portrait of the English, while drawing frequently on the other, contrasting national stereotype of the English as being polite 'gentlemen' who value 'fair play' above all.

It is worth considering the differences in patterns of English support at Wembley with experiences away. At Wembley there is a much more varied set of fans. It is common to see women, children and family groups. The atmosphere is very different. We only need to think back to Euro '96 to visualise the sea of red and white, the flags, the replica shirts and the painted faces as everyone participated in orchestrated singing and contributed to a carnivalesque atmosphere. The ambience was one of an enjoyable day out rather than the tense nerves, apprehension or excitement associated with most crunch matches. There was atmosphere without overheated passion, attended by a wide cross-section of society but who nevertheless shared a certain togetherness for the duration of the match. The anthem 'Three Lions' was one which succeeded in bringing together different strands of support by playing on past glories in a self-mocking, almost optimistic way. English football fans seem to be on the way towards creating a new identity but cannot quite relinquish the old values and these are particularly salient when England play away. So can it be claimed that the role of masculinity in the construction of the nation's identity is in decline? Is the English notion of national identity becoming 'feminised'?

Although there has been an increase in the number of female fans and 'New Fans' who turn up for home games at Wembley, and similar processes appear to be taking place there as in the domestic game, there is little to suggest a 'feminisation' of England fans abroad where nationalism is strongest. It seems that it is a very English trait to link so closely nationalism and masculinity. Perhaps it is a legacy of former imperialist values which link patriotic nationalism with military/warrior values. Certainly this is reflected in the militaristic terminology employed in football writing. Professor J.A. Mangan in his book *Tribal Identities* demonstrates how close the links are between the language of sport and militarism. In recent years football has been the catalyst for a renaissance in English nationalism. As preparations for Scottish and Welsh political devolution gathered momentum, the notion of Englishness came increasingly under examination as the realisation dawned on some that the English lacked any positive national characterisation and they began to seek an identity. It has been well documented that sport, and in particular football, provides one of the most potent symbols of national identity. Union Jack flags formerly a common sight at England games were gradually replaced with those bearing the Cross of St George.

There is currently a search within the English for a new national identity, one which draws on positive values and looks to the future rather than wallowing in past glory. This seems to be proving hard to achieve, perhaps reflecting the artificial nature of the notion of an English nation given the diversity within it, perhaps because there is little cultural distinctiveness which marks the experience of following England as being something special.

If by supporting the national team an individual can feel part of the nation, then equally lack of identification can lead to exclusion. Any glance at England's following abroad gives us a clue as to who is included in the construction of the nation's identity: young, white males. Minority groups, including women, are vastly under-represented. England's support abroad has not become 'feminised', except that there probably are a few more fans travelling who actively reject the masculinised notions of nationhood. But these fans are the silent minority.

As notions of masculinity and femininity in society in general are evolving all the time, some of the results of these changes are filtering into football culture. We are experiencing a period of transition and some are resisting the change in the form of a backlash, sometimes under the guise of 'laddism', sometimes as more blatant sexism. It seems that England as a footballing nation is searching for a new identity, but part of it refuses to reject its legacy of masculine devotion to pride and patriotism which all too easily degenerates into xenophobia and demonstrations of masculine insecurity.

Structural changes within the domestic game which have affected pricing policies and the infrastructure of football grounds led to a certain degree of gentrification as well as the introduction of 'New Fans' who might not share the same notions of masculinity as many more traditional fans. This has all contributed to changes in the atmosphere within football grounds. As with all change, there is resistance. Resentment of female fans is one sign of this resistance to change. Some would prefer women to become 'masculinised' so that they would blend in with the male atmosphere rather than dilute it. Others would simply prefer us not to be there. Football – and laddism – represents a certain nostalgia for more traditional social networks in which segregation of the sexes was the norm.

It is over-simplistic to classify female fans as one single group. Not all females are the same. Similarly, it is inaccurate to treat all men as though they were all prime examples of 'geezers'. Clearly they are not. To a certain extent within the domestic game there is greater freedom for both men and women to challenge gender stereotypes and reject traditional attitudes yet this is proving more difficult where England is concerned, especially following the team abroad. With England old values of masculinity still prevail and a last bastion of cherished maleness reasserts itself to maintain its exclusivity. If this last bastion digs its heels in and the next generation of England away fans refuses to evolve with the rest of society, then the self-image of the English will continue to alienate many fans in the way it has done in recent years. In the domestic game and at Wembley, the limits of English masculinity are being pushed and to some extent at least redefined. It is increasingly possible for anyone to become part of football culture. This trend will not be reversed. However, it is unlikely that feminisation or gentrification of football will continue to spread on the national level without a helping hand to guide the process along in the way it did domestically. Whether or not it extends to influence the England following abroad in future years could well depend upon key factors such as how the media portrays England fans abroad and how the Football Association distributes tickets for away games. There is some evidence to suggest that a change of image has already begun as we witness England fans (in Italy, for example, following the World Cup '98 qualifier) being defended by the press and politicians. This could be the helping hand that is required to convince those back home that you don't need to be a thug to follow England abroad. England fans are no longer vilified automatically. Most importantly, however, a new, positive English identity needs to emerge, and in order for men and women of all backgrounds to be able to identify with this image the old values of masculinity must continue to erode at the national level.

Too Many St George Crosses to Bear

Ben Carrington

> Following England is all about pride and history. Our place in the pecking order. For centuries we've been kicking shit out of the Europeans. They start something and we finish it. We're standing on the White Cliffs of Dover singing: 'Come and have a go if you think you're hard enough.'
>
> John King, England Away

It's a warm and sunny Sunday afternoon on 14 June 1998 in the picturesque old port, Marseilles. An over-weight, slightly balding, white bloke, wearing a short-sleeved Ben Sherman shirt, flaunting a tattoo of the St George's Cross, Levi jeans and trainers, stands three feet away from a French policeman. The riot-policeman is dressed in an all-black uniform, wearing a helmet and gas mask, with CS Spray and a semi-automatic gun in his belt strap, holding a riot shield and an extendable baton. He looks nonchalantly straight ahead, ignoring the English abuse he is receiving from this curious monstrosity in front of him which he doesn't quite understand, but the intent is clear. The English lad (probably a baker, plasterer or postal worker – it matters not) is goading the French *gendarme* to come and 'have a go'. To a backdrop chorus of 'In-Ger-Land' and 'It's Coming Home', his mates behind him are lobbing bottles of cheap French lager into the massed ranks of the police, whilst Tunisian flags are set alight around them. But the police force's main attention is with the North African-descendant French youths with whom the English are having a pitched battle. English lads are running up and down the streets hitting anyone stupid enough not to look 'English'. The *gendarmes* look on, not quite sure whether to charge the English fans or simply let them fight it out with the locals, who are often themselves on the receiving end of brutally racist policing methods. A no-lose situation for the French police. The fighting continues, more bottles are thrown, shop windows are smashed, cars are set on fire, and a few French locals are sent to hospital before the police finally move in to mete out their own violent control. The English have arrived.

The next day's papers retell the story for all it is worth with their usual moral indignation: 'England fans on rampage' (*Daily Telegraph*); 'England fans battle with French police' (*Times*); 'Shamed again by the louts' (*Daily Mail*); 'A bloody disgrace' (*Mirror*); 'A disgrace to England' (*Sun*). One image dominates the British TV screens and newspapers. It is of a large, shirtless, white man, with the St George's Cross tattooed across his stomach, with short cropped hair and sun glasses, smiling as he is led away for arrest by the French security forces – handcuffed but defiant. Later tabloid papers will be confused when they try to expose this lunatic 'thug' only to find out he is a 'respectable family man' with a wife and kids living in a suburban semi. A typical Englishman if ever there was.

Two crises came together in Marseilles, and violently expressed themselves through football. They were the crisis of English nationalism in a rapidly changing world and the crisis of masculinity at a time when the meanings embedded within traditional forms of masculinity will no longer be relevant to the twenty-first century. The four hundred or so rioting English supporters made a futile gesture against these changes and provided a statement at the end of the twentieth on the state of English masculinity. It didn't look nice.

Nationalism is increasingly defined by sociologists, not in terms of biology, or genealogy, but in terms of the cultural processes and representations through which nations attempt to tell stories about themselves – the popular fables, legends and images that come to be seen as telling a nation who they are. Nations are, as Benedict Anderson famously phrased it, imagined communities, that rely on notions, and perhaps more accurately myths, that serve to position people as belonging to certain shared communities in the imagination. Thus nations are not only political entities, but also, more importantly, complex cultural communities, and hence important sites for the production of identities for millions of people. As we are never likely to meet even a fraction of those whom we deem to be fellow nationals, it is through shared public displays and mass-mediated spectacles of nationhood – and few cultural events do this better than the hyper-mediated events such as the World Cup or the European Championships – that people come to see themselves as belonging to the same country.

Because our sense of nationhood seems so obvious and natural, it is often difficult to conceptualise our sense of self without a national identity. The 'naturalness' of these feelings towards arbitrary geographical units, which we call nation states, has, of course, to be constantly worked at. The very notion of national cultures is a relatively recent formation – the majority of European nation states, at least in their present geographical location, are less than a hundred years old – tied as they are to the emergence and growth of nation states in the eighteenth and nineteenth centuries. However, nation states had to overcome the problem of cultural diversity that inevitably existed within the arbitrary boundaries of the state. In order for states to become legitimised, nation states sought to obliterate all notions of 'difference' and construct a uniform cultural mass in order that the nation could identify around a singular set of shared values, customs and, invariably, invented traditions. In most cases the project of nation building was successful, but as we see today in examples like Quebec in Canada, the Basque and Catalan regions in Spain and, of course,

Northern Ireland – and also in the more violent reactions against the imposition of nation states in settings ranging from Rwanda and the Congo, to Kosovo and Chechnya – many regions were able to resist the processes of cultural uniformity and have sought to assert their own independence.

It is impossible to talk about British identity without also having an understanding of the central role of Empire. From the seventeenth century onwards, Britishness became increasingly synonymous with Empire in the minds of both the political élite and the populace. At the heart of this imperial national identity lay a profound contradiction. On the one hand the British came to see themselves as the world champions of liberal democracy, civilised governance and humanitarian enlightenment, whilst at the same time conquering, exploiting and enslaving non-Western nations as they did so. This was justified, as the inherently superior values of the British were thought to override all other concerns about other nations having universal human rights of self-determination, especially as black populations were seen to lack the basic prerequisites to fully enter into the modern world. It was only through submitting themselves to British rule that the colonies could gain acceptance as civilised societies. What this meant was that British identity became racialised. To be British was to be white – a coloniser of others and never, as 'Rule Britannia' reminds us, to be slaves.

Sports were central to these ideological processes of cultural and imperial indoctrination. The spread of Empire was intricately intertwined with the promotion of sports as a way of not only ensuring some form of symbolic sporting superiority over the colonies but also through the educative and moral values that competitive team sports in particular were thought to have. Given the decreasing centrality to public life of two of the key institutions that have traditionally helped to foster a sense of national belonging – war and the Royal family – sport, and football more than any other sport, has increasingly occupied a central role in symbolising English nationalism.

The cultural critic Kobena Mercer has noted that: 'Identity only becomes an issue when it is in crisis, when something assumed to be fixed, coherent and stable is displaced by the experience of doubt and uncertainty.' With the decline of Empire during the first half of the twentieth century, and the processes of de-colonisation, the central tenets of Britishness came increasingly to be questioned. Britain could no longer claim to have an inalienable right to govern countries that increasingly neither wanted, nor needed, British rule.

Any discussion about what constitutes Britishness therefore needs to be situated within this historical context of the decline and disappearance of Empire, and the more recent wider changes that have arisen from globalised economic restructuring which challenge the ability of all nation states to control their own financial affairs and political destinies.

These issues are also related to the increasing internal fragmentation of Britain itself, at the start of the twenty-first century, with the re-emergence of regional, in opposition to central governmental, desires for political control and the moves towards increasing forms of national devolution and independence in

Scotland, Wales and Northern Ireland. Whereas previously Englishness had subsumed itself within a definition of Britishness over which it had an all-powerful dominance, these multi-faceted changes have meant that the idea of Englishness itself is in dispute. The English centre has been challenged and started to shift and fragment, as the periphery itself moves away. Thus as the notion of Britishness is increasingly questioned, what is left is an Englishness that is unable to articulate a coherent, mature and confident sense of self without recourse to a mythical British imperial past. But this Englishness cannot be convincingly defined in any narrow way that privileges the myth of England as a green and pleasant land of paternalistic governance – essentially a middle-class, patriarchal, and white imagining – not least since the cultural and social changes involved with the migration of those from the former colonies since the Second World War have decisively reshaped the cultural landscape of England.

The crisis of Englishness is heightened by the fact that there are few English social institutions. There is no English State or parliament, no English passport, and most of the major cultural institutions have separate Scottish, Welsh and Northern Irish sections, but no comparable English equivalent. This is because of England's historically dominant position within these institutions – meaning that Britishness was merely a substitute for Englishness – which camouflaged England's power base. The other nations were merely seen as a deviation from the English norm. Recent changes have allowed right-wing commentators like Simon Heffer and Richard Littlejohn to appeal to a spurious populist mandate suggesting that the English are now the only ones without political institutions to support their aspirations. This fraudulent positioning – by any objective measurement England still remains the major player within the United Kingdom with all current political governance still taking place within its remit – means that far from these changes decentralising Englishness, as some had hoped, a more reactionary and dominant form of Englishness is increasingly being asserted by those claiming to speak on behalf of the 'oppressed majority' in their own land. These arguments have been central in producing a white-victim masculinity that sees itself under perpetual threat from women, blacks and other minorities who form part of the mythical politically correct movement. This type of English nationalism is seen as respectable and legitimate, and increasingly occupies the centre ground in the political debates over British nationalism.

Sport, and by that it is normally meant élite-level, male competitive team games, is seen in many countries as central in symbolising the key characteristics of a nation's identity. The symbolism of national sporting sides, and sport itself, has therefore acquired huge political significance in trying to not only promote particular notions of what British identity is and should be like, but also as a way of trying to put the 'Great' back into Britain at a time when Britain, economically and politically, is no longer a major player in world affairs.

The attempt to use the symbolic power of sports to communicate particular points to voters is a now well-known strategy for political strategists. It was cricket – symbolically representing the core 'English' values of fair play and decency – that provided the context for John Major's 1993 St George's Day speech in which he invoked the essence of 'Britishness' by describing Britain as a country of 'long shadows on county grounds, warm beer, invincible green suburbs, dog lovers and pool fillers and old maids cycling to holy communion through the morning mist'. Similar forms of association were also in evidence when the Labour Party used the Man Utd manager, Alex Ferguson, in their 1999 European Election broadcast just a month after United's historic treble, to demonstrate the benefits of being at the 'heart of Europe'. Indeed with the creation of the Department of Culture, Media and Sport (replacing the Tories' Department of National Heritage) and the general high profile embrace of sport, evidenced in the government's support for England to host the 2006 World Cup, New Labour has been keen to embrace the New Football Culture as a symbol of its new 'Cool Britannia' image of a young, dynamic and modern country.

The *Daily Mirror* provided one of the crudest examples of how sport is supposed to be a metaphor for the state of the nation, and how this has been, and continues to be, used politically. In June 1997 it asked the British public, a month after Labour's General election victory and on the day when England had bowled out Australia for 118 runs in the first Ashes Test of that summer, 'Don't you feel just great to be British?' The front-page leader exclaimed, next to a full-colour photograph of an England cricketer, arms aloft in exaltation:

Feel that Fieldgood Factor! It was great to be British yesterday as our hero cricketers bowled out the Aussies for a pitiful 118 runs in the first test. The exhilarating triumph – led by Andy Caddick – came after England soccer stars beat Italy and Poland, and the British Lions roared to victory in South Africa. *But it's not just sport – EVERYTHING feels better. You can feel it in the air, a sense of optimism and hope that at last something is happening to our country.* Tony Blair was revealed yesterday as the most popular Premier in history. He promised he'd make things better – and he has already. *So make the most of it. Get up this morning, smile, give a little cheer and do something positive. The Great is back in Britain.*

Given sport's central place in many nations' sense of self it is not surprising that sport, and in particular football, the world's most popular sport, has not only been seen as providing a sense of collective identity, but also, paradoxically, seen as reflecting some of the debates about the 'crisis' of English identity as well. Nowhere can this confusion over the points of demarcation between what constitutes Englishness and Britishness be more clearly seen than in national sports events. Indeed it is not so much that sport has reflected these changes happening 'out there' in society, as much as sport has actively contributed to the confusions over national identity. This is best encapsulated by the fact that there is no British team in football, despite there being a British state. Sporting nationalisms therefore reveal the schizoid nature of British identity – we are British in most, but not all, athletic events, with a separate Republic of Ireland squad, five nations in football, yet four when it comes to rugby union, and one team – though sometimes four – if it's rugby league, and one team called 'England', plus whoever else is good enough to play, and a separate Scotland team, when it comes to cricket.

Sport is therefore an important political site for national and cultural contestation, especially for racists, in their attempt to reconstruct sporting sides as symbolic markers of white English nationalism. In 1993, Dudley Wood, then secretary of the Rugby Football Union, was complaining that the increasing number of black athletes would drive away spectators – it did not occur to him that black Britons could be spectators of athletics. Then there was Robert Henderson's infamous 1995 diatribe in *Wisden Cricket Monthly* where he argued that black cricketers lacked commitment to the Test team – the two cricketers mentioned in the article, Devon Malcolm and Philip DeFreitas, both won substantial damages against the magazine – and that therefore the numbers of blacks, according to Henderson, should be limited to two per team to stop the inevitable 'racial tensions' that would apparently result in destroying team morale. And of course there was Norman Tebbit's 'cricket test', which sought to extend the questioning of black players' national commitment to questioning the identifications made by spectators as well. In all these instances we can see how sport continually acts as a metaphor for wider discussions about the place of black Britons within the nation more generally, which seek to question the loyalty of black migrants to Britain and their place within the country.

A clear example of these shifts over the re-emergence of English nationalism was seen in the 1996 European Championships held in England, and in the 1998 World Cup held in France, where the abandonment of the Union Jack for the St George Cross was seen by many as a positive re-affirmation of an English nationalism in response to the collapse of a coherent British identity.

Euro '96 was seen as signalling a major shift in football fandom leading some to talk about a new 'post-hooligan' fan culture – it was interesting how quickly the events of Dublin in February 1995, when the England versus Ireland game was abandoned after rioting by far-right groups, has been exorcised from the collective memory. These changes and shifts within aspects of football fandom reflected some of the internal changes within football such as the injection of BSkyB money into the game, the introduction of all-seater stadia and the corresponding rise in ticket prices, and the increasing middle-class and female attendance at games. The argument supposes that the racist, violent and aggressive footballing cultures of the 1970s and 1980s have somehow, magically, been eradicated with the advent of the New Footballing Culture, which everyone is now a part of.

However, in reality Euro '96 failed to project a national identity that many sections of the black community were able to identify with, and still reproduced many of the same problems that have haunted English identity in its recent past. As the survey reported in Britain's leading black newspaper *The Voice* demonstrated, the majority of black Britons actively supported 'anyone but England' during Euro '96 due to the unease with the overt nationalism and jingoism expressed during the tournament. The theme of the tournament itself, 'football's coming home' showed the small-mindedness of a dominant Englishness that assumes, no matter what others may say about football being a world game, that as the rules of football were written in England over a century ago, the game is, and always will be, ours. The chance to represent a multi-cultural version of England and English football was lost, as everything from the pre-tournament FA promotional film, to comedians Baddiel and Skinner's 'Three Lions' anthem which helped to popularise the ethnocentric anthem 'Football's coming home' and which amazingly failed to include any black faces at all, be it players or spectators, in the accompanying pop video, to the commemorative poster stamps and street posters, portrayed the entire history and contemporary reality of English football as a white affair. Mark Perryman argued in the *New Statesman* at the time, that despite the welcome changes within football fandom in recent years, much of this had failed to be reflected in the tournament's coverage and promotion:

> Euro '96 in its marketing and presentation, goes with the grain of petty-minded Englishness, rather than celebrating England's coming of age as part of Europe. The marketing slogan says it all: 'Football Comes Home'. Let's reassert all that history, those far off days when we invented every game known to mankind, then taught Johnny Foreigner how to play it. The banners draped over all eight host-cities portray the game as a solely English product, and the portraits used pass off our sport's history as a white thing too.

Whilst there was clearly less trouble inside the grounds than many 'experts' had predicted, there was, in a sense, a sort of 'displacement' of the violence to outside the stadiums themselves. The rioting that took place in Trafalgar Square, particularly after England's traditional loss to Germany, and the attacks on German cars, as well as on Asian, black and foreigner visitors that night – as reported in the Institute of Race Relations document *Monitoring Racism in London* published that summer – clearly showed that English nationalism had not smoothly re-invented itself as an anti-racist, non-sexist, post-imperial cultural formation. What became clear from the tournament was that despite the hype, English nationalism had not managed to come to terms with its real world position, and that football nationalism could not provide a panacea for this situation.

Significant too was the way in which 'New Laddism' became intertwined with the nationalist discourse allowing for an assertion of an aggressive and macho form of English nationalism. During the build-up to Euro '96 the distinctions between the separate cultural fields of Britpop music and football began to disappear. What Steve Redhead has referred to as the 'holy trinity', at least for young men, of fashion, pop music and football converged in ways unknown before. Thus during Euro '96, footballers appeared on front-covers of indie music magazines such as *NME*, comedians became singers and appeared on New Lad magazines, such as *Loaded*, and pop stars were falling over themselves to be involved in celebrity football matches – pop, footy, and New Lads had finally fused into one indistinguishable cultural form in order to promote English nationalism.

'New Lads' themselves were supposed to be a reaction against the 1980s creation of the caring, sharing and socially reformed man – the so-called 'New Man' who fully respected the rights of women to be his equals, and even superiors, and did not mind adopting roles previously considered 'feminine' such as child-rearing and house-keeping. The New Lad then was a partial reversion back to the traditional sexist masculinity of old, although the New Lad was now supposed to have accepted the basic claims of feminism and so any behaviour, gestures or actions that appeared to be sexist were now 'ironic' and playful, and not, therefore, meant to be taken literally. Tim Southwell, who along with James Brown was one of the founders of *Loaded*, has been quite explicit about *Loaded*'s politics in this regard, when he stated: 'Although no one ever sat down at *Loaded* and said this is going to be the agenda, we knew we were redressing the balance against the New Man.' 'Addressing the imbalance' is of course coded wordplay for suggesting that the achievements of feminism over the past 30 years have gone too far. This argument – which parallels those made by the right against anti-racist measures – suggests that men and women are now equal in every sphere of social life, thus 'preferential treatment' for women is 'reverse discrimination' against men. Such views are nonsense. Women still only earn between 70 and 80 per cent of the equivalent income for a male employee; are more likely to be the victims of domestic and sexual abuse – reporting of rapes has increased by 165 per cent over the past decade with the attacker being known to the victim in nearly 90 per cent of cases, yet the number of actual convictions has fallen; women are still hugely under-represented within the judiciary and the legal profession, not forgetting the political establishment, civil service, police forces, academia and senior management positions within blue chip companies and media organisations. Put another way, it still pays in this society to be born white, male and middle–class.

Promoted, often by middle-class males who suddenly found themselves able to engage in sexist jokes and comments, TV shows like *Fantasy Football* and *Men Behaving Badly* became huge successes. There is now a plethora of wannabe working-class heroes whose mock cockney accents give them entry into the New Lad world, despite their own privileged middle-class backgrounds, and who often claim to speak on behalf of the 'ordinary man in the street'. Comedian David Baddiel is an Oxbridge graduate and TV presenters Johnny Vaughan and Jamie Theakston are both public school boys. Even TV's original urban warrior, Ali G, is a public-school and Cambridge graduate.

A reflection of the growth of the New Lad as a consumer group can also be seen in changes that have taken place within publishing. Recent years have seen a phenomenal increase in the number and volume of magazines aimed primarily at young men/New Lads from general interest magazines such as *Loaded* to a number of new football and sport magazines, to health and fitness magazines. The volume sales of these magazines is quite staggering – *Loaded*'s sales figures have come close to 500,000 and *FHM* at the end of the 1990s was selling *in excess* of 750,000 copies *per month*. These figures are all the more significant when you consider that a decade ago this market simply did not exist.

Most of the men's magazines now stick to a format of sport, usually football, fashion and women, preferably naked, with feature articles on issues ranging from how to make your own porn video to stories about the violent criminal underworld. *Loaded*, which was the first of the men's magazines to make money from this format, is often accused of having shifted the content of the serious men's style magazines downwards to the extent that it is increasingly difficult to distinguish such magazines from so-called soft-porn 'girlie magazines'. Revealingly, recent figures have shown that soft-core pornography magazines have been losing sales quite heavily over the past few years. It is quite apparent that many of the same clientele who would normally have bought *Razzle* or *Fiesta* are now buying *Loaded* and *FHM* instead – why risk social embarrassment reaching for the top shelf when you can still get your masturbatory fantasies from a mid-shelf men's magazine? *Fiesta* was selling a quarter of a million copies in the first half of 1995 – soon after *Loaded* was launched – but by the end of 1997 was selling less than 180,000 copies – nearly a 30 per cent fall. Conversely, *FHM* increased its circulation by 326 per cent, from around 182,000 copies per month in 1996, eventually overtaking *Loaded*, to sell around 775,000 in 1999. One of the main shifts in men's magazines from the 1980s to the 1990s is that the covers of men's magazines in the 1980s actually had men on the front cover. Today, standing in any newsagent and surveying everything from men's magazines to 'girlie magazines', women's magazines, to health and fitness magazines, it is evident that the female form is subject to a voyeuristic gaze unprecedented in recent cultural history.

Despite the protestations of the publishers and editors themselves, what such magazines have done is to bring the objectification of women and the use of pornographic images to the mainstream. The defence that because B-list celebrity women consent to their own objectification, it means that this form of sexualisation is legitimate, is irrelevant. Power, male or otherwise, works most effectively when those subject to its effects consent to their own subordination, and more pertinently, actually work to reproduce this situation. The fact is that it is still, overwhelmingly, young women who have to be measured and valued according to their physical attractiveness to men to advance their careers. The form of body control that this invokes in young women – many of whom are, increasingly, experiencing all too high rates of illness such as bulimia and anorexia – is one of the side effects of this.

Any suggestions that masculinity might be reconfigured to meet the demands of the twenty-first century without resorting to such puerile expressions of male identity – based on sex, violence, sport and homophobia – have been lost. Men increasingly seek to insulate themselves against their changing gender roles in post-industrial societies, which are no longer founded on the need for hard manual labour and the masculinities that went along with this, by their consumption of such magazines.

The pretence that English football fandom after Euro '96 had somehow managed to resurrect itself from its associations with hooliganism, aggressive masculinity and xenophobic expression was shattered during the 1998 World Cup when large numbers of English fans fought with locals and the police when England played Tunisia in Marseilles.

The tabloids, and most politicians, argued that 'these thugs' were ruining the good name of English football, and by default therefore the nation as a whole, and saw their actions as being atypical compared to the 'real fans'. The Conservative politician, the late Alan Clark, however, proved to be the exception in arguing that the rioters themselves were actually the victims in all this as they had been typecast and targeted by the police and, far from disgracing the nation, should be seen as the bearers of some of our finest characteristics. Clark argued: 'If you are English you are targeted, particularly if you are English and tough-looking, and are wearing an English flag. In a sense it is a kind of compliment to the English martial spirit I suppose. But they really haven't got a chance, these guys, everyone is out to get them.' New Labour's response was predictably authoritarian, though the main concern for the political élite was less to do with what the riots may or may not have said about the condition of English nationalism and masculinity, but more to do with what this would do to England's chances of successfully bidding to host the 2006 World Cup. Tony Blair described the rioting fans as a 'mindless minority' who had brought 'disgrace' upon the good name of Britain – they were British fans now, not English! He declared: 'We have to encourage employers to take strong action against those people that are convicted of football hooligan offences abroad.' Blair offered no sociological or rational argument as to how making large numbers of men unemployed would prevent future episodes of violence. Clark and a few fellow mavericks apart, what such analyses tended to do was to treat the rioters as a fringe element on the margins of normal fandom, which was seen as essentially honest and patriotic.

The truth is that most of these fans were not the special 'Category C' hooligans who were known troublemakers but 'ordinary fans'. As the *Mirror* put it, somewhat perplexed: 'Only three Category C thugs – the most feared organisers of violence – were held in Marseilles. In an alarming twist, the vast majority of troublemakers are not even known to the police. But officers say 400 were behaving like hard-core hooligans.'

Nick Lowles, in *Searchlight*, has argued that:

> The stereotype of the Englishman throughout history has been of a short, stocky, and quite ugly working man seemingly quite prepared for a ruck. From John Bull to Winston Churchill, and even our national mascot, the British Bulldog, the image is the same . . . Two factors were responsible for the events in France, both very much part of English culture – a propensity to drink followed by a desire to fight, and a nationalism that is both aggressive and xenophobic.

It was just such an image that *The Sun* invoked on the Friday before the Marseilles riots. Its front page had the header 'LET'S HAVE IT OFF FOR ENGLAND' next to a picture of Chris Evans in a *Sun* 'bowler hat', in the St George's Cross colours, dressed in an England shirt, fist and teeth clenched in an aggressive pose. It was meant to be part of *The Sun's* campaign to 'give every worker in England next Monday afternoon off to cheer on our soccer heroes'. However it was also, of course, a play on the term's working-class meaning of fighting –'having it off'– for England. The lads across the Channel duly obliged the following week, having apparently failed to realise that the comments weren't meant to be taken literally. The tabloids, having stoked up the emotional feelings of aggressive nationalism could hardly complain when it really did 'kick off'. The tabloids naturally poured moralistic outrage on to the fans, quickly distancing themselves from their own complicity with the jingoistic climate they had been fostering only a few days before. Interestingly, the *Mirror*, quick to position itself as the moral voice of Britain, used a front-page montage of various white male England supporters rioting in the streets, some wearing the same *Sun* bowler hats Chris Evans had been wearing the week before while encouraging the England fans to 'have it off'. The *Mirror* header bellowed: 'TOUGH ON CRIME PRIME MINISTER? THESE MORONIC, LOATHSOME YOBS ARE HUMILIATING OUR COUNTRY AND THEY'RE MAKING YOU LOOK WEAK.' Of course, it is precisely this macho reaction to being 'hard' as a way of dealing with such issues, with the predictable calls for more authoritarian and punitive measures to correct the behaviour of 'the thugs', that lies at the root of contemporary problems concerning masculinity and the politics that arise from it.

As Suzanne Moore put it in her critique of the New Lad embrace of footballing culture: 'The yobs are back. As if they ever went away. If anything proves that the cult of middle-class football is an all-played out fantasy, it's the pathetic, sickening scenes from Marseilles. Hornby, Baddiel and Hancock, where are you now?'

It is worth remembering that not all English fans that travelled to France '98 engaged in the sort of actions witnessed in Marseilles. Many black Britons, for instance, travelled to France, particularly when Jamaica played Croatia at Lens, and this aspect was significantly under-reported within the mainstream media. As the editorial of the August 1998 issue of *Searchlight* put it:

> Football says much about a country. France '98 was no exception. The French nation found a new togetherness, both on and off the field, and as a result undercut the current strength of the *Front National.* That large numbers of black Britons decided to support another team, be it Jamaica or Nigeria, said much about the lack of inclusiveness in this country. Conversely the outbreak of English hooliganism again demonstrated that an aggressive and xenophobic nationalism still maintains a firm grip among many in our society.

Whilst it is undoubtedly limiting to view football fandom only through the lens of hooliganism, as some commentators have tended to do, thereby downplaying other aspects of football spectatorship that cannot be reduced to a propensity for violence, the Marseilles events showed that there are still worrying elements within 'normal' football fan culture. The novelist John King has argued that:

> In the seventies, the Union Jack became this right-wing symbol – now it's all Cool Britannia. The right-wing thing at Chelsea was always greatly exaggerated. It's the same now. English fans are seen as extreme right-wing fascists yet the far-right never get any support to speak of in England. The French press portrayed English fans as a marauding army, yet there's more right-wing extremism in France – they get about 25 per cent of the vote. Who's fooling who here?

By comparing the political success of the far-right in France to their British counterpart, King manages to construct an argument that downplays the real problems inherent within contemporary football fandom, and by extension within British society. By distorting these arguments he dismisses as exaggerated those attempts to criticise English fan culture that result in events like Marseilles. It is not that all English fans are fascist or racist, and neither that it is just a fringe on the edges of good spectatorship. The problem is that most English fans tend not to be aware of race as an issue, with a small element being actively, and politically, racist and perhaps a similar small number who could be described as actively anti-racist. This means that the vast majority tend to see themselves as not being racist, and would certainly deny the charge. Yet it is this 'non-racist' majority who will often engage in certain banal forms of racism and, under certain circumstances, join in more overt expressions of racial and xenophobic abuse and violence. Defences of traditional football fan culture rarely address the degree to which such latent racism is pervasive, seeking to argue their case by pointing out that organised racist activity is minimal, as if that in some way justified the casual everyday racism that does exist.

One of the most worrying developments in this mix of New Laddism, English nationalism, and football, is the way in which the centrality of class has been invoked by those seeking to either justify or defend such expressions of violent English masculinity. According to this view any critique is merely a liberal, middle-class, intellectual reaction to a working class, that such critiques know nothing about. This defence of certain forms of white English masculinity gets dressed up as a form of heroic working-class resistance.

Take the semi-fictional writings of the Brimson brothers who have themselves created a mini-industry in counter–cultural football 'hooli' books. They have been central in helping to foster a sense of white-victim masculinity against, as they put it in *England, My England*, 'the dreaded PC movement' which has 'made any show of national pride shameful' and destroyed the 'English culture and spirit'. The violent elements of football fandom are celebrated in these 'authentic' accounts, giving a supposed glimpse into the world of Britain's growing 'underclass'. Dougie Brimson in *The Geezer's Guide to*

Football: A Lifetime of Lads, Lager and Labels paints a fantasy world where gender roles are absolute, where women know their place, and the middle-class infiltration of football culture, seen as a feminising process, is to be resisted. He states that football, contrary to popular misconceptions, is no place for women. Thus to be a true working-class man – or 'geezer' in Brimson's terminology – is to adopt the attitudes of a traditional patriarch – 'forget all talk of "girl power" and sexual equality; to be a geezer you must be a bloke, and there are absolutely no exceptions to that'.

The appendix to the book has a section explaining the various 'geezer' gestures such as 'the wanker sign', 'giving it "the biggie"', and 'come on then!' – the last 'used primarily to goad opposing fans and to invite them to come and have a go at you if they think they are hard enough'. Anyone wanting to know what a geezer would look like should recall the pictures of a smiling Neil Acourt leaving the Stephen Lawrence inquiry in 1998, arms out wide in the 'come on' gesture. Whilst the Brimson brothers would no doubt distance themselves from the actions of Acourt, and the other four white men suspected of the Lawrence murder, the problem remains that such young men are clearly not extreme neo-Nazi thugs. They are representative of a large section of the white male working-class who genuinely, though mistakenly, believe themselves to be victims of a 'politically correct' society, who are, to a large degree, disenfranchised by the circumstances of modern capitalist societies, and who have resorted to an aggressive and reactionary 'geezer' attitude as a way of dealing with their situation.

Whilst the blurb on the cover jacket for Dougie Brimson's book meekly tries to claim that the book is 'tongue-in-check' it is clear that the sense of irony – so beloved of the middle-class lads who have embraced the New Football Culture – is very thin on the ground. The misogyny evident in Brimson's writing is merely indicative of the general cultural shift within contemporary English masculine culture towards a culture that celebrates aggressive and violent masculinity, homophobic sentiments and the systematic objectification of women. The defence of this culture is predictable. Tim Southwell has claimed the portrayal of women in *Loaded* is somehow an expression of working-class desire, upholding the bastions of working-class culture against the evil dictates of 'political correctness' – that spurious invention of the right which was created to discredit progressive feminist, anti-racist, and lesbian and gay politics by trivialising their political demands. Southwell has claimed:

> No one seemed to complain too much when *Dazed & Confused* or *I-D* or *GQ* or *Esquire* used pictures of barely dressed women. The reason is simple. It's a class thing. *Loaded* portrayed women in a very mainstream fashion and had no shame about the fact that this basic element would appeal to our readers, most of whom would be men and most of whom would, if they were anything like us, appreciate the inclusion of such pictures.

Exactly the same arguments are often made, usually by the same white middle-class males, in attempting to defend the overt racism of comedians such as Bernard Manning on the grounds that this is an expression of 'real working-class culture' and is therefore somehow beyond reproach. What all of these accounts have in common is a misrepresentation of working-class life. Many of these apologists forget that blacks are part of the working class too. The mythical working-class invoked by such commentators assumes that it is universally white and heterosexual, and overlook that many white working-class communities have, at certain times, been vociferously anti-racist as demonstrated over the past hundred years or so by radical working-class anti-imperial and anti-colonial politics. As the last Census data revealed, with between 30 to 40 per cent of black people having white partners, talk of separate black and white communities within Britain is misleading. Further, expressions of sexism and homophobia are not intrinsic to working-class life – as though these communities were incapable of articulating politics other than those associated with sexism and homophobia. Such arguments actually say more about the 'class tourists', as Jarvis Cocker so accurately put it, who live to sample a bit of the exotic other in contrast to their own restricted middle-class cultural lives, than it does about the communities such people claim to be speaking on behalf of.

After Robbie Fowler taunted Chelsea's Graeme Le Saux for supposedly being gay during a game in the 1998-99 season some tried to defend Fowler on the basis that he was a working-class lad from Liverpool, as if that automatically meant he would be homophobic, and therefore any criticism of his 'humour' was a form of middle-class prejudice. The episode was framed by many commentators as expressing the last stand of the old traditional footballing culture against the feminising and emasculating influence of the new. 'Class warfare is the key to soccer "gay taunts" row' as the *Daily Telegraph* dramatically put it. In *The Guardian*, journalist Jim White noted:

> In the blue corner was Le Saux, educated, middle-class, renowned as a collector of antiques and a reader of broadsheet newspapers. In the red corner was Fowler, unreconstructed Scouse scally, renowned as a collector of purple Porsche Carreras and friend of sacked dockers everywhere. It was old football against new football, the terraces against the family enclosure, the hot-dog stand against the executive dining facilities.

The uncritical acceptance of New Lad/'geezer' culture as somehow being an organic expression of working-class life allows for reactionary expressions to emerge, and then be defended as being in some way an expression of authentic English nationalism. Take for example this defence of *Loaded* by one of its editorial staff:

> A bloke who punches a woman in the face does so not because of something that they have seen in *Loaded*, but because their Meccano-like brain will have possibly reached some dismal cycle where he thinks it's time to do something

bad to a girl. The fact that there are still people like that around isn't my fault and I don't think that by having magazines like *Loaded* around makes things worse. This is England and it's not a particularly sophisticated country.

New Lad culture claims that its critics simply don't understand the essentially honest character of the pragmatic, 'down-to-earth' Englishman. Reading *Loaded* does not lead men to abuse their wives, but it does form a central part of a wider cultural space that cannot comprehend women in any guise other than that of sexual objects available for male gratification. As psychologists have constantly told us, it is not just that this is precisely the distinction many wife-beaters fail to make between the fantasy of women portrayed in this way and how real women behave, but rather the culture that condones such behaviour as just 'lads having a laugh', that is at issue. Paul Gascoigne's violent abuse of his wife did not result in his 'lad' status decreasing. Arguably, it actually increased as his apologists sought to defend him against the 'politically correct' and argued that he shouldn't be dropped by the England manager as first, England needed him and second, this was a 'domestic affair' and not something for which 'the nation' should be punished by losing his footballing services. Sheryl Gascoigne just being an unfortunate victim, collateral damage if you like, of the nation's desire for footballing glory.

One of the central problems with both English nationalism and the position of English football is an inability to objectively analyse the actual state of the nation, on or off the pitch. The 'myth of 1966' actually serves to hold back any serious discussions about the deficiencies within the English game, allowing a delusion of footballing strength, where none has existed, and allowing for the 'English style' to be applauded even when it patently fails. The notion of the hard-working, industrious and 'honest' Englishman is contrasted with the skilful, but naïve, foreigner who only ever beats the English by luck – penalties, unfair dismissals – or cheating – hands-of-God, play-acting – thus leaving England with the perennial 'we would have won, but for . . .'

But it needs to be pointed out that by any objective criteria England is not a major player in international football. England has yet to win a European Championship and normally struggles to even *qualify*. It has won the World Cup once – on home soil – and has never, since or before, made it to the final. Argentina, Brazil, France, Holland, Italy and Germany are all clearly way ahead of England in footballing terms – with England, one of the best of the rest, and likely to be overtaken by the so-called 'emerging nations' over the next decade, in particular by the likes of Nigeria and South Africa. Even at club level, German and Italians, and also Spanish and French teams, continue to dominate European football in a way that English clubs, except for occasional surprises, have not for almost twenty years now. It is not surprising then that English identity, if aligned so closely to footballing victories, is always so wrapped in existential angst and seen to be in a state of crisis, the 'thirty years of hurt', as Skinner and Baddiel termed it in their Euro '96 anthem 'Three Lions', demonstrates.

There is also the further problem that success in male competitive sport in general, and football in particular, should be taken as marker of the nation's identity anyway. As Chas Critcher argues:

> The ideals which the triumph of '66 confirmed are precisely those which now stand in the way of the needed transformation of the game – and indeed the inability of British society more generally to adjust itself to the modern world. As long as there is a sustained belief that foreigners have little or nothing to teach us, that sport is an arena for the realisation of a recalcitrant sense of masculinity and that football should express the values of a class once nurtured on the experience of hard manual labour, then English football will not be able to take what should be its rightful place amongst the top nations of the world.

But England has no 'right' to be among the top nations of the world in any sphere – despite popular versions of cultural and historical amnesia, we do not have an Empire any more! Football is so marked by a racially exclusive, sexist and homophobic culture, that it both feeds off and itself helps to promote, despite what the apologists and New Football recruits may wish, that it cannot, at least for the foreseeable future, function as a model for what English identity could, and should, look like in the twenty-first century, in a modern, democratic and egalitarian society. The English often look down upon those countries – the Scots in particular – that lack a footballing team that can truly stand on the world stage. Rather than pitying a nation that lacks such footballing heroes, we should perhaps pity those who still feel the need for them.

They Thought It Was All Over

D.J. Taylor

The connection between football and the writings of William Makepeace Thackeray is perhaps a fairly marginal one. Thackeray died in 1863, long before the faintest stirrings of the modern game. One can assume, perhaps, that sometime in the 1820s, when not being pursued by the cane-wielding Dr Russell or lascivious sixth-formers, he kicked a ball around the playgrounds, if not the playing fields, of Charterhouse. Cambridge, where he went in 1828, had only just discovered rowing, and 'sport' to the mature Thackeray meant horses or rat-catching or cock-fighting. In all the thousands of his letters I examined over a five-year stretch prior to writing his biography, I searched in vain for that revealing sign-off in which the writer would suddenly declare himself: 'By Gad, madam. This Saturday last I stepped up to Brompton Green to see the gentlemen of Kensington, and can report that the new centre forward is devlish fine' – something like that. So, nothing then. And yet, Thackeray's chief obsession towards the end of his life – before it, too – was *nostalgia*, which means that the mental distance between the nineteenth-century novelist sorrowing over his lost childhood and the average fortysomething of today who can account for each minute of that tense Saturday afternoon back in the summer of 1966 is less cavernous than it may seem.

Like many another Victorian novelist, Thackeray had complex feelings about his childhood. In many ways his whole adult life was a journey into the past and an attempt to recover its sights, sounds and tastes. Simultaneously the voyage conceals, or fails to conceal, a determination, first, to recapture this lost time, and, second, to compensate himself for something that was missing from it. In reading the accounts of his schooldays, boyhood holidays, college escapades, all the shot inner debris of 40 years assembled in a series called *Roundabout Papers* just before his death, one often feels that something has slipped away out of them, that the recollections would be less intense had the reality itself been more fully realised. It is the classic literary man's pursuit of lost time. You start off in search of an apparently roseate past, because that past is precious to you, and yet both your motives and the object pursued are shot through with fractures and uncertainties. Perhaps any attempt to recreate past time implies some dissatisfaction with its present equivalent. Equally, the imagined constructions of middle-aged nostalgia have a habit of falling far below what really happened. My final biographer's conclusion on the *Roundabout Papers* is that Thackeray was trying to find something that wasn't there, and that the real importance of this 50-year-old's elegisings is what they tell you about the 50-year-old elegist, not his former self. The same may be true of dozens of elements of our national life, but it is unquestionably true of football: an obsession with ancestry that fails to disguise both an enormous amount of present unease and the lurking suspicion that the past, that rolling, goal-strewn vista of men with short hair striding across pitches like billiard tables, was not as we imagine it.

Here at the start of the twenty-first century, bathed in the final glimmer of the post-Imperial twilight, nostalgia infects our national consciousness like a kind of leprosy. Our institutions, by and large, have been dragged towards something approaching modernity, along with all kinds of goverment-sponsored nonsense about the new millennium – but what might be called our inner lives and the way in which attitudes to our past and its capabilities manifest themselves in areas such as art and sport remain hopelessly wedded to the past. To look at practically any serious or sub-serious art-form is to find its practitioners consciously, and sometimes delightedly, trading off past glories. Just as the English novel has never really got over the paralysing brilliance of Dickens, Thackeray and Jane Austen, so native pop music has never truly recovered from the influence of the Beatles. Nowhere, perhaps, are these myths and legends, this reliance on bygone exemplars, so resonant as in the field of English football, and specifically its national team.

Already, you see, the sense of some shared heritage, a collective memory of white-shirted figures romping over endless greensward, hangs over what I write. It is not going too far to say that the 1966 World Cup supplied some of my first proper memories, though even here one has to separate out what one really remembers from the false recall of photographs seen many years later. But I can remember the Argentine players crowding the referee prior to Rattin being sent off, my father leaving the result of the Portugal game under my infant pillow, Weber sliding forward to equalise in the last minute of normal time. All this is interspersed with yet more minute details: Nobby Stiles' head; an undersized World Cup Willie T-shirt that I could barely pull over my shoulders. Afterwards, too, the England team stopped being professional footballers and metamorphosed, unbidden, into mythical figures, caught eternally in the moment of their triumph. It was impossible to imagine Banks, Moore and company having any further life post-1966. They became quite unreal. I remember bumping into Geoff Hurst once in a culvert beneath the main stand at Carrow Road in about 1973 – he might then have been unsuccessfully managing Stoke City – and registering first awe, and then a sense of mild dissatisfaction at this jowly thirtysomething who clearly enjoyed a pork chop or two and didn't give autographs. Martin Peters ended up playing for Norwich in the late 1970s, but it was hard to connect this useful veteran midfielder with the fresh-faced harrier of 1966. Martin Peters? No, he died on a soccer pitch in

North London when I was five. The other guy just happened to share his name.

Worse even than this – far, far worse – was a BBC documentary from summer 1986 entitled *It Was Twenty Years Ago Today*. There they all were, a line of vaguely arthritic middle-aged men – the distinguishing mark of a retired professional footballer is a faint uneasiness in the knee region. Banks, one eye gone after a car smash, was some kind of celebrity golf PR man. Cohen was a builder recovering from several operations for stomach cancer. Wilson – Ray Wilson, the classiest left-back of the 1960s – was an *undertaker*. Stiles, track-suited and still a stranger to his dentist, was coaching somewhere. Jack Charlton and Alan Ball had graduated to management. The forward line was a nightmare of insurance salesmen. Only Bobby Charlton – the one serene, Olympian figure of the bunch – still seemed to be himself, somehow detached from the workaday realities that had gathered up the others and deposited them in undertakers' parlours, cancer wards and beaten-up training grounds. Ghastlier still was the discovery that there were further depths to be plumbed. One of the saddest things I ever saw in a newspaper – or something that described itself as a newspaper – was a mugshot of Bobby Moore wearing a World War One aviator's bonnet and in the guise of 'tailgunner Moore' reporting in words of one syllable on some game he'd been sent to cover. This was followed by the news that our man, in his capacity as the *Sunday Sport*'s 'sports editor', had been taken ill in the office while supervising the putting together of the next day's pages. Christ! An England captain labouring on one of Fatboy Sullivan's porn sheets! It's hard to convey just how upset I was by this, the thought of that tall, graceful figure, the expression on his face as he lifted the ball off Pele or Eusebio one of quiet seriousness, reduced to scanning layout grids while the plump goblin next to him reckoned up the nipple count and wondered if they could squeeze in another loanshark ad.

All this is hugely unreasonable, of course. It ignores the fact – a very common oversight among football supporters – that players have lives to live off the pitch, and livings to make; ignores, too, the limited financial rewards available even to internationals 30 years ago. A false distinction, inevitably, but the average Premiership teenage superbrat already on £5,000 a week might care to spare a thought for Ray Wilson counting the bottles of embalming fluid. If there is one thing that any prolonged study of past time teaches us, it is perhaps that people's lives can rarely sustain the weight of the myths that we create above them. At the same time, to ignore the effect of the '66 World Cup victory on a whole generation of pre-teenage children is to ignore something fundamental about mass perceptions of the English game, and of England itself, over the past 30 years. Broadly speaking, if you are a white English male aged around forty, your initial interest in the game will almost certainly have been sparked off by July 1966, extended through the near-miss of Mexico 1970 and maintained until the Poland defeat of 1973 which effectively ended Sir Alf Ramsey's career. Localised perceptions, too. The so-called 'soccerati' – Nick Hornby, Pete Davies, Giles Smith, Harry Pearson and others – tend to be men in early middle age whose pre-adolescent lives more or less began with the sight of Bobby Charlton, head down ominously over the ball, about to strike one of his 40-yard screamers, or Nobby Stiles – small, gap-toothed and ferocious – niggling away at some lofty forward like a terrier worrying a mastiff. There is a particular type of modern English soccer writing that, whatever the glories currently before it, can never quite forget the age before wall-to-wall TV, stupid haircuts and telephone number salaries, when it didn't seem fanciful to think of Bobby Moore as some kind of role model and epitome of the Corinthian spirit. This was why the job on the *Sunday Sport* really hurt – like Roy of the Rovers being found in a massage parlour.

There is a paradox here, too, and not merely the usual one about a present interest disguising a backward projection. The second stage of the Ramsey tenure was what lured all us bright young pre-teens in our sober provincial homes towards football in the first place. At the same time it was also what closed the game off for us, combined with the vast stock of parental opinion on display to suggest that this was the end of an era, not a beginning. For my own part, I can't detach what I thought and assumed about English football in the late '60s and early '70s from what my father thought and assumed about it. My father was born in 1921, which means that his memory extends back to the early 1930s. Although his consuming interest, understandably enough, was the local side – Norwich City – his adult perspective on England and English internationals was extraordinarily wide. During the war, despite various RAF postings to Ireland and occupied Europe – he was actually *playing* football on a blasted heath somewhere in Germany when strafed by a Messerschmitt – he managed to attend any number of matches between Services XIs that just happened to contain internationals as conscripts. After the war, and back in Norwich, he was the kind of man who found it a pleasure to make the 240 mile round-trip to Wembley to watch internationals. Basically, between around 1946 and the mid-1950s, Dad saw the lot. He was there in 1953, of course, when they went down 3–6 to Hungary, and was so overwhelmed by the sight of Puskas and Hidegkuti nutmegging Billy Wright and his puzzled companions that he came to use the Hungarians as a yardstick with which to measure teams from the glittering present. The upshot of this wholesale immersion in the professional game of the '40s and '50s was that the names which floated through my youthful imaginings included Lawton, Matthews and Mannion as well as Hurst, Banks and Charlton. Predictably, this absorption was reinforced by literature. There was a row of '50s sports books on the downstairs shelf – items such as Billy Wright's *Football Is My Passport* – and by the time I was ten I could tell not you not only what Bobby Charlton ate for breakfast but also that waggish Len Shackleton had advertised a chapter of his autobiography as 'What the Average Director Knows About the Game' and then left the rest of the single page that followed blank.

What my father really thought about 1966 I've never quite been able to fathom. Inevitably, it was a whole lot more than football. Having had five years of his early manhood spirited away by the war, seen his house bombed out and several of his friends die, he hated Germans. The final, consequently, was invested with a vast symbolic significance. I can remember him jumping out of his armchair in a paroxysm of delight when the final whistle went, and, such was his exultation, presenting me with a pound note, the first time that I'd ever had such a thing. But though he certainly rated Charlton, R., Hurst and Moore, I think they paled a bit before the lurking behemoths – Lawton, Mannion and Frank Swift – of his youth, and curiously enough I never recall him being quite as interested in the national side after that. Such passion as he cared to expend on the game was reserved for Carrow Road. Perhaps, in a small way, he saw the Jules Rimet trophy as a line drawn under his own early life – he was in his mid-forties in 1966 – a period that had coincided with a golden age of English football. Then there was the fact that he disliked Sir Alf, in much the same way that he later disliked Bobby Robson, on account of the Ipswich Town connection. But whatever the spur, the conclusion was the same. By the early '70s the Golden Age was gone. Bobby Charlton had proceeded to dignified retirement. Ramsey was back cultivating his Suffolk garden. In their place a succession of no-hopers and makeweights struggled gamely yet fruitlessly and, ultimately, embarrassingly on.

Wheeled under the arc-lights of forensic analysis, Golden Ages typically end up being pitilessly exposed. So literary critics who expound on the ability of the Victorian novel to knock anything our pallid scribblers can produce into a cocked hat nearly always overlook the mountains of bygone rubbish that crowd out the second-hand shelves alongside Dickens, Thackeray and Trollope. Predictably, it takes only the merest glance at the appropriate reference books and participants' memoirs to show that it wasn't like that at all. Take, for example, the performances of the national side between the end of the war and the 1958 World Cup (where we ended the first round table all square with the Soviet Union and went out in the play-off) – roughly the period covered by Billy Wright's *Football Is My Passport*. As a child the book and its author were rather favourites of mine. The blond quiff, the climb over the barriers of his own physique to become a five-feet-nine-inch centre-back who regularly outjumped men three inches taller, the being told about his England captaincy by the conductress on the Wolverhampton bus – all this somehow accorded with my juvenile notions of what football was and the spirit in which you should approach it. Thirty years on from a first reading, much of *Football Is My Passport* is hard to swallow – the deference and the reluctance to find a bad word for anybody. At the same time it is a book whose sociological interest outweighs the reminiscences of stout chaps and 'real comedians' who graced England touring parties in the 1950s. On the one hand, Wright has no doubt that England teams of the period harboured some superlative talent – one of the photos shows him standing in the line-up of the team that steamrollered Portgual 10–0 in 1947, including Matthews, Mannion, Mortensen, Lawton and Finney – and there are any number of references to patriotic pride and duty. Yet at the heart of the book lies a deep uncertainty. Wright lingers over the great disasters of the immediately post-war era – the 0–1 defeat by the USA, the Magyar fiasco of 1953, the

Yugoslavian drubbing shortly afterwards – with desperate unease. What had happened? Where had it all gone wrong? There was a symbolic moment early on in the Hungary game, with the score at 1–1, when he went into a tackle with his eye fixed on the ball lying at Puskas's feet. Ninety-nine times out of a hundred he would have got it. This time Puskas whipped it back like lightning, our Billy found himself 'in contact with nothing' as he puts it, and a half-second later the ball was in the back of the net.

Who to blame? Marvelling at the speed of the Hungarians, and their awesome dexterity with the ball, Wright is uneasily conscious that the England players weren't quick or penetrative enough – for the record, the England forward line in 1953 was Matthews, Taylor, Mortensen, Sewell and Robb. To this is added a belief that England was falling behind the commitment and enthusiasm of overseas competition. Every time that he travels abroad, Wright compiles a dutiful little file of statistics – so many thousands of registered players, so many hundreds of certified coaches – and worries a bit over the implications. Abetting all this evidence of decline, he feels, is the affluent post-war world of Harold Macmillan's Britain (Wright started as a teenage apprentice in the 1930s and thought himself lucky to get a job), that soft, comfortable life of TV, armchairs and the Light Programme rising up to distract England's youth from the call of the football pitch. It's a strange sensation, this, to find the exemplar of soccer's Golden Age accusing the youngsters of the 1950s of being a gang of degenerate stop-at-homes, but no one could doubt the depth of Wright's sincerity. Watching the street boys in Brazil juggling tangerines on their insteps, he is forced to admit that the country that taught the world to play 20 years before is in serious danger of being overtaken.

In the rush to mythologise the decade that followed, the Wright prognosis is rather too easy to set to one side. Banks, Cohen, Wilson, Stiles, Moore, Charlton, J., Ball, Hunt, Hurst, Charlton, R., Peters. You can't argue with that, not with a team so wantonly decorated with talent that it can't find a space for the extraordinary versatility and pizzazz of Greaves. On a technical level, the class of 1970 – which included newcomers Bell, Lee and Mullery with '66 veterans Moore, Ball, Hurst, Charlton, R., and Peters surviving for the quarter-final, were even slightly better. And yet students of Ramsey's 11-year reign tend to forget some of the embarrassments that preceded 1966 – the 2–5 thrashing by France in the 1963 Nations Cup, the 1–5 humiliation courtesy of Brazil on the 1964 South American tour; forget, too, Ramsey's inflexibility, the arguments with Moore and Greaves – whose larkiness Sir Alf had considerable trouble in accommodating – the apparently inexorable drift back to 4–4–2. To read contemporary, or near-contemporary accounts of the six 1966 games is a curious experience. The 0–0 draw against Uruguay was generally held to be an abysmal exercise in mutual imagination loss. Come the quarter-final against Argentina, the midfield, ringside testimony insists, had no idea. Only in the semi-final against Portgual, with Stiles marking Eusebio out of sight, did the machine start to whirr smoothly into gear, the passes connect, the assumption hold that here, finally, was a team rather than 11 extremely nifty lads stuck on a pitch together and told to act in unison.

And afterwards? The 1970 quarter-final mess-up, which probably wouldn't have happened had Banks not downed the bottle of local beer and rearranged his stomach a couple of days before, we know about. Last four in the 1968 European championships. Last eight in the 1972, ditto. 'One splendid success and eight years of anti-climax' is Brian Glanville's stark conclusion in *The Story of the World Cup*. For all the pull of memory, the light shining off the trophy held in Moore's outstretched hand that far-off summer day before exams, jobs and responsibilities, back when the world was green and promising, it's hard to disagree.

Some statistics. Not long ago, on the eve of Kevin Keegan's début as England manager, *The Independent* sports pages ran a spread entitled '50 Years of England' – nothing less, in fact, than an exhaustive analysis of every game contested by an England XI since 1950. The whole thing was subsumed into two tables of managerial performance – one computed on the three points for a win, one point for a draw formula, the other by way of a slightly more abstruse 'ratings' system – and a decade by decade analysis of team performance. How did past time turn out? Past time turned out to be not as one remembered it. Best manager on the three points for a win, one for a draw system (Walter Winterbottom wasn't included among the candidates, by the way, on the reasonable grounds that he never had full managerial control)? Ramsey, of course, but with Greenwood not that far behind and Hoddle a very creditable third. Best manager under the ratings system (based on quality of opposition and venue)? Ramsey again, with Greenwood an uncomfortably close second and Venables zooming up to third. The bottom berths in each table were occupied, respectively, by Revie and Taylor and Robson and Revie. In terms of chronological spread, the best decades for overall team performances were the 1960s and 1950s. The worst was the 1980s, and the second worst the 1970s. The lowest point ever reached in the post war era? The 1 2 defeat by Switzerland in Basle in 1981, when the captain was, ah, a certain K. Keegan. Historically, then, one can sketch a gradual rise to a mid-'60s plateau, followed by a 20-year decline leading to a modest '90s recovery. This doesn't mean, however, that 1950-70 constitutes some kind of golden age when we taught those frightful foreigners their sporting business. Neither does it provide an adequate yardstick by which to judge the serial indignities, the pious hopes and false dawns of today.

More than 30 years on, the spirit of 1966 still hangs over English football in the way that the memory of a prize fellowship at All Souls sometimes hangs over a tiring 50-year-old academic who still hasn't managed to produce that ground-breaking book on the Schleswig Holstein question: a memory of youthful promise which may console but is also, given that it hints at powers that were never fully developed, ambitions that were never wholly fulfilled, faintly irritating. One of the ghastliest, though at the same time most predictable, spectacles of the build-up to any World Cup in which England are involved is the regularity with which the ghosts of Moore, Charlton and Hurst are brought out to cast metaphorical blessings on the proceedings. The detachment of the average tabloid newspaper from any kind of observable reality is a feature of the modern media circus, of course, but oh dear me, the rubbish that was peddled in the papers prior to France 1998 – peddled in serious newspapers, too, if it comes to that. The barefaced lies that were spun around England's prospects and the awful xenophobia that accompanied it all! The traditional technique of mean-spirited newspapers – say you disapprove of an individual or a situation while simultaneously inciting it – has particularly grim results when applied to football. Soccer hooligans are scum, but let's hope we can get some really good pictures of them throwing things! Thus lads in St George's Cross T-shirts are trailed endlessly round foreign shopping malls in the not quite openly expressed hope that they'll give someone – some foreigner, of course – a really good kicking, managers are relentlessly scrutinised for signs of incipient weirdness, the slightest player-on-player or player-on-coaching-staff disagreement is seized upon and magnified to the nth degree, and to what purpose? Did anyone seriously believe that we were going to win the 1998 World Cup? Or that we deserved to win it? But, oh dear, the recriminations when we failed and the beetle-browed intimations of public disquiet. Of all the nonsense that was spoken or reported of France 1998, the worst case of all was the news that David Beckham had received hate-mail after his second-round sending off. Think about it. What kind of person is stupid enough, or mean-spirited enough, or thinks the time well-spent, to send a hate letter to a professional footballer? One could just about contrive a justification for harassing a politician in this way, but someone as unimportant and essentially innocuous as David Beckham?

Worse, perhaps, is the media's delight in jumping on a particular player and deciding that here, superabundantly, is where the national sporting spirit, the pale elusive scent of '66, resides. At the moment Michael Owen plays this talismanic role, but for almost the whole of the past ten years such perpetually glowing iconic status has been reserved for Paul Gascoigne. No offence to the man himself, but if ever a player epitomised the deficiencies of the English game and its enslavement to well-intentioned myth-making, that man is our Paul: a kind of emblem for the stupidity and wishful thinking that governs the workings of England plc. Rather a lot has been written about Gascoigne in the past ten years – a surprising amount of it by senior literary critics of the Ian Hamilton/Karl Miller school – but not too much, perhaps, on his enormous symbolic significance. *What about Gazza?* ran the headline throughout the '90s whenever some hapless incoming manager was trying to put a side together from what remained of the Premiership when you took away the foreign players. Was he fit? Was he sober? Was he sane? What on earth was it all about? Like most supporters, I first became properly aware of Gascoigne around the time of Italia '90. 'The best young player of the tournament,' Bobby Robson later opined, and bang right too.

When in doubt about the merits of some exceptionally talented and flamboyant sports star over whose general usefulness some kind of question mark hangs, I invariably refer the matter to my father. 'Ian Botham, Dad?' 'He's a yob . . . But you'd like to have him on your side.' 'Linford Christie, Dad?' 'He's a yob . . . But you'd like to have him in your relay squad.' And Paul Gascoigne? Taken to watch Norwich play Spurs at White Hart Lane in the autumn of 1990 – a game enlivened by the sight of squeaky-clean Mr Gary Lineker palming the ball downward and subsequently propelling it into the Norwich net with his back to the referee – Dad duly obliged. 'He's a yob . . . but you'd like to have him on your side.' Bang right again too, provided, that is, he was fit/sane/happy/not about to be had up for wife-beating or whatever. And yet – some magical moments like the Euro '96 goals excepted – he was never really the same player after the 1991 Cup final horror, which occurred, ironically enough, at a time when a less charitable ref would already have had him off the pitch for dangerous conduct. But then excessive charitableness was always Gascoigne's undoing. A Ramsey or Greenwood – even a Robson, when the going got tough – would have taken our Paul to one side at a very early stage in the proceedings and said – not in so many words, but the inference would have been clear even to Gascoigne – 'Look, son, that's as far as it goes. This is a football team, not a branch of the entertainment industry. Blow it again and you're out. *For ever.*' However, this being the 1990s, and the level of misguided sentiment about the national side which has been reached, no one ever did, or at any rate not until it was too late, and the result has been possibly the greatest squandering of God-given English talent in post-war soccer history.

Quite apart from comparatively minor irritations like newspaper hysteria and player worship – the wrong sort of player, inevitably, and for the wrong reasons – there is a wider context in which all this rapt national self-consciousness, nervously focused on something as trivial as a game, needs to be fixed. Of all the years in which we could have won the World Cup, there is a rather dreadful significance in the fact that it had to be 1966. Look at the 1960s from the vantage point of the late 1990s and they are the decade in which Britain first became fully aware of the consequences of having lost the Second World War. Suez, perhaps, is the first symbolic intimation of fading influence, but the 1960s, to the modern historian, is a procession of ominous marker flags: devaluation, Wilson sucking up to President Johnson, the economy patently starting to disintegrate, smoke-filled rooms full of trades unionists readying themselves for the great industrial showdowns of 1972–74. The winters of discontent, the 1976 IMF meltdown, the discovery that Europe was a Franco-German run gentleman's club just itching to avenge itself for past slights – all these had their origins, took root and grew in Wilson's Britain.

At the time, though, it didn't seem like that. We were basking in the midst of the Swinging Sixties, a kind of blur of rising hemlines and expectations, the white heat of the technological revolution and a stupendous optimism about our future that now seems altogether ludicrous. In these circumstances, winning the World Cup was a spectacular demonstration that England still mattered, an eternal validation of 'Englishness' and 'English character' played out on native soil and against a time-honoured English enemy. Harold Wilson. The Beatles. Bobby Moore shaking the Queen's hand and lifting the World Cup. These are characteristic '60s images, melded together into a little time capsule of purpose and pride. As we know, it wasn't like that at all, and the following decades confirmed the fractures in our institutions and self-belief that the '60s had only hinted at. But whereas our political and economic life in the past 30 years has been an endless series of readjustments and admissions of declining power and influence, our sporting life still exists in this quaint never-never-land where bygone achievements are somehow ripe for duplication if we can get the right players, the right manager, the right attitude. Maybe we can. In the meantime, though, it's a whole third of a century since anything really happened in English football. The red-shirted boys who wove their way past Beckenbauer and company are touching sixty now, and Bobby Moore is dead.

The Making of Saint Michael

Philip Cornwall

Michael Owen's Signed England Shirt To Win! (Unwashed!)
Sugar magazine, March 1999

Michael Owen's Million Pound Book Deal
Apparently he's signed up with a company to produce three books in the next two years – including an autobiography. That should be good: 'Got born, went to school, scored against Argentina . . . err . . .
'Supersub', *Football365.co.uk discussion forum*, May 1999

At the beginning of May 1997 Michael Owen was a largely unknown Liverpool youth player without a first-team game to his name. By the end of June 1998 he was the toast of the England team, on the front pages of papers from Saint-Étienne to Beijing. When the 1998 World Cup started, Owen was already a phenomenally successful footballer for an 18-year-old, especially an English one; but his life changed irrevocably when he put England into a 2–1 lead with what was, neutrals seem to agree, the second best goal of the tournament. In 14 months a footballer yet to win a medal as a professional, so small and slight you could almost mistake him for a mascot, had gone from being an unknown to becoming perhaps the most famous teenager in the world: a footballer, a sex symbol, a marketing tool to sell everything from Swiss watches to crisps.

By the end of the 1998-99 season, Owen was still without a trophy to his name – unless you count the 1998 BBC Sports Personality of the Year award, or the other personal triumphs he accumulated. Indeed, those who gave him his breaks for club and country, Roy Evans and Glen Hoddle, have moved on under equally painful, if very different, circumstances. Lilleshall, the élite football academy at which he was educated, has been abandoned in favour of a policy of broadening the search for new stars. Steve McManaman, the player who provided the passes which launched his club career, and gave him his first England goal, had opted for Spain after yet another season where things just didn't quite go right for Liverpool, and has been written off as a failure by many. Owen is one of the greatest success stories in football, but only against a background of failure.

When it was reported in May 1999 that Owen had signed a deal to produce three books, there was a degree of cynicism about it – footballer's autobiographies are renowned for being amongst the least interesting forms of publishing yet invented. At his age, honestly, what was going to fill the space between the covers?

What is it about Owen – both on and off the pitch – that marks him out? What is it about the game in the 1990s that will make his experience different from that of his predecessors? And can those around him cope with the implications of his talent? Will he be a shooting star both literally and metaphorically, or has he got what it takes to fulfil the enormous expectations That Goal placed on his shoulders? Is he a saint, a messiah, or a false prophet?

The first time I saw Michael Owen play was at Selhurst Park on the first day of the 1997–98 season. I saw him play for Liverpool against Wimbledon just fleetingly, for seven or eight minutes through a gap between two gates after neither love nor money proved enough to secure a ticket. It was a ridiculously hot day, and the idea of standing still in bright sunshine for 90 minutes to watch about half a football pitch palled in due course. So I wasn't there in the second half when, after a brief discussion with a team-mate about whether he was old enough to handle the responsibility, the 17 year old stepped up to calmly equalise from the penalty spot.

With two matches to go in the previous season, he had scored there against Wimbledon as a substitute on his début, as Roy Evans's side surrendered their chance of winning the Premiership with a 2–1 defeat, but nonetheless it took remarkable calmness to secure a point on that boiling hot day. Though few that day understood quite how much that confidence was to become an Owen trademark through his first full season. Indeed it was something which he'd already demonstrated breaking schoolboy records for clubs and country. Gary Speed's appearance record and Ian Rush's goalscoring mark went for Deeside; and he'd bettered the total shared by Kevin Gallen and Nick Barmby for England schoolboys.

On his European début against Celtic he found himself in the clear 40 yards from goal in front of a hostile crowd of 50,000 with only a dozen minutes gone; the ball ended up in the back of the net. This was a crucial staging post in his rise to public prominence, coming live on BBC television, and around this time – early September – questions started to be asked about whether he should make the step-up at international level. Not to the first team, but from the Under-18s to the Under-21s. The conclusion was, no. Not yet, too soon – and as it was he got himself suspended. The verdict was reversed by the end of October, and while his Under-21 début saw his team go out of the European Championships on away goals, Owen scored. Four months later, in February 1998, Michael Owen became England's youngest full international this century.

The previous record had stood since the 1950s, when the tragic figure of Duncan Edwards, one of the Man Utd stars killed in the Munich air disaster, had set a new mark. For years since, England managers have been criticised for not giving youth its chance. Owen's dead-eyed calm not only landed himself a shot at the national side – but significantly has altered the way we look at young players. It will not be a surprise if his hold on the record is a brief one. Joe Cole, for instance, the West Ham midfielder with a handful of Premiership matches to his name, is widely tipped to break the record.

It is important to acknowledge the role that other people's bad luck played in Owen's sudden rise. Robbie Fowler, another youthful goalscoring phenomenon, had been sent off just before the end of the 1997 season, creating the vacancy that prompted Roy Evans to hand Owen his début. Injury to Fowler meant he was unavailable at the start of the next season, too. Injury to Alan Shearer meant that there was a spare slot in the England team for the first half of the next season. Andy Cole was due to play against Chile until he too was injured. Then Fowler was again injured, this time seriously, and so for the last three months of the 1998 season Owen was Liverpool's undisputed lead striker, which not only removed a serious rival for a World Cup place but showed Glenn Hoddle yet more evidence of how well he could handle the spotlight.

It is also worth remembering that the much-criticised Hoddle had pitched Rio Ferdinand into the top ten youngest England players the previous November, against Cameroon. But it was Owen's phenomenal maturity which suddenly lowered the barrier. It wasn't just That Goal. In the second game of the tournament, against Romania, he came on at 1–0 down and immediately equalised. In the last few minutes England let in a second goal; Owen then struck the woodwork from 20 yards. And against Argentina, he scored his penalty in the dramatic shootout conclusion; a task beyond two of England's senior players, Paul Ince and David Batty. The new motto was, if you're good enough, you're young enough, and the effect has not been confined to football. Within a few weeks of the World Cup, the golfer Justin Rose was being hailed as that sport's equivalent, and countless articles have referred to how much English cricket could do with its own Michael Owen.

Of course, it's not just for playing ability that the English cricket team could do with its own Michael Owen. What was once the national summer sport is under attack on all sides. It's being squeezed by an ever-expanding football season. The pre-eminence cricket's Sunday League enjoyed in the 1970s and early '80s has been usurped as tennis, motor racing, horse racing, whatever, have moved from Saturday. The England team have, with the odd blip, been consistent losers, and there's no doubt that they could do with the inspiration a cricketing Owen would add on the pitch.

But in this world where it's not the message, it's the packaging – an Owen would be just as valuable in marketing the sport. For Owen's fresh face sells.

He reaches out to teenage boys, who want to play like him; teenage girls, who want to go out with him; and their mothers, who would like to mother him, and can feel confident that he's the kind of role model/imaginary boyfriend who's not going to lead the kids astray. His name or picture are on the front page of *Shoot* and *Match*, and *Sugar* and *It's Bliss*. Walkers Crisps, who shift bucket-loads to this market, have earmarked him as the successor to Gary Lineker, and honoured him by renaming Cheese and Onion, 'Cheese 'n' Owen'.

But he's not restricted to the youth market. One of his first endorsements was with the Swiss watch makers, Tissot, not a brand which targets those whose disposable income accrues from paper rounds and babysitting. Owen appeals across the age groups and the sexes, an achievement few other sports stars or entertainers can achieve.

Owen was interviewed at length in the April 1999 edition of *GQ*, on sale at the same time as his name was on the front of *Sugar*. *GQ* described Owen thus: 'As pin-up material goes, he's more Boyzone than Robbie Williams.' But Owen straddles this gap. Indeed Ronan Keating's management have tried to place an interview with the boy-band leader in *GQ* as they try to establish him in a more adult market, but the magazine see him as being too young for their readership. And look at Geri Halliwell's difficult transition from a Spice Girl for the teenies to an AOR solo artist.

Owen's breadth of appeal is a product of his fame, but also of how he handles himself. Credit is due to Tissot and to kit manufacturers Umbro, who both made major investments in him before he went to France. It's hard to imagine the watchmakers attaching themselves to the star of England's last World Cup campaign. Paul Gascoigne's big endorsement after Italia '90 was for the aftershave, Brut.

However half-baked the devil/saint comparison Walkers Crisps made between Lineker and the youngster, Owen's wholesome image is an important part of who he is, and what he means to football. Walkers hope, of course, that he is the successor to Lineker as the nice man of English football as well as its top striker. When it comes to on the pitch, that is a moot point at best, but off it there are important similarities.

Lineker was made by a World Cup, and as Golden Boot winner in Mexico in 1986, he moved to Barcelona. The former Leicester and Everton man proved remarkably receptive to new cultural experiences. In 1992, as he moved into sports presentation, he was part of the BBC's coverage of the Barcelona Olympics. When the opening ceremony took a particularly weird turn, Des Lynam turned to Gary with a 'these Spanish, funny chaps' remark and was amazed as the son of a greengrocer who refused to serve Argentinians during the '86 World Cup launched into a lengthy appreciation of the architecture of Antoni Gaudi and the art of Joán Miró.

British footballers abroad were famous for their refusal to embrace their surroundings; when West Brom went on a tour to China in the late '70s, one anonymous player famously refused the chance to go and visit one of two man-made objects visible from the moon (the other is the Staten Island rubbish dump) by saying, 'When you've seen one wall, you've seen them all.'

Owen, through his family and his attendance at the FA's Lilleshall School of Excellence, has learnt all this at an early age. His father Terry, a professional with Everton, Rochdale and others in the '60s and '70s, inspired in his son a rare dedication. Perhaps because his own career was spent around the lower divisions with just the briefest top-flight spell at Everton, Owen Senior drummed into his young son the importance of doing everything to make sure that if the chance came your way, you took it.

While Owen is too young and too dedicated to the game to have developed a cultural hinterland, there is still time. He has absorbed the right attitudes to diet and training which are only just being embraced by professional clubs thanks to the introduction of foreign coaches, and their success. He doesn't drink, and watches what he eats. Phil Thompson, Liverpool's recently appointed coach, played for the club in an era when you drank as hard as you played, and plenty of Owen's teammates subscribe to a similar philosophy. Owen's success, though, is as the first of a new generation of players who grow up knowing the kind of things players like Lineker only learnt abroad. There is still a battle going on in the English game over its culture; Owen, along with the imported coaches and players, should help the forces of enlightenment win it.

Owen has, of course, benefited enormously from the changes in society's attitudes to football in the 1990s. From being reviled by the government in the hooligan years, when every innocent fan was portrayed as being a thug, and few companies would dream of getting involved with the sport, an amazing transformation took place, starting with Lineker, Gascoigne and Italia '90. The result is today's situation where no self-respecting player is without his endorsements.

The risks of sports star endorsements are many. Umbro may have Owen, but they also have Alan Shearer, a man whose career was changed by an injury in a friendly in the summer of 1997 which cut him down at the height of his powers. No one disputes his determination to recover from injury – he's done so remarkably well in the past – but now he seems to have lost his spark irrevocably, and Umbro have a very expensive contract with a has-been. Lawrence Dallaglio, England's rugby union captain, had his world turned upside down by the *News of the World* undercover investigation team, ironically pretending to represent a shaving firm considering using him for their adverts in order to wheedle a damaging confession about drugs out of him.

GQ asked Owen about his future after football, posing the question as to whether he'd end up another George Best, while knowing full well that the very idea was preposterous. As Owen said: 'I've got at least another ten years of football in future of me. Nearer the time, I'll start thinking what else to do with my life. I certainly won't end up in the gutter. Or turn into an alcoholic or anything.'

But you can never write injury out of the equation. And there are other factors which may affect Owen's future.

On the first day of the 1996-97 season, it was Man Utd who were playing at Wimbledon, rather than Liverpool. A goal at Selhurst Park launched another England career, indeed if David Beckham has an equivalent of That Goal, it was the one he scored that day. With time running out and his side 2–0 to the good, Beckham saw that Wimbledon's keeper was off his line, and chipped him. From the halfway line.

The goal helped Beckham into the England side two weeks later, and he became the only ever-present during the qualifying campaign for France '98. Dropped for the opening matches after Glenn Hoddle expressed doubts over his temperament, Beckham bounced back with his first goal for his country, a free kick to help beat Colombia. Playing for a successful club, unlike Owen, and with his pop star wife, Beckham was the other rising star in the side. It was his dinked pass to Owen that set the striker on his road to the Argentine goal.

But just as Umbro must have been celebrating Owen's personal celebrity while they were mourning England's departure, so the UK division of Adidas had a double reason to mourn that morning. On the eve of the game, they had placed an advert in the papers reading, 'After tonight, England v Argentina will be remembered for what one man did with his feet.' The next morning, while Owen's star was in the ascendant in relation to his team-mates, David Beckham's position was best summed up by the front page of the *Mirror,* one of the papers that had carried the Adidas advert: '10 heroes and one stupid boy.'

With the game in the balance at 2–2 early in the second half, Diego Simeone brought down Beckham just inside the Argentine half. A free kick to England; and a yellow card for the miscreant. But as Simeone walked past the prone 23-year-old, the Englishman kicked out. Not violently, but enough to merit a red card, to prove right the doubts about his temperament. Simeone had leant down to say something as he walked past Beckham, and he had snapped.

Beckham recovered from that experience, playing a major role the next season in winning for his club the unprecedented treble of league, FA Cup and European Cup, in the face of some of the most hostile crowds an English player has ever faced. He was taunted for three reasons: first, jealousy of him and his team; second, because of what he did; third, because of his refusal to admit the error of what he did. He dealt with it by making sure that his team won.

He could have made life easier for himself with an admission of guilt; instead, the only one offered, by his agent, was contradicted by what Beckham actually said. When asked in Norway whether he had put the World Cup behind him, he said: 'I didn't do anything wrong, so I haven't got anything to put behind me.' Instead he did it the hard way, by playing better and better, and rarely rising to the bait: for the most part, efforts to wind him up cost you dearly; the sight of Beckham cupping his ears to listen for the abuse after setting up or scoring yet another goal silenced the taunters. In a later interview, he was asked whether the World Cup experience had made him stronger: 'Definitely, because I've had to grow up a lot and it's made me realise a lot of things.' For those of us who argued that he should be taunted precisely so he would learn to cope with it, and been lambasted for it, this was a source of quiet pleasure.

Beckham remains crucially important to England's future, and therefore Michael Owen's future. After all, Owen is a goalscorer; he needs a goal creator. The story of Beckham's career asks some important questions of Owen.

For a start, whatever it may say on crisp packets, Owen is no saint. Many Man Utd fans sprang to the defence of Beckham by pointing out that Owen had been sent off not once but twice: for England Under-18s in September 1997, and then in March 1998 at Old Trafford, when he picked up two yellow cards for tackles that could have merited red. The first was on Peter Schmeichel; the second finished Ronnie Johnsen's club season. Owen hadn't calmed down even when he scored, in between the two cards, and his team played an hour without him. Wasn't that the same as Beckham's offence?

Up to a point. The context for Owen's offence at Old Trafford was different, and so was his reaction to it. It was not the last 16 of the World Cup; his manager had not felt the need to publicly warn Owen about his petulance; on each occasion that he earnt a card it was in a reckless attempt to reach the ball, with no attention to the consequences of his actions but nonetheless with the ball in play, rather than out of it with a free kick awarded to his team. And afterwards, in every interview, Owen said that he regretted it, that he wished it hadn't happened, but that now that it had happened he hoped he would learn from his mistake.

Beckham has succeeded in laying the ghost in the best possible way, with an outstanding season and a massive role in Man Utd's historic treble. Yet there lurks within him the desire for revenge beyond what he can exact within the rules, and so the doubts are still there. One moment early in the season, when he risked a red card during United's 3–0 defeat at Arsenal – Stephen Hughes fouled Beckham on the halfway line, bringing a free kick and a booking for the Arsenal youngster. But that was not enough. A couple of minutes later, Roy Keane fouled Hughes, and as the Arsenal player lay on the ground, Beckham deliberately stepped on his thigh. Luckily for him, it wasn't noticed by the referee, and the moment passed.

Owen's regret seemed sincere, and while his tackling earnt him the odd booking in 1998–99, including one with England away to Sweden in the very first match after the Argentina game, it seemed that he pulled back subsequently. One nasty incident in Liverpool's 4–2 defeat of Aston Villa in November 1998, which culminated in Stan Collymore being shown a red card for retaliating, showed that the temper and the poor tackles are still there, but he never really looked close to a repeat.

Beckham and Owen finished the 1998–99 season the same way, though. While Owen was on holiday, recovering from injury, David Beckham was limping off at Wembley. Both were knocked out by hamstring problems.

Owen had struggled with a niggling problem until it finally went against Leeds in March 1999. Perhaps for the last time, Steve McManaman played a ball into the channel for his team-mate to run on to, and Owen looked at first to be getting there. But he pulled up suddenly, and went to ground. (It is worth recording that even though he missed his club's last seven games, Owen still finished equal top-scorer in the Premiership, with the same number of goals, 18, it had taken him to achieve the same feat the year before.)

Beckham was playing for England against Sweden at Wembley, in early June. With the game already going badly – goalless, two substitutions already made, and Paul Scholes sent off for two recklessly late tackles – Beckham, the one England player who looked as if he could turn the game, pulled up and limped off.

A footballer's career is a fragile one – especially for a player like Owen. So much of what he does is based on speed. He has skill, but he lacks strength and height. Which makes him vulnerable.

Owen is very lucky that he is playing today, rather than 20 years ago, as the protection offered to forwards is far better. But it will still take luck if he is to get through his career without a major injury.

Of course, being injured didn't stop David Beckham making headlines in the summer of 1999. He was facing a fixture which emphasised another difference between him and Michael Owen. His wedding.

By a narrow margin, readers of *The Sun* voted the marriage of Prince Edward and Sophie Rhys-Jones as being more important than that of Beckham and Victoria Adams, but the paper drew attention to a late flurry of calls from London's SW1 area, from similar phone numbers. *OK* magazine paid a reported seven-figure sum for the pictures of the event, clearly believing that the hugely successful footballer and the pop star mother were going to help sell piles and piles of copies. The pictures were the *OK* cover story across three successive weeks, with a book thrown in for good measure. The only time Michael Owen's private life has garnered many column inches was when his mother blubbed as he became the youngest-ever winner of the BBC Sports Personality of the Year; Beckham has been regular tabloid front-page fodder from the moment he started going out with Posh Spice.

Beckham had a certain glamour about him from the first. He was seen in the fashionable clubs and bars, and took great care in his appearance, his clothes but also his hair. The floppy dyed fringe seemed almost designed to obscure his vision, but was clearly something his eventual wife valued a great deal. A Spice Girls documentary showed her calling David after the fateful red card against Argentina, and she seemed as concerned to point out that his roots needed doing as to commiserate on his and England's respective exits.

When they first started going out the news broke a thousand teenage hearts, but the way the couple subsequently acted, notably over the birth of their child Brooklyn, won back many to the idea that this was a fairytale romance. Some teachers and child psychologists provoked a brief media storm by suggesting that teenage girls would seek to emulate the couple with children of their own.

This was just one example of the price you can pay for being in the limelight: getting branded 'irresponsible' by the *Daily Mail* for having children before you're married. Others included a storm over an Easter 1999 interview with the London listings magazine, *Time Out*. The magazine decided to draw a parallel between Beckham's verbal crucifixion following his World Cup red card and the crucifixion of Jesus Christ, which was their business. But when they persuaded Beckham to dress in white transparent clothes, decorated with the odd cross and holding his arms out wide, his desire to embrace the world of fashion photography back-fired. And, of course, all through his relationship there has been the scurrilous song with which rivals fans taunted the United player, 'Posh Spice takes it up . . .' Even those of us who regard Beckham's temper as one of his worst characteristics have to feel sorry for him when forced to listen to that while going about his daily business (indeed if Diego Simeone muttered something along those lines then I take back all my criticism).

Owen has never had to put up with anything more detailed than analysis of his game: abuse from rival fans in the stands but nothing like that endured by Beckham, and the odd critical piece on the sports pages. Papers have tried to fill a bit of space with descriptions of his family life and his long-standing girlfriend, but his failure to fall into any of the traditional football traps – alcohol, fast cars and nightclubs – protects him. Time might change him – and who knows what might happen if he meets the right pop star. But for the time being the clubs he is best known at are golf establishments, and his private life is just that.

Many would say the longer that holds true the better. There is enough pressure for a young footballer from the day job, and from the fact that the every day attention from well-wishers can be hard enough to deal with, without seeing your every personal move discussed in prurient detail. Beckham has to some extent bought in to this culture, with the *OK* deal and a Channel 4 documentary about the wedding. The *Time Out* shoot was of course voluntary, one of a series of interviews way off the beaten track, all the way to *Elle*. Which begs the question of the standard of advice he is getting, given that he apparently was unaware of the implications of the Jesus poses. Footballers are icons, but this was perhaps going a bit far.

All this off-the-pitch activity has lifted Beckham above Owen in the fame stakes; not that Michael seems bothered by this. But there is another, perhaps crucial, question in which the best way to consider the striker is in relation to the pop star's consort. Providing that he avoids injury and suspension, Beckham will be England's primary creative player for the foreseeable future. In one important way, he and Owen are incompatible. Beckham is widely acknowledged as the best crosser of the ball in Europe. But Owen, not least because of his height, is weak in the air.

What Owen has is a potential every bit as great as Beckham's, with the advantage of being five years younger; though dependent on speed of foot, his speed of mind is getting better all the time as he practises. However, you won't have to look far to find a Liverpool fan who would argue that Fowler is currently the better all-round player. Only Alan Shearer of today's players has reached 100 goals faster, and Fowler's greater experience is embodied in a man who, after all, is only 24. It's too late for Robbie to learn common sense, and Owen's potential is greater, but in pure footballing terms he's not yet his partner's equal. Meanwhile, David Beckham's lead over his peers is so great that the pressure to conform may well fall on the forward line. Owen must try to score for his country while unable to capitalise on one of its principal weapons. There is a strong possibility that Owen will see those bigger than him promoted to the England starting line-up ahead of him, which may be a disaster for Owen, but also for his country. For not only would they be losing the services of a talented individual, but also throwing away a chance to change the pattern of play in this country.

For Owen's talent is a challenge to a football culture which has long prided itself on the power of its centre-forwards. The purr in Andy Gray's voice every time the Sky pundit describes a headed goal sums up the place that aerial power occupies in the British game. Brian Clough may have said: 'If God had meant football to be played in the air, he'd have put grass in the sky,' but his 1978 Nottingham Forest side won the league championship in large part due to the goals of Peter Withe, as old-fashioned as centre-forwards come. The terrible fact is that while the tactic is effective at club level, at international level headers are a rarity. The best defenders and keepers deal with high balls with relative ease.

The worship of the high ball reached its peak in the late '80s and early '90s, with Wimbledon, Sheffield United and others playing the ball in the air towards the penalty area from anywhere, playing the percentages, hoping that for every x balls that were easily headed away, y would result in goals. In the league, it worked for a time; unfortunately at international level $y=0$, all too often.

Beckham is not in any way a representative of the old long-ball philosophy. His touch is superb, he isn't hoofing the ball forward on the off chance, instead it is played in from the right flank with a wicked curl and dip that first commits then leaves the keeper stranded off his line. And it worked to good effect for England against Poland in March 1999, setting up his club team-mate Paul Scholes for a vital goal as Kevin Keegan sought to restart his country's Euro 2000 qualifying campaign. When they work, they work well. Beckham's crosses are an important part of the armoury he offers his country.

But the challenge Owen represents is this: to get the best out if him, to get anything out of him, he needs the ball played on the ground. Beckham, as well as being the best crosser England has, is for many people the best passer. The argument about whether he should play inside or outside ignores the fact that playing one of England's two most talented players on the wing deprives the other of service, unless he is given a freer rein and can come inside, closer to Owen, catching his runs as he pulls the defence and playing the ball through the gaps between the obstacles, rather than over them.

This should not be a problem, would not be a problem in most of Europe, or indeed the football world. If the challenge is given to Beckham and he rises to it, then he and Owen will have done their bit to drag the English game away from the sterile tactics that have yielded so little. Owen will be 22 in 2002, just 26 at the time of a possible 2006 World Cup in England; he is a player around whom England could build not for one major competition, but if you count the European Championships then for five or six. Beckham is appreciably older, but will still be just 31 in 2006.

At Anfield they are building around him already. Time will tell whether a French revolution will turn Liverpool around. Gerard Houllier, the technical director of the French FA credited with playing a large part in their 1998 World Cup triumph, first partnered then succeeded Roy Evans when another season went wrong by early November. He was left with the task of rebuilding a side that lost its principal playmaker, Steve McManaman, when the 27-year-old opted to further his career in Spain. Owen and his attacking colleagues were only outscored by Man Utd; the boy wonder retained a share of the Premiership top-scorer position, matching his 18 goals in 1997–98 in spite of his injury. But the defence was a shambles, and Houllier was forced to rebuild it near enough from scratch, buying in from abroad the players who he hoped would turn things around, and shipping out the surplus whenever possible. But if there was one player who he wouldn't dream of letting go it was Owen.

Owen is not the only star at the club. Robbie Fowler and Jamie Redknapp are the leading English players but with plenty of young talent coming through, including England Under-21 captain Jamie Carragher, already a full international. Patrik Berger and Vladimir Smicer were amongst the first qualifiers for Euro 2000, with the Czech Republic. Yet there is added pressure on Houllier to deliver with such a star as Owen in his squad. He is on record as wanting to stay at Liverpool and win trophies there – but what if they don't come, and he seeks to leave? No manager could easily survive his departure under such circumstances.

The difference between failure at club and country level, of course, is that Michael Owen is stuck with England, but if Liverpool do not improve then he will look elsewhere. Should England fail to qualify for Euro 2000, then Owen will not be able to move on similarly.

He could get injured, too, and find himself unable to leave Liverpool. He'll have his fortune, of course – the contracts he's already signed will see to that. But he'll have more, thanks to six seconds of magic on 30 June 1998.

It might not be the best goal he has scored – in his own view – but is certainly the best known. What made it so special?

The best goal Michael Owen has ever scored was also in an England shirt, according to the man himself. But it came in a schoolboy international. Scotland had scored a sloppy equaliser, incensing the then 15 year old so much that he demanded the ball from the kick-off, waltzed around the entire opposition and restored the lead. By those standards, receiving a pass in the middle of the pitch and beating three men before powering the ball home seems relatively low-key.

But perhaps part of the magic of the goal was that it was not that magical. He got the ball in enough space to be able to pick up speed before an opponent could get near him, and from then on no one knew what to do. It wasn't the kind of intricate dribble which is more or less unrepeatable: the power of Owen's pace seemed to say, 'Give him the ball and he can do this again.' Earlier in the match England had equalised from the penalty spot after a defender made the mistake of trying to tackle him; and this was what happened if you didn't.

England – a country whose footballing record falls well short of its people's expectations – had a player who looked unstoppable, and yet was just 18. And the goal had been scored in the last 16 of the World Cup – against Argentina.

The extent to which sport is, in the words of George Orwell, war minus the shooting offends plenty of football fans. The two teams that England fans would most like to beat are undoubtedly Argentina and Germany, and neither the tabloid press nor many supporters can resist bringing the Falklands or World War II into the discussion around such matches.

And yet it is undeniable that part of the reason why these games have meant so much is down to the footballing, as well as the military, history. With the Germans, there are now two semi-finals lost on penalties in the '90s, two lost quarter-finals in the '70s, and lurking behind that, one match won in 1966 that casts the longest shadow in the English game. The 4–2 victory at Wembley in the 1966 World Cup final is still earning people knighthoods after more than thirty years of hurt.

With Argentina, there was a match in that same 1966 World Cup, a famously violent contest in which England committed the most fouls but the Argentine captain was sent off. The result was an England victory, but 20 years later Argentina won a return match at the same stage of the 1986 Mexico World Cup, with two of the most remembered goals in World Cup history. The first was punched in by Diego Maradona, with what he later dubbed 'the hand of God'; the second was stroked in by the same player after an astonishing dribble from inside his own half. The latter was a contender for the greatest goal ever in the tournament; Barry Davies, commentating for the BBC, immediately swallowed his bitterness at the first goal, pronouncing: 'You have to say, that was magnificent.' But few England fans see past the first goal, claiming that as Gary Lineker pulled one back the game should have been a draw, or Argentina should have been thrown out.

For the England coach in France, Glenn Hoddle, that 1986 match was a bitter personal memory. He had seen the handball clearly, and remonstrated with the referee at length after the goal was awarded, an understandable if unusual action for a player whose well-mannered determination was so often criticised. For Hoddle, and the whole footballing public, this match represented a chance for sporting revenge; Owen's goal and the skills he used in scoring it seemed to promise just that, and even better the chance to match Maradona's legitimate goal, or at least have one that was worth discussing. As we all know, and in circumstances too painful to relate, every England football fan was living a dream.

Whatever does happen to Michael Owen, he and we will always have that moment.

Chants Would Be a Fine Thing

Andrew Blake

Music and football have shared a lot ever since the origins of the organised game in the mid-1850s. But is there, or has there ever been, a national music for the 'national game'? When we lie back and sing of England there are many options. The national anthem, Elgar's 'Land of Hope and Glory', Queen's 'We Are the Champions', or 'Football's Coming Home'. But all these are pretty functional answers, covering a very wide range of music. Is there an English football music?

The basic answer is no; the more complex one, yes. In a simple sense there is very little identifiable 'English' music. Elgar and the other early twentieth century composers wrote German symphonic music combined with a little holiday spirit. Folk is easier to identify as Scottish, Welsh or Irish than English. Pop since the early 1960s has been an Anglo-American hybrid, with America the dominant partner; the same goes for jazz. Yes, there are inflections – a mode here, a turn of phrase there, vocal accents perhaps, but most of all a readiness to mix and match. Located at the hub of imperial and trading relationships dating from before the Roman invasions, and easier to settle in than the 'Celtic fringe', England has been culturally and ethnically hybrid for the last 2,000 years. 'Do you put the kettle on?' asks Fat Les. Yes – to make tea, grown in upland India and Africa from the descendants of plants stolen from the Chinese by British imperial adventurers. Likewise with music, and as with tea the theft is often the product of admiration. But that doesn't mean English music doesn't exist. Far from it: the secret's in the mix.

Where does it come from, that organised singing, chanting and cheering while paid professionals entertain and represent us? Of course there's a long story here, from caves and hunting rituals onwards, but let's just stay with that key word ritual – which is what we're dealing with at football, when worship combines with confrontation. The obvious sources, the ones where music is used to achieve communal solidarity of purpose, are religious and military. Football chants, however much they deviate in lyrical content, are all similar in melody and rhythm to the chants used in European churches since the dark ages. We talk about football 'anthems' – an anthem is sung by a church or cathedral choir, but as used in popular culture the meaning is closer to the church hymn, which everybody sings at various points during the service.

Hymns have a clear melodic curve, usually with a high point just before the final line of the verse to encourage the participants' continuing effort. 'Rock anthems' are songs with a similar melodic curve, though not in the verse but the chorus, and the audience – often enough in a football stadium – joins in: that ubiquitous Queen number, or Bon Jovi's 'Living on a Prayer', and plenty more. A football song in which the terraces can't join very easily – such as 'World in Motion', with its very one-dimensional attempt at a chorus – may be good music, but it's not an anthem; 'Football's Coming Home', which just about manages to produce a high point, or 'Land of Hope and Glory' for that matter, are both usable as football anthems despite their different origins.

Elgar's overstated imperialist ditty, however, is also a march – the original version, 'Pomp and Circumstance March No.1' was a full-scale military march; the words were added later. The form makes it a far more usable patriotic effort than 'God Save the Queen', by the way – not so much because the latter exists in French and American versions as well as British, but because it is in three-four time (with one strong beat followed by two weaker ones, and so on: pom ching-ching) You could waltz to it, but not march. It isn't military music. And the military march remains the single most important source of football music. The first hundred years of the organised game saw both the high point and the decline of the British Empire, which continued sport's association with military training and discipline, as promoted by the Greek Olympics, medieval tournaments, the tragi-comic First World War battles during which troops went over the top kicking footballs ahead of them, and so on up to John King's ambitious and ambivalent treatment of the theme in *England Away*. The fans chant 'Kevin Keegan's Barmy Army', until the tabloids decide it's time for him to be sacked. Incidentally this chant combines both prime sources. It's in march time: two bars of two-four time (i.e. two strong beats per bar, pom pom; a beat for each leg), repeated *ad nauseam*. And it uses the very simple pitch relationships employed in churches since the eighth century appearance of Gregorian chant – a level tone, then down, then up, and repeat.

So football music is often written and played, chanted, or sung in medium tempo two-four time. Media theme music, for example the opening bars to Radio 5's *Sports Report* and television's *Match of the Day* and *Grandstand*, are all marches, though the latter two are in various stages of parody. As are many of the anthemic songs made by football teams: the 1970 England classic 'Back Home', and Chelsea's 1972 'Blue is the Colour' were meant to help fans and teams alike march to victory. The more ironic contemporary cash-in song, Fat Les's 1998 World Cup offering 'Vin-da-loo', parodies the march both in its music, complete with military snare drum, and in the song's promotional video, which revolved around a carnivalesque and socially inclusive march through the streets; the tune is also, very deliberately, anthemic. And the theme tune of *The Great Escape*, the England fans' anthem of the 1998 World Cup, is also a march.

Of course those religious and military sources aren't the only ones, or the most immediate. Football emerged at exactly the same time as the male voice choir and brass band. And music hall, a form of professional entertainment revolving around comic songs, with audience singalong participation built in to the scheme of things (unlike in classical concert music, or sports like tennis, where the crowd's role is merely to respond). The football-comedy link continues: Baddiel and Skinner, and Fat Les, as professional comedians, are the natural inheritors of the music-hall tradition, which can be traced back through the work of people like George Formby and Gracie Fields. The official 1966 World Cup song, 'World Cup Willie' (a typically thoughtless appropriation of the British Lion for an English occasion) was sung by a Scot, Lonnie Donegan, a musical comic best remembered for 'My Old Man's a Dustman', who worked in music hall's 1960s descendant, cabaret.

There's a particularly important point in this connection. Music hall, like football, was and remains popular culture, aimed at a very wide audience, but it was never in any simple way by 'the people'. Urban and industrial, both forms underline the division of labour in modern societies, which means among other things that despite the prevailing ideology of individualism, individual people and communities alike are not self-sufficient in anything, but must combine together either as performers, audiences or both. And at the same time, that leisure industries exist to provide entertainment as commodities for people whose lives do not permit them the time and energy to make their own. So music hall, like football, was a popular culture provided for people as entertainment, by an industry owned by the middle-class. But its potential meanings are open to very different kinds of interpretation: audiences aren't passive, they choose, discriminate, and intervene in what is provided.

The brass band and the male voice choir brought a lot of this together. Male voice choirs, now associated with Wales above all, were once also common in the industrial areas of England and Scotland. Brass bands emerged when Victorian technology was able to mass produce instruments which were relatively versatile, cheap, and easy to play. Choirs and bands were often, then as now, amateur and communal, and therefore the opposite of the leisure industry entertainment of music hall: people were doing it for themselves. But by the time the Football League emerged in 1882, there was also a network of semi-professional bands and choirs in the North and Midlands. Based around communities and workplaces, just like football clubs, and usually likewise sponsored by employers, these institutions competed against one another, as they still do; the film *Brassed Off* was about a real world. And they evolved a new hybrid popular music ('light music' for want of a better word) which mixed church, classical, opera and operetta, military march and naval hornpipe, folk song and dance, and music-hall sources, and from the turn of the century American music like ragtime and jazz. Just as late twentieth century football music does. Most football clubs employed the services of a local brass band, which would typically play light music for an hour or so before a game, lead the crowd in a popular song or hymn or two, play the home team's song as they ran on to the pitch, and often provide a marching display at half-time. Military bands might still be seen at Cup finals, and occasionally at other important matches; though their presence at England games is no longer routine, the pre-match national anthem ritual over which they once presided remains, it seems, immutable.

Are there characteristic, identifiable forms or musical trademarks beyond these modes of organisation? Can we say more than: it's a football song when people agree to use it in that context? Is there a distinctive national voice in all or any of this? Yes and no, again. Looking at some music in detail emphasises the continuing paradox: to identify an English musicality means acknowledging the debt to music from many different local and global sources. In other words, the Englishness is in the mix, the way in which for example north and south American influences inflect a local tradition. Take two television themes. The classic BBC *Match of the Day* tune dates from around 1970. In tempo and rhythm it's a march, bubbling along in two-four time at about 120 beats per minute, with a bass guitar line emphasising every beat, just as a bass drum would do in more recent dance music; there's no emphatic backbeat, as there is in most African-American derived pop. The drum patterns aren't military, but they're crisp and even. You can imagine marching to the rhythm happily enough, and you can imagine the tubas of an Edwardian brass band puffing away on the bass. So far, so *Sports Report*. But the melody is an altogether different thing. It's a brass sound all right, but far from military: a cheeky tune played by two perky trumpets, in some recorded versions doubled by violins – in other words a strong hint of the Mexican Marriachi style, as pioneered in 1960s pop, in very diluted form, by Herb Alpert's Tijuana Brass.

There are similar levels of reference in another early 1970s television show theme, Tony Hatch's *Sportsnight*, though this is an altogether more complex piece of work, by the highly versatile and professional composer of middle-of-the-road themes for soaps *Crossroads* and *Neighbours* among much else. Again the tempo is right, but the *Sportsnight* theme isn't much like a march; it's four beats to the bar instead of two, though that in itself wouldn't stop you marching to it. Instead it's a mixture of mainly African-American-derived forms. A middle-pitch line on clarinet, doubled by guitar, with bass guitar an octave lower, suggest a Blaxploitation-style disco workout, while an urgent repeated pattern on xylophone and strings hints at the formal seriousness of the 'news'. Meanwhile the melody interest is carried by a classic jazz big-band arrangement, choruses of trumpets, saxes and trombones swopping licks before the lead trumpet reaches for the sky at the final cadence. If there's any sense of musical Englishness here it is in the hints of an update to John Barry's music for the early James Bond movies, in which the hedonism of the swing-era big band was joined by the cool, definitely post-Rock 'n' Roll, modernism of the electric bass and lead guitars. Barry's music, a radical departure from anything written for an Ealing or *Carry On* comedy film, signalled an Anglo-Americanness which has been renegotiated in many different ways since the appearance of Bond on film in the early 1960s, especially in pop. On reflection there is yet another source for English football music: the 1960s, in just about all senses appropriate to that magical symbol of hip liberalisation.

When, led by George Best, footballers began to acquire media-friendly 'personalities' and matching paypackets, and when within a few years England won the World Cup and Man Utd emulated Spurs and West Ham and won in Europe, they left the dour, UK-internalised artisanal world of the Football League and joined an entertainment industry which was modernising itself like silly on the back of the international success of the Beatles, exemplars of Merseybeat. Liverpool's best-known male voice choir, the Kop, adopted a 1963 pop cover version by Liverpool band Gerry and the Pacemakers. But this was not a march or a pop song, but an anthemic American ballad, Rodgers and Hammerstein's 'You'll Never Walk Alone' (from the 1945 musical *Carousel*). Other terrace songs adapted from 1960s pop charts included Pete Seeger's 'Guantanamera', which had been covered by the Sandpipers in 1966 – still in use today as 'Sing when you're winning' – Jim Reeves' 1966 'Distant Drums', and two Lennon-McCartney numbers from 1968, 'Hey Jude' and the Mary Hopkin feature 'Those Were the Days'. But note the Anglo-American hybridity in action here; even terrace songs are not a lexicon of English self-assembly but part of the mixing of cultures which has occurred throughout a century of high speed travel, broadcasting, and recorded sound.

The people on the terraces were adopting chart material. The game was part of pop now, and pop returned the compliment. As brass bands were replaced as pre-match entertainment by DJs playing pop records, and the new wave of terrace songs used pop tunes, pop records themselves used the sounds of the terraces. The deservedly little-remembered 1968 Dave Clark Five number 'Red Balloon', like Pink Floyd's 1971 'Fearless' (from the album *Meddle*) included the sounds of chanting or singing fans. The terrace chant, initiated and sustained by groups of young men, was one of the sounds of the 1960s. Call-and-response chants, rhythmically strong but even simpler than terrace anthems, can also be sourced back to the Church, where they can still be encountered daily at the Anglican Evensong; but what was happening here was a bottom-up rebuilding of the football event, using ritualised chanting of players' names and hate songs for opposing teams and fans to produce a more intense experience of football and the time which surrounded it.

Looking back from the edge of the millennium, when even average Premiership footballers earn pop-star salaries, we can overdo the similarities, and the symbiosis, which existed in the recent past of the 1960s. Even in the glamorous Man Utd squad, for every George Best, boutique owner and public womaniser, there was a Bobby Charlton, a 'model professional' who had nothing to do with pop stardom or pop culture. And pop, for all the success of the Beatles, was not and is not British but Anglo-American, a product of an Atlantic culture in which the key advantage of shared language enabled the British reworkings of rock and roll and its derivatives to succeed in America and then worldwide. That *Sportsnight* theme indicates how deeply embedded American music had become in post-war Britain; but the Atlantic communication did not extend to sport. Aware of the lack of interest in the key American market, British pop kept its fascination with football low-key. The international success of British football in the 1960s was comparatively fragile;

the dominance of English club sides in Europe after the mid-1970s was not replicated by the England side. Far from it. Pop, on the other hand, remained a key British export. Partly as a result, football followed different trajectories almost as soon as that mid-1960s moment passed. But they were never completely divorced. In the early 1970s, paradoxically, reggae was celebrated on the terraces in skinhead subcultures well before Spurs fan Bob Marley's mainstream impact. Laddish 1970s stars like Slade's Noddy Holder and Rod Stewart (whose 'Sailing' remains a terrace anthem), proclaimed their club or country allegiance with pride, while in the 1980s Phil Collins' interest in Spurs was matched by Glenn Hoddle and Chris Waddle's self-conscious attempt at pop stardom.

Meanwhile there was one key similarity, from the late 1960s onwards. Like pop itself, football chants, and the semi-structured young-male gangs which invented or adapted and used them, became international exports. Chants originated in Britain were, and still are, common currency at football stadia worldwide, sometimes in English, sometimes in translation; the addition here has often been the fans' band, a small gathering of drummers and brass instrumentalists who lead the fans through the repertoire of songs. As you'd expect, this repertoire is at its widest in Brazil, where samba schools often provide a rhythmic vigour as sublime as the players' skills. So it's not just the chants and songs as musical structures, but also the functional role they play, which are at the same time English in origin and international in current practice.

This, the chief English contribution to the game's culture following our original invention of the game, has been an ambivalent legacy. Chants and songs are often inventive and amusing. But as with military songs and marches, part of the idea was to raise the communal emotional temperature before a physical confrontation; from the 1960s on these became increasingly important, semi-structured parts of fan culture, paralleling the match itself. The emphasis on chants such as 'you're gonna get your fucking heads kicked in' (yet another vestigial military march, basically the same Gregorian riff as the 'barmy army' chant) and the accompanying subculture of violent confrontation, led to two decades when football gradually grew apart from pop culture. Neither the music business nor many bands, proponents of international communities and sales rather than local particularism, wished to be associated with nationalist male violence. Even punk's unpent fury had stronger associations with Rock Against Racism than with many football fans' late-1970s drift towards the National Front. And there were ambivalences here within the apparently progressive punk mix – its legacy included the extreme right underground music scene which can be traced through Oi! Music and White Noise to Skrewdriver. Meanwhile the end result of all the hatred stirred up by terrace chanting over some twenty years was death, at Heysel, and indirectly, because of fences installed against 'hooliganism', Hillsborough.

After the Holocaust, it was said, art is impossible. Wrong, of course; pop itself emerged, as did various forms of abstraction, and holding them together was an increasing sense of self-aware playfulness, irony, far from the pompous realism which served the fascist cause. This is what is called post-modernism. After Hillsborough pop has reclaimed football, with its sanitised stadia and corporate sponsors, as its own. But now it's increasingly on pop's terms. The 1990 England team song made with New Order, 'World in Motion' is mixed-genre pop. Featuring the rap of John Barnes, it's close to dance music, lacking the melodic curve of the anthem. Nonetheless, fans appreciated it, and especially felt happy that this was real pop; there was no ghastly team singalong that year. But team songs or not, the pop-football relationship in general has increasingly been one of cash-in. The European Championship and World Cup finals are accompanied by the release of pop songs by well-known major label artists, 'On Top of the World' by 'England United' and the like, which are just slightly better sung versions of the basic team singalong. 'Football's Coming Home', another more thoughtful effort, realised a fortune in royalties from sales on the back of its Euro '96 terrace success, and was unsurprisingly remixed and re-released for France '98. Football, in this sense, is another commercial opportunity, and finals have become an extra Christmas, which now seems to exist principally for record companies to release tacky tunes in a race for the seasonal number one.

This doesn't mean that the football-pop relationship is merely down to the dictates of an industry with an eye for the main chance, or that it's alien to the stadium cultures of the 1990s. There's no questioning the devotion of Oasis to the beautiful game, or at least to those bits of it which can be viewed from Maine Road; indeed, the whole Britpop celebration of New Laddism rode on a wave of post-Taylor Report rehabilitation which was more than just opportunism. Football has been celebrated in 1990s songs and videos alike. And the celebration goes well beyond the nostalgic field of guitar rock. Even rap (unsuitable for terrace use because it is impossible to perform without backing tracks to wrap the words around) has made an impact, in the form of Collapsed Lung's 'Eat My Goal'. And as Steve Redhead has claimed, there were from the start of acid house in the late 1980s, strong associations between Ecstasy-based dance music cultures and the fans' side of the response to Hillsborough. The *Boy's Own* fanzine was as keen on dance music as on football, and it was directly associated with DJs such as Paul Oakenfold and bands including Underworld, whose production company is called Junior Boy's Own. Doubtless, especially in the crucial late-1980s moment, the benevolence given by Ecstasy use helped to prepare the way for football's general cultural reformation; as did the fans' movement. The youngish culture based around fanzines has argued, with some success, for the transformation of many fans' and administrators' routinely misogynist and racist attitudes; and the fanzine writers are usually living inside a pop-based awareness – if often, again, 'ironic' – of the possibilities for expression and transformation of football cultures. They have helped to save the game.

As football has been simultaneously rehabilitated and commodified, as the new small but perfectly formed out-of-town stadia replace the Goliaths built before the age of mass car use and television, and as the presentation and analysis of the game have become both more hi-tech professional and more blandly ubiquitous, music's functions within the game and its representations have broadened. The role of music in sports broadcasting, meanwhile, has changed from the call-to-attention of the march-time theme tune to provider of a versatile poppy background; for analysis, highlights, or comedy cuts – even as background to highlights of radio commentary. For years the BBC cut the *Match of the Day* 'goal of the month' slot to a loop, without vocals, from the Lightning Seeds' 'The Life of Riley', with its folkish accordion and cheerful violins. The repetition of this trick means that for many of a certain age, witnessing a good goal brings this tune to mind in a mental reflex action. Thanks to this tendency to underscore extracts with music, and the increasingly powerful digital control of image speed, televised football becomes ballet, a magical dance almost unimaginable without music; our expectations of the game inside the stadium therefore change. Sure enough, there's an increasing tendency for stadia PA systems to provide a brief clip of appropriately celebratory music when a home goal is scored. Perhaps the terrace chants under threat from the all-seater stadium's 'bourgeoisification' will eventually be challenged by American style matchplay accompaniments. A nightmare, perhaps, though stranger things have happened.

There's still a strong association between football and song, but this, too, has been commodified through the influence of the broadcast media. If digital technology makes football more like ballet, then in 1990 the emotionally overwhelming combination of Puccini's music, Pavarotti's voice and Gazza's tears made it more like opera. The Three Tenors also made their début at Italia '90, and have so far managed to keep coming back. Misunderstanding this connection as a move towards popularity for classical music in general (which was happening in parallel, though for different reasons and for a non-football-specific audience), broadcasters and the music business have tried to replicate this 1990 moment, so now the football faithful are offered albums of 'terrace classics' (as well as Three Tenors albums). The Virgin/EMI 'Best Footie Anthems in the World Ever' album, released in 1996 to coincide with the Euro '96 tournament, contained choral music from Beethoven's Ninth Symphony alongside the Cockerel Chorus's rendering of 'Nice One, Cyril'. Pop commodity, then, but this is not pop music, more a remaking of that hybrid category 'light music' which was created at the end of the 19th century by male voice choirs, brass bands and so on.

Meanwhile, back in the stadia, the displacement of 'the game itself' by pop, opera, ballet, and so on proceeds with a new audiovisual settlement, thanks to the Jumbotron screen. Using player and manager interviews and footage from previous matches, usually with soundtrack music of various sorts echoing the new televisual techniques of sonic background, the Jumbotron previews the game and provides entertainment not only at half-time but during the match itself, including replays of controversial incidents in ways which can undermine both the authority of the referee and the concentration on real-time play of the spectator. Here, it seems, is a move to provide passive audiovisual entertainment from the time the gates open, as was the case when those brass bands were around, but which disappeared when pop records became the pre-match entertainment and terrace chants dominated the match.

And yet in the case of England, the brass band is also with us once more, reinvented in a subversive way which is part straight protest and part, again, a post-Hillsborough, 'ironic' appreciation of the identity of the fan which is increasingly acknowledged by the broadcast media and sports authorities. From the fans' side, the march made a return with the *Dambusters* march as a football stadium anthem in the early-mid 1990s. This Elgar-style military march written by prolific light-music composer Eric Coates for the 1955 film had been repopularised by its use in witty advertisements for Carling lager, which played on national stereotypes such as the supposed German tendency to hog the poolside at holiday hotels. The ads had parodied the film's image of the bouncing bomb, the Englishman bouncing his towel over the pool to claim a place in the sun before the Germans can get there, in a magical evocation of the British victory over Germany which obstinately refused to manifest itself economically after 1945 or, after 1966, on the football pitch.

The Great Escape emerged as a football song at about the same time. Like the *Dambusters* tune it is a reference to the Second World War, a march, and a film theme, but this time American in origin, taken from a Hollywood-produced version of a very British subgenre of the war movie, the escape film. Sung and whistled by fans of teams which have escaped or were on the verge of escaping from relegation, the tune had been adopted by the Sheffield Wednesday supporters' band, one of the very few English manifestations of the stadium fans' brass band, a phenomenon widely present elsewhere in the world, and one of the few examples of terrace culture imported back into England. The Hillsborough band was named the Official England band of the 1998 World Cup, and featured in a television documentary as they led the fans through countless renditions of this tune during the campaign. Unfortunately for England there was no escape for the team or its manager, who was then hunted down by a vengeful press convinced of England's divine right to win.

The Hillsborough band was designated 'official' by officials – of the Football Association, keen to make more efforts to bond with the fans. Partly because this was simply the right thing to do; partly because of the media's interest in fan organisations such as the Football Supporters Association; partly because good fan behaviour in 1998 was crucial to efforts to bring the World Cup finals back to England. What the band were doing, under this official label, was in effect cheerleading, taking a crowd through a semi-official repertoire of supporting songs, rather than leaving vocal support to those in the crowd themselves. Cheerleading – American in origin – refuses to rely on the crowd, invoking a safe (if not strictly passive) model of crowd behaviour. But however much we deploy notions of irony here, the effects go beyond those of the new social organisation of the crowd and its responses. An American march, from an American-made war film, celebrating in a very complex way victory over

Germans, 'The Great Escape' inhabits the same ideological world as the chant 'Two World Wars and One World Cup' – which is also American music, Stephen Foster's 1850 tune 'Camptown Races'. English feelings of a certain sort, sung to American-derived music – that sums up much of twentieth-century English popular music.

Pop now is all in the mix, and that's where football music always has been. There was never a dominant form, no musical hegemony on the terraces, and there isn't one now. England is still a crossroads, now a post-colonial-Atlantic culture, its football Anglo-European, its music a mix still accumulating as it has done throughout the history of this often-resettled island. Manchester City fans singing Rodgers and Hart's 1934 ballad 'Blue Moon', or Leeds fans adopting local anarchist band Chumbawumba's 1997 anthem 'Tubthumper' are continuing this line of mix and match. Hopefully this will remain the case in the future, the right mixture of 'official bands' and terrace innovation incorporating the vestiges of a hybridising culture, rather than the straight pop feed such as 'Football's Coming Home'. As the new Wembley's 175-foot aerial-towers wave proudly in the breeze, may the mix continue without Jumbotronic passivity.

Fighting Talk from the Press Corps

Emma Poulton

Football provides a powerful arena for the construction and representation of national identity by its very obvious identification of the nation with the national team. While it may be difficult adequately to define what 'Englishness' is in this multi-cultural, multi-national society at the start of a new millennium, it becomes a lot easier when a football match between 'us' and 'them' is in progress.

Success and failure in football is commonly seen to reflect on a nation's superiority or inferiority in its political, economic and cultural world standing. The 'feel-good factor' after a victory usually generates a sense of national pride and unity. Defeat in international competition has a rather different effect, yet can still ignite a passionate identification with the nation, albeit of an often more defensive, sometimes aggressive nature. Results and performances then, matter. The treatment of England managers over the years who haven't produced the goods is testimony to that: most notably with Graham 'Turnip-Head' Taylor and Glenn Hoddle's acrimonious plummet from grace. There's a history to this too: Don Revie was treated as a national pariah after deserting the job for the tax-free riches of the United Arab Emirates and even the late Sir Alf Ramsey's reputation was rubbished after England failed to qualify for the '74 World Cup.

The media plays a crucial role here, both in terms of playing judge and jury on the team and manager's success rate and, more importantly over the long term, the construction and representation of national identities through images of unity and cohesion. Television and radio commentary and press reporting emphasise the *whole* nation as embodied in its representatives in the national team.

One of the most common ploys in this process is the tendency to present 'England' through an all-embracing language. The national identity of Ingerland and supporters of the national team are referred to as a unified whole. This is clearest when commentators or journalists claim 'the *whole* nation are on the edge of their seats' or 'the *nation* is in mourning following the penalty shoot-out defeat'. Whatever we as fans may think, these are distinctly tenuous claims. A British audience of 23.28 million people – from a population of almost 60 million – watched England's televised match against Argentina during France '98. This means that considerably less than half of the 49 million English population can have tuned in, especially if we allow for any Scots, Welsh, Irish and other nationalities living in England who may have watched the game. The Euro '96 semi-final against Germany attracted the most viewers ever for a British sports broadcast, 26.2 million. This surpassed the previous record audience of 25.21 million for the Italia '90 semi against West Germany. These figures are put into blunter context still when noting that 31.8 million Brits tuned in to watch Diana, Princess of Wales' funeral. Ironically the *whole* nation was also said to be *united* in grief following her death, although this figure would also suggest nearly half were not sufficiently bothered enough to switch on the television.

Ingerland is usually portrayed as essentially white, male and heterosexual. Women and ethnic minorities are often subtly excluded from the representations of Englishness in most of the media's football coverage. The black community newspaper *The Voice* claimed as much during Euro '96, printing a poll showing how large sections of the black population had chosen not to support England, opting instead for teams with a visibly higher number of black players like Holland or France or even remaining completely indifferent to the tournament's outcome. A columnist for *The Voice*, Tony Sewell, saw the problem as being that 'English patriotism is based on putting someone else down'. He explained: 'I don't think I'll ever be able to support the country of my birth because it can't express its pride without hate. Those of us who live in that nowhere-land of liking and hating England, can never find comfort in the red and white of St George or the Union Jack.' Similar accounts were given with regard to France '98, with sections of the English black population following teams with whom they had family links, most notably Nigeria and Jamaica.

Women also are often excluded by the tabloid press in particular, especially during attempts to mobilise 'the nation' in support of the national team. It is only when the media has helped to instil a feel-good factor across 'the nation' that the 'other half' of the population are invited to join the ranks of football's 'family'. All of a sudden female columnists, who up until this point have taken the 'poor neglected football widow' line with guaranteed 'football-free zones' headlining their pages, profess to undergoing something of a conversion having been swept along with the occasion. Jane Moore, *The Sun*'s 'Woman' editor, on the eve of Euro '96, campaigned for the removal of the phrase 'football season' from the English language on the grounds it was a misleading description since it actually meant 'one long turgid cycle of league matches, championships, friendlies and never-heard-of-them games'. However, as the tournament, and more importantly England, progressed, she announced in a headline: 'EN-GIRL-AND – NOW EVEN I'VE STOPPED HATING FOOTIE AND GONE EURO '96 LOOPY.' *The Sun* subsequently advertised a 'super England supporter' bra set complete with 'a St George Cross on each cup' and step-by-step instructions for a 'cut-out-and-keep *Sun* Soccer Appreciation Kit', as it encouraged women to 'Give 'Em a Cheer Girls'. Similarly, self-professed former 'soccer hater' Mary Kenny, in the

Daily Express declared: 'I Repent! I Recant! It's Not So Bad a Game After All'. Most of these female journalists who undergo such apparent 'conversions' write without any genuine enthusiasm or knowledge of the game. Lynn Truss's column in *The Times* exemplifies this. Her column adopts an apparently 'typical female' attitude of ambivalence and apathy to football and sport more broadly. This was evident especially during Euro '96 as she appeared to reluctantly attempt to come to terms with the way she was becoming caught up in the patriotic fervour which began to envelop the tournament. Throughout however, she remained somewhat reserved and above it all: 'Football's coming home, la, la, la. Football's coming home, dee-dee-dee. Honestly, what on earth am I doing here? What has happened? *The Times* sent me out and about to Brighton pubs on Saturday to watch the England versus Scotland match on television . . . and now I wander in a state of identity amnesia, trying to pull my old football-ignorant self safely around my shoulders again, like a – well, like a slippy old cardigan. I try saying "Euro '96? What's that?" but I can't get the words out any more.'

Rare exceptions to this style are reports written by the minority of regular female football correspondents such as Alyson Rudd, of *The Times*, Olivia Blair of *The Independent*, Amy Lawrence from *The Observer* and Vicky Orvice and Janine Self from *The Sun*. Indeed, these female writers can often provide an added dimension, broadening the base of what Ingerland is through their observations and sometimes alternative perspective. Amy Lawrence for example noted during Euro '96 how: 'The Wembley crowd has had a noticeably different flavour during the tournament, the almost exclusive image of the young, white male replaced by a welcome cross-section of age, sex and colour.' But, overall, the media coverage of football ensures it is framed in highly gendered terms, maintaining the game and Ingerland as very much a white, male preserve.

A further part of the process of constructing Ingerland is to do this in contrast to the representation of the opposition. The treatment of opposing nations, their teams, players, supporters and homelands, is central to the championing of our own national team and, by implication, England and Englishness, however idealised the construction of our identity may be. The emphasis is put on 'them' being *different* from 'us'.

The press, especially the tabloids, often use the personal pronouns like 'us' and 'them' to denote allegiance and accentuate rivalry. The Euro '96 headlines say it all: 'Blow *Their* Jocks off!' (*Sun*); 'Go Give *'Em* a Clogging England!' (*Sun*); 'We Kick *Them* in the Castanets' (*News of the World*) and 'Herr *We* Go, Herr *We* Go, Herr *We* Go!' (*Mirror*).

Radio and television commentary teams also use personal pronouns to emphasise their partiality. However, television's preference for a more cosmopolitan collection of pundits, reflecting the 'foreign legions' of the Premiership, does help temper the more populist, partisan tone of the press. The presence of Ruud Gullit and Alan Hansen alongside Jimmy Hill brought a new British/European balance to television commentary during Euro '96. For France '98 the BBC's new recruit, David Ginola, brought his continental perspective to the panel and enough Gallic charm to almost rival Des Lynam's popularity as the ultimate in smooth operation.

The sense of 'them' against 'us' is also achieved through the perpetuation of stereotypes that are usually complimentary about 'us' and disparaging about 'them'. Preconceived notions of what particular nations and nationalities are like are stored deep within the national memory bank, alongside our shared histories of success and defeats, all learnt as we grow up. In the run-up to internationals old national stereotypes are brought out, dusted down and displayed. Some of these crude images may well be inoffensive, like the clichés about the 'samba-crazy' Brazilians. Others, such as those referring to 'naïve' or 'happy-go-lucky' African nations can carry more obvious racial undertones. During Italia '90, ITV's Elton Welsby referred to Cameroon as 'just happy to be there'. His colleague John Helm, added to a shot of a fan wearing a T-shirt signed by the Cameroon players, with: 'Well, they can all sign their names.'

A striking example of national stereotyping was before the Euro '96 quarter-final against Spain. Perhaps as a consequence of the distant historical naval hostilities and the more recent controversy over the EU's fishing quotas at the expense of the Cornish fishing fleets, a series of irreverent stereotypes as well as puns and 'jokes' about the so-called 'paella-eaters' surfaced: 'For the nation that nicked our fish, there will be no *plaice* in the semi-finals' (*Sun*). There were 'costa crackers' in abundance in the *Daily Mirror* about Spanish women being overweight with excessive facial and armpit hair and about promiscuous Spanish men. Recalling such unpleasant historical episodes as the 'Spanish Inquisition' would seem to have little relevance to a late twentieth-century football match, yet this was highlighted by both *The Sun* and most notably the *Daily Mirror* in its list of 'Ten Nasties Spain's Given Europe'. The list also included syphilis; Spanish flu; carpet-bombing; bullfighting; and 'pavement paella because of its habit of repeating'. On the radio meanwhile, Jonathan Pearce, imitated that famous piece of Norwegian commentary by screaming after Seaman's decisive penalty save: 'Salvador Dali, Pablo Picasso, José Carreras, El Cordobés, Don Quixote – your boys are out! And you can stick it up your Julio Iglesi . . . ASS!'

All in good fun? Part of our 'unique English sense of humour'? Or derogatory, offensive and xenophobic? The cultural denigration and antagonistic lampooning of certain national traits, customs and symbols can all too often go beyond a joke. A nation which constructs its own identity at the persistent expense of others does not project a very positive image of itself. In fact, it suggests a nation with a low self-esteem and rather fragile sense of national identity of its own.

The stereotyping of other nations is not just a technique unique to the tabloids. Broadsheet writers toy with such stereotypes while castigating the tabloids' excessive use of them. Writing about Holland in Euro '96, a *Daily Telegraph* writer noted: 'For a nation of cyclists, the Dutch should be used to back-pedalling.' Such techniques employed by broadsheet journalists allow for this subtle playing with stereotypes and is as potentially effective in perpetuating the images as the tabloids' more pejorative use of them.

The media representation of Ingerland through the emphasis on 'them' rather than 'us', aided by the use of national stereotyping, is contentious and insensitive. It essentially involves a balancing act between healthy, robust patriotism and xenophobia. It is a fine line which commentators, pundits and journalists tread in not veering too near the latter in their reporting. National pride is a vital part of the game today. Displays of patriotism are only right and proper, but manifestations of xenophobia and overtly nationalistic rhetoric do nothing but sell football short.

Patriotism is the positive assertion of your own nation and national identity. A patriotic person takes pride in national achievements, footballing or otherwise, and in the values which represent what is best about the nation. This is quite different to xenophobia. Xenophobic sentiments are exclusively disparaging and hostile toward other nationalities, seeing no virtue in any other nation except your own, and forever seeking proof of national superiority. The xenophobe defines his/her own nation in terms of another's failings. There is always plenty of patriotism and a crusading upbeat spirit urging the England team to success in the media's coverage of international campaigns. During Euro '96, the *Daily Express* demanded 'ROAR US ON!' while the *Mirror* attempted to generate public support with the plea: 'Make a Noise for Our Boys!' Similar mobilisation techniques were employed in France'98, with the *Mirror* proclaiming: 'We Are the Top Dogs – Roar Hoddle's Boys to Victory!' However, we also too often see the nastier face of xenophobia. This is contemptuous and jingoistic, the principal characteristics of much gung-ho tabloid reporting over the years.

Why do sections of the English media have to invoke negative images of opponents rather than positive ones of England? It seems there is a defensive arrogance about the English and a need to harp on about the good old days when '*Britannia* ruled the waves'. This is also part of a common English tendency to anglicise and hijack a sense of 'Britishness'. A *Daily Mail* editorial after England's Euro '96 defeat at the hands of the Germans attempted to gain some satisfaction from the outcome by arguing that England had been defeated at our 'own game', not at Germany's:

> We must regard last night's defeat as another sort of victory – not a moral victory, but a historical victory. For surely we British have achieved nothing more admirable this century than teaching the Germans how to beat us at our own game. It was in 1863 – 133 years ago – that the Football Association was born. At that time, Germany did not even exist as a united state. And although the game had caught on in Imperial Germany by the time of World War I – so much so that on Christmas Day, 1914, British and German soldiers played football together in 'No-Man's Land' – it continued to be regarded as an English import . . . Nor is football the only thing we have taught the Germans this century. We have – after two great conflagrations – taught them economic liberalism and parliamentary democracy too. Not bad going. True, no teacher likes it when his brilliant pupil gets the better of him.

But there is surely some satisfaction in seeing how well the pupil has been taught.

Such sentiments are the epitome of a nation lacking in confidence in its current world standing. This is England. Sections of the English population and many politicians are in large part struggling with a post-imperial, nostalgic hang-up. This is reinforced by the Scottish, Welsh and Irish succeeding with their calls for devolved governments. Many of the English are also failing to come to terms with a minor role in a Franco–German-driven Europe, sensing an increasing loss of sovereignty to Brussels. Right-wing sections of the press in particular have long championed the anti-Europe cause. The *Daily Mail* has run scare stories with headlines like: 'EURO WAR: Brussels Targets Britain Over Fish, Beef and Even Baby Milk'. The same newspaper celebrated the John Major Government's offensive over the banning of British beef on grounds it was allegedly infected with BSE with: 'Major Goes to War At Last!' The *Daily Star's* perspective has been similarly direct: 'Eff EU Lot!'

The Sun has led the way with calls for a referendum on the 'Euro' and numerous campaigns, such as 'I'm Backing British Beef' and 'Save Our Pound'. *The Sun's* sentiments towards European politicians have been explicitly negative, most infamously with their front-page message from November 1990: 'Up Yours Delors!' which was followed by four pages of anti-French 'jokes' and stories. Having 'exposed leftie German finance chief Oskar Lafontaine as the biggest threat to Britain since the war' and demanding he 'Foxtrot Oskar', the newspaper hailed his subsequent resignation with the war-film style headline: 'We haf vays of making you QUIT!' *Sun* columnist Gary Bushell's call to arms articulates some of the most common fears:

> . . . Let's call a halt to the softly, softly process that seeks to strip us of our national identity. Even the teaching of our history is under question. Inch by inch, the very essence of England is being eaten away. The Pound will go next . . . Miles, pints and stones will follow. It will even affect our language . . . we are trading our identity for provincial status in a corporate centralised Euro-superstate . . . As we count the cost of Europe with losses to our fishing fleet, our beef farmers, and even our gold reserves which are to be moved to Germany by 1999, the English will come to realise what we have lost and will seek to reclaim it.

These perceived attacks on an already fragile English national identity encourage a hostility towards opposing nations who appear to threaten it. If only the media could cast off this mindset and start promoting the nation and national team on more positive grounds, asserting 'us', but not at the expense of 'them'.

George Orwell's famous belief that sport is 'war minus the shooting' is regularly demonstrated by the media in their efforts to hype and dramatise football matches through the use of militaristic images and war-time terminology. Given some of the press coverage of international football, Euro '96 most vividly, the only thing missing from the reports is, indeed, the weapons. Witness the *Mirror*'s headline during Euro '96 before England's semi-final match with Germany announcing that 'Football War Is Now Declared'. While the tabloid press in recent years have been notorious for such war-mongering sports reporting, this is not new. On the eve of the 1966 World Cup final, a broadsheet editorial commented: 'If, perchance, on the morrow Germany should beat us at our national game, let us take comfort from the fact that twice we have beaten them at theirs.'

Tabloid reporting of real conflicts perversely almost reduces war to a game. Headlines like 'CLOBBA SLOBBA: Our Boys Batter Butcher of Serbia in NATO Blitz' during the Kosovo crisis and 'GOTCHA!' from the Falklands are typical of this. The *Daily Star*'s play on this infamous *Sun* front-page with 'OUTCHA!' after Argentina had knocked England out of France '98 illustrates this cross-over in the coverage of sport and war. During Euro '96 a *Mirror* back-page banner headline stated: 'Ve Are Not Fooled Fritz! Who do you think you are kidding Mister Hitman?', challenging the German camp's announcement that their striker Jürgen Klinsmann was injured and would miss the semi-final.

By making a sport–war connection through likening a football match to war with the use of militaristic words and imagery, the contest is framed as if something more than a game of football is being played. This 'greater game' can involve past hostilities or contemporary rivalries, not just from the football pitch, but from the political and military arenas as well. Indeed the more antagonism, past or present, footballing or otherwise, associated with an adversary, the more mileage the media can get from the reporting of the game itself and the more of a grudge match it becomes.

The partisan, jingoistic character of the tabloids means they frequently portray matches in this way. The sport–war connection and the language and imagery of war, was a feature of the media coverage of Italia '90 where England and Germany met in the semis. A *Sun* headline at the time claimed: 'We beat them in '45, we beat them in '66, now the battle of '90.' Given this kind of headline and the incendiary historical baggage between the two nations, on and off the field, it was perhaps only to be expected that this theme would surface again in press coverage of the England v. Germany semi in Euro '96, especially given the intensified political antagonisms between the two nations over Europe since 1990. However, nobody could perhaps have anticipated to what extent, especially given the fact we were hosting the tournament. The organising committee, the FA, the government and police were all hoping for a successful, smooth-running tournament. But the *Mirror*'s cry of 'ACHTUNG! SURRENDER – For You Fritz, Ze Euro '96 Championship Is Over' hardly suggested a friendly host nation welcoming guests to our shores. Illustrating this front page statement were the faces of Paul Gascoigne and Stuart Pearce, with tin helmets superimposed upon their heads. Also on the front page was a Piers Morgan editorial in the style of Neville Chamberlain's declaration of war in 1939:

I am writing to you from the Editor's office at Canary Wharf, London. Last night the *Daily Mirror*'s ambassador in Berlin handed the German Government a final note stating that, unless we heard from them by 11 o'clock that they were prepared at once to withdraw their team from Wembley, a state of soccer war would exist between us. I have to tell you that no such undertaking has been received and that consequently we are at soccer war with Germany. It is with a heavy heart we therefore print this public declaration of hostilities . . . May God bless you all. It is evil things that we shall be fighting against – the brute force, the high tackle, the unfair penalty, the Teutonic tedium of their tactics and the pretence of injury after a perfectly legitimate English tackle. Against these evils I am sure that inside right will prevail.

The paper also ran a cartoon of a father and son accompanied by a rewording of the famous war-time propaganda slogan: 'What did you do in Euro '96, Daddy?' Such a cartoon makes an explicit sport-war connection by giving the idea that the mobilisation of the nation, in support of the national team, was akin to that of a war-effort. This was actually a somewhat surprising agenda for the Euro-friendly, Labour-supporting tabloid, especially since it had stood alone in presenting a pro-European stance during the press-led 'Beef War'. However, the editor Piers Morgan explained: 'We have flown the European flag for some time, but for football we decided to make an exception.' The *Star*, more predictably, joined in with front-page headlines exclaiming: 'Mein Gott! Bring On the Krauts!' and depicting Terry Venables as Earl Kitchener from the First World War. *The Sun*, unusually somewhat moderate in comparison, settled for a headline demanding 'Let's Blitz Fritz!' This appeared several pages into the newspaper and fronted a comparatively more light-hearted article reporting how it had 'signed up Jake the Lion to maul the Germans' as a lucky mascot. Unusually in this instance, *The Sun* did not take the war-fixated line found explicitly in the other tabloids.

While the tabloids as a whole received criticism from all quarters, with the *Mirror* in particular singled out, this is not to say other media were entirely innocent of playing such war games. Radio 5 Live, usually associated with the more moderate commentary of Alan Green, Jimmy Armfield, Roddy Forsyth and John Inverdale, couldn't resist the opportunity as the station advertised their coverage of the semi in the newspapers with the caption: 'Prepare for some aerial bombardment.'

Broadsheet writers attempted to claim the moral high ground by condemning the tabloid excesses. However they themselves utilised the war vocabulary and military imagery they were criticising, thus serving actually to reinforce the same sport-war connection. The press reporting of the Euro '96 England v. Scotland game by both *The Sun* and *The Times* framed the match as 'the Battle of Britain' between the 'Auld Enemies'. Both sets of correspondents made repeated references to the battles of Bannockburn and Culloden. *The Sun*, celebrating England's defeat of the Scots, remarked: 'Dates are everything in

Anglo-Scottish history – 1314, 1746 and now 16.39. Forget Bannockburn and Culloden. In years to come students will be schooled in the precise moment Scottish forces were so heroically repelled by Lord Admiral David Seaman at Wembley on Saturday.' Likewise *The Times* was keen to point out how the contest against Spain was 'the most important between the two countries since 1588', the year of the Armada. Some of the broadsheet writers tried to elevate themselves above this mire of historical off-field encounters. David Lacey in *The Guardian* castigated his fellow journalists: 'People who remember dates and battles will already be comparing England's advance to the quarter-finals of the European Championships with a potted version of English history. Having settled the marauding Scots and quelled the Low Countries, Terry Venables' hearts of oak are about to take issue with Spain. Germany and France, moreover, could lie ahead. Even if the sequence is historically awry it cannot be long before the spirits of Drake, Wellington and Montgomery are called upon to support our boys.'

Other broadsheet writers similarly appeared to claim the moral high ground, but in doing so indulged in militaristic imagery of their own as they extensively reported on the tabloid excesses and condemned them for their jingoism and xenophobia. *The Times*'s lofty observation that each game was 'Another Day and Another Enemy for the Press Corps', was accompanied by the headline: 'Sammer Leading the Battle on Two Fronts'.

In this way, broadsheet writers still flag up the sport–war connection while they vilify their tabloid colleagues for doing the same. In heralding Seaman's decisive penalty save against Spain, a *Sunday Telegraph* headline echoed the historical nautical connection to the Armada that had been a prominent feature of the tabloid reporting and proclaimed: 'Spain still can't beat an English Seaman.' Meanwhile *The Observer* declared: 'Seaman Sinks Armada'. On the eve of the semi-final against Germany, David Lacey was still advising readers to 'Beware of the Hun in *The Sun*' predicting, correctly, the forthcoming tabloid coverage: 'The spirit of the Blitz and El Alamein will be invoked . . . Spitfires will once more do battle with Messerschmitts in the skies over Wapping. And much, much worse.'

In the broadsheets, journalists and politicians alike complained of the tabloid 'Hun-bashing' and of 'xenophobic triumphalism'. Yet in doing so they continued to toy with militaristic imagery as they lambasted the tabloids' warmongering. *The Times* noted that the 'mobilisation against Germany is well and truly under way', referring to the 'heavy artillery of the tabloids' and branding them 'the advance shock troopers of modern tactical warfare'. Similarly, despite David Lacey's own advice and mocking of the tabloid coverage, he and other *Guardian* writers were writing elsewhere of England being 'led by Shearer rather than a Sherman' and describing the controversial kit change to grey as being 'kitted out like the Waffen SS'.

The *Daily Telegraph*'s Henry Winter was one of very few journalists to suggest that 'putting the bomb in bombastic is both offensive and potentially inflammatory' and in a considered criticism claimed:

The sad irony is that yesterday's 'Achtung!' headlines do not reflect the reality of Euro '96 which has been an international knees-up, not punch-up . . . By bringing the imagery of war to a sporting event, by perpetuating grievances and exaggerating stereotypes, the Fritz-blitzers do football a disservice. The emphasis should be on promoting national pride, not prejudice. If England lose to Germany, the fear is now that a whipped up resentment may come seeping out of the small-minded . . . The practice of imposing jingoism on football also ignores the changing face of the English game, now a multicultural, multilingual success.

Unlike media coverage of England games prior to or since, the sheer scale and content of the reporting on the Euro '96 semi-final against Germany prompted a backlash that involved not only broadsheet journalists, but politicians, the Press Complaints Commission (PCC) and the police. Lord Healey, the former Labour cabinet minister, commented: 'The grubby little men who write this sort of trash should remember that our monarchy are krauts.'

The controversy was the leading story on television news programmes and became the subject of many talk-shows and radio phone-ins. *The Times* reported how Vauxhall, one of the official sponsors of Euro '96, protested by 'waving the red card and withdrawing its advertising from the *Mirror* and *Daily Star*' for the remainder of the tournament. Ironically, the Vauxhall advert was not without nationalistic sentiments itself. In an apparent jibe at the EU's ban following the 'Mad Cow Disease' scare, the message read: 'Germany: Prepare for Some Good Old British Beef!'

Urged by the cross-party National Heritage Committee, the PCC – the regulatory body charged with protecting press standards – considered claims that articles in the *Mirror*, *Sun* and *Daily Star* in the lead up to the semi-final against Germany 'contained references to England's opponents that were pejorative and prejudicial in breach of Clause 15 (Discrimination) of the Code of Practice'. The actual Discrimination clause states that:

> i) The press should avoid prejudicial or pejorative reference to a person's race, colour, religion, sex or sexual orientation or to any physical or mental illness or handicap.
> ii) It should avoid publishing details of a person's race, colour, religion, sex or sexual orientation unless these are directly relevant to the story.

The PCC itself had received some 300 complaints from the general public – a substantial amount considering that the Commission receives an average of only 2,500 complaints in a whole year. On top of which, of course, there had been the uniformly negative reaction in other sections of the media to the tabloid coverage of the match.

The PCC found there was no breach of the Press Code of Practice Discrimination Clause. Having considered various factors in light of the complaints, the following conclusions were issued:

• . . . In these circumstances a considerable amount of nationalist fervour and jingoism from football supporters themselves was inevitable. Without making any judgement about the emotions which football matches excite, the Commission took into account that the coverage reflected at least in part the tone of comment and humour traditionally found in partisan support of football fans for their teams . . .

• . . . The Commission believed that the coverage – although shrill and poorly misjudged – in reflecting this partisan national support, was clearly not intended to incite prejudice directed at specific individuals on grounds of their race; furthermore, the comments made against Germany and the German people in particular could not be taken as serious threats or incitement to discrimination, particularly in view of the generous comments by the German Football Association . . .

• . . . Members of the Commission recognised that while there is a long and proud tradition in the British press of robust and nationalistic comment in support of British sportsmen and women competing in international sporting events, this has always been combined with an equally proud tradition in such reporting of tolerance and fair play towards others.

• Although there were no grounds for formally censuring any newspaper for a breach of the Code, Members of the Commission reiterated that some of the coverage departed significantly from those journalistic traditions. They wanted to place on record their own concern about the lapses in editorial judgement which had occurred, and trusted that all editors would take into account the public reaction to the coverage of Euro '96 – as evidenced by the large number of complaints the Commission had received – when covering future international sporting events.

When called before the Commission to answer the charges against them, the tabloid editors defended themselves. Piers Morgan of the *Mirror* explained that he had been aware of the criticism and had promptly apologised. While acknowledging that his newspaper's coverage had been regarded as offensive and overtly jingoistic, he rejected suggestions it had breached the press Code of Practice: 'To interpret it otherwise would be to prohibit highly critical articles about the conduct of nations as a whole or their people.' The *Daily Star* claimed its coverage was 'not malicious and the jokes were tongue in cheek and designed to raise a smile'; while Stuart Higgins of *The Sun*, maintained the line that the reporting had been 'jingoistic, robust and designed to bolster national pride, but not xenophobic or racist'.

These responses, and the Commission's conclusions, raise sensitive ethical and legal questions and lead to debate over censorship, sanctions and the appropriate extent of the freedom of speech. Such issues are highly important when it comes to considering what is acceptable journalism when media coverage is so focused on 'them against us'. Matthew Engel writing for *The Guardian*, rebuked the *Mirror* for its 'second-world-war-style-German-baiting-edition', branding it 'coarse and demented journalism' and suggesting that there was a strong case for saying the newspaper should be prosecuted under the Public Order Act of 1986 for the incitement of racial hatred.

Euro '96 in fact marked something of a watershed in terms of the future coverage and indeed the monitoring of future sports reporting. Following the controversy caused by the tabloids' coverage of Euro '96, Lord Wakeham, chair of the PCC, took an unprecedented measure on the eve of France '98. He issued a statement to newspaper editors attempting to prevent 'a repeat of such undesirable headlines' and instructing that newspapers had to be vigilant and ensure that they did not over-step the line between robust comment and racism. Wakeham's concern came in the light of the row over the French organisers' ticket allocation which had prompted a *Daily Star* headline: 'Frogs Need a Good Kicking' and an editorial slating the French nation: 'French history is littered with acts of plunder, greed and cowardice. The way they have grabbed the lion's share of the tickets is typical of their slimy continental ways. They need a good kicking in their Gallic derrières!'

While the PCC did not uphold the complaints made against the newspaper for its headline and accompanying editorial, Wakeham issued the warning to temper their nationalistic language in future coverage, with the imminent 1998 World Cup in mind: 'We want to have robust reporting of the World Cup, and we don't mind people being partisan – of course not, we want British teams to win. But I don't want newspapers inadvertently or in any other way inciting fans to violence and to cause trouble.'

In reply, Stuart Higgins, editor of *The Sun*, assured readers that their World Cup coverage would be 'jingoistic', but not 'xenophobic', the distinction he had tried to make during Euro '96 in defence of his 'Let's Blitz Fritz!' headline. Higgins elaborated: 'According to the Oxford English Dictionary, jingoism means loud and blasting patriotism. I'm proud of that. Xenophobia is a deep antipathy to foreigners and foreign things.' Piers Morgan, editor of the *Mirror*, added: 'Wakeham is preaching to the converted . . . Language such as *Hun* and *bosche* is passé. That was old style tabloid humour perhaps to a big degree. We have all probably realised the appetite for that kind of thing has changed.'

England's qualification from the group stage paired them in the following round with another, more recent adversary from on, but also off the football field, Argentina. During Mexico '86 a *Sun* headline declared 'It's War, Señor!' While not as explicit this time around, some newspapers brought the past events between 'them' and 'us' into the framing of the France '98 contest, by referring to both the 'hand of God' goal and the Falklands conflict. Memories were also evoked, especially by television commentators, of the bruising encounter of 1966 when Antonio Rattin was sent off and Ramsey prevented his team from swapping shirts, branding the Argentinians 'animals'. *The Mirror* ran a front-page headline: '8pm Tonight: PAY BACK TIME – At Last! England's Chance to Avenge the Hand of God'. Ironically, beneath this was a plea from Simon Weston, the Falklands veteran, to England supporters maintaining that the match should not be seen as a continuation of the war and to dismiss thoughts of revenge through giving the Argentinian fans a hammering. A rather clumsy attempt to police the emotions and bitter memories the newspaper seems aware it could actually be unleashing.

What have military conflicts to do with football? Everything, yet nothing it would seem. This sport-war theme is likely to pervade the media whenever England is drawn against an old adversary from the history books' battlefields. Indeed, in February 1999, Michael Naumann, the newly appointed German government minister for culture claimed: 'There is only one nation [England] in the world that has decided to make the Second World War a sort of spiritual core of its national self, understanding and pride.' He added that this obsession with the war, the centrepiece of English national identity, was most evident in relation to football, citing terrace chants, xenophobic headlines and the general use of language as revealing an inability to think of the Germans without reference to the war. This British 'mythologising' about Germany has been extended, Naumann claimed, to the depiction of its modern politicians. Citing *The Sun*'s portrayal of Oskar Lafontaine as 'the most dangerous man in Europe', Naumann said: 'It's not as if poor Oskar goes to bed crying about this, but to call him a *gauleiter* goes to the gut. People do not understand what a personal offence this is to people who have spent their lives rebuilding this nation and are truly anti-fascist.'

Anti-German sentiments are commonplace in much of the English media. After England were knocked out of France '98 by Argentina, the *Mirror* ran a banner front-page headline declaring: 'Come On Everybody: CHEER UP! It Might Have Been Worse. We Could Have Lost to the Germans Again'. Likewise, an article by Richard Littlejohn in *The Sun* on St George's Day, 1999 only served to support Naumann's observations about an alleged English preoccupation with past conflicts. Littlejohn, contentiously calling for club allegiances to be put aside to support an English club side in Europe and thereby controversially equating club competitions to international contests, argued that it was 'fitting that in the final of the European Champions League, Man Utd will face Bayern Munich'. He went on: 'Britain versus Germany. Two World Wars and one World Cup. Don't mention Euro '96. I mentioned it once but I think I got away with it.' Given the offence such insensitive and jingoistic anti-German comments clearly cause, as Naumann intimated, to the German nation which is trying to put its past behind it, isn't it about time we didn't mention the war?

Since footballing success or defeat has come to be seen as indicative of a nation's superiority or inferiority in the broader, global scheme of things economically and politically, it follows that hostilities between nations find expression in football. This provides nations with an accessible arena out of the political domain to settle scores. The media readily draw on the sport-war connection to frame matches when the opposition has been a past military foe. Contemporary political rivals provide a similar reason for the media to call for scores to be settled, both on and symbolically off the field.

England in recent times has not enjoyed much footballing success, which has compounded a general sense of threat to the nation's identity and therefore status. The move towards ever-closer European union has confirmed the fears of some over the further loss of national sovereignty to Brussels. While sections of the English attempt to come to terms with this and the loss of the British Empire, they face the re-assertion of Scottish and Welsh national identities. These factors have given rise to an exaggerated sense of anxiety and dislocation amongst sections of the English. This does not sit comfortably with defeats on the football field, perceived by many as the last remaining cultural realm in which to salvage some national pride.

Euro '96, played against a backdrop of political tensions in Europe at the time, made it easy for the media, the press in particular, to transfer the political antagonisms over fishing quotas and BSE to the football pitch. Radio One DJ, Simon Mayo, was quoted in *The Sun* calling for some English revenge before the quarter-final with Spain: 'They've been stealing English fish in their Spanish nets – now let's put some English balls in their nets!' *The Sun* also selectively featured readers' faxes in support of the England team and maintained its own Euro-sceptic agenda in the process, such as: 'They ban our beef; They take our fish; They try to change our law; Let them step on Wembley's turf and feel the lions roar!' Indeed the tournament became increasingly interwoven with the 'Beef War', especially when England progressed to face Spain and then of course, Germany. Jimmy Greaves, also in *The Sun*, wrote: 'Our football team finally gets the chance to do what our politicians are too scared to try, and stuff it right up Europe.'

The broadsheet writers also used England's Euro '96 matches to set their respective agendas on 'Europe' and in doing so, often promoted and reaffirmed an assertive sense of Englishness. The *Daily Telegraph* reinforced its traditional anti-Europe stance, by remarking: 'Euro-sceptics will be delighted that the invasion of fans has not led to an upsurge in Federalist fashion. The separate identity of nation states is a key theme in these Championships.' The tournament organisers meanwhile, were trying to promote the tournament as some kind of celebration of 'internationalism', with the unifying message, courtesy of Simply Red's theme song, 'We're in This Together'.

Banners and chants in the crowds suggest that the 'Beef War' which was being waged at the time actually had resonance with some fans not just the newspaper editors. 'Gazza Eats Beef' read one and as German fans provocatively 'moo-ed', sections of the English crowd responded with a re-worked: 'No surrender to the BSE!' – a mildly refreshing change to the far-right's 'No surrender to the IRA!' Chants of 'Shearer, Shearer!' were met with 'Chirac, Chirac!' Similarly during the England v. Spain match, English fans demanded of their Spanish counterparts: 'Can we have our fish back?' and after the final whistle sang a re-worded 'Cows are coming home!'

The indications are that Ingerland is suffering from some kind of hang-up about the nation's lost European and indeed global standing. The fortunes of a nation over the centuries can deeply affect and reflect the identity of that nation. A key feature of English identity is that it is backward-looking. There is a tendency to project a picture of the nation's greater past into the present. There is always an unfounded expectancy that England should and will do well. Writing Sir Alf Ramsey's obituary, *The Guardian's* David Lacey wrote: 'The abundant optimism, albeit unfulfilled, which accompanied Glenn Hoddle's team to France last summer owed much to what Ramsey had achieved eight tournaments before.' Lacey suggested Ramsey had 'taught England the art of the possible' and that ever since 1966, 'the idea that another England side might win has never quite gone away'. The editorials and headlines on the eve of international competitions, echoing the immortal words of Nelson before the Battle of Trafalgar, of 'England Expects' epitomise this sense of anticipation. This is despite the fact that in international competition since the momentous victory of '66, we have failed to qualify for two World Cups and failed to beat any of the major forces in the game, like Italy or Germany, Brazil or Argentina. Indeed, Matthew Engel of *The Guardian*, lamenting the warmongering tabloid headlines aimed at Germany during Euro '96, remarked upon this deluded English arrogance and expectancy: 'The Germans can probably take it. They will assume this is yet another British tragedy: the fact that we have achieved so little since 1945 and hark back for solace.'

France '98, mainly due to the draw, meant that there were fewer opportunities than during Euro '96 for the media to frame the games as an opportunity to settle any scores. The *Daily Telegraph*, however, still tried to bring their European political agenda into play by asking: 'if England – angels and ministers of grace defend us – should fail to make the quarter-finals, to whom should we transfer our allegiance?' After rejecting Scotland, Germany and Argentina as possible candidates, their conclusion maintained the newspaper's line of Euro-scepticism: 'No, there is only one nation which, in the event of an England defeat our readers should support – the plucky little country that voted no to Maastricht and came so close to felling the Amsterdam Treaty. A country so Anglophile that its main football chant "We are red, we are white . . ." is sung in English. Come on, Denmark!'

What we are witnessing is a vain fumbling search for a real definition of 'Englishness'. The crux of the problem concerns the foundations on which the sports media represent the nation: with a continual emphasis placed on knocking 'them' rather than promoting 'us'. This is the inescapable evidence of a nation's faded glory. The problem is that too many people refuse to see it and continue to rest on the laurels of our imperial past. Back then we had global power and status – in politics, in economics and in sport – but we are no longer the top dogs in Europe, let alone the world, no matter how tightly consecutive British governments try to cling to the USA's coat-tails. This has led to an insecure, Little-Englander mentality.

The English have an illegitimate superiority complex, born out of an inferiority complex. This misplaced superiority, which reveals itself in the grand assumptions that we are still as influential as we used to be, comes from knowing deep down that these are nothing more than dreams based on the greatness of our past to block out current insecurities and fears stemming from the lost global standing. There is an arrogance about Ingerland which manifests itself in the aggressive assertion and defence of 'us' and our national identity coupled with a hostility to anyone seen as a threat, for whatever reason. This is further tinged with a post-imperial hangover and other nostalgic hang-ups. There is a certain Anglo-British propensity for nostalgia in a knee-jerk response to contemporary inadequacies. How does the song go now: thirty-odd years of hurt?

Part of the broadside against the tabloid reporting is the concern that such press coverage leads to public disorder. Indeed, after the 1996 defeat by Germany, German-branded cars, garages and businesses became the target for attack. *The Guardian* reported: 'In Trafalgar Square there were outbursts of violence until well after midnight, as officers tried to keep crowds out of the West End. Hatred of Germany and its products blossomed. A Volkswagen Golf was smashed and a passing Audi was stoned and battered. Altogether 200 people were arrested in central London, 40 cars damaged, six overturned and two set alight. At least seventy-six people were injured across London.'

There were similar disturbances across the country. *The Times* headlined with: 'Russian Stabbed For Sounding Like a German', confirming also that 'two German tourists were attacked and robbed in Basingstoke' and how 'vandals smashed the window of a BMW dealership and the German-owned Aldi supermarket in Birmingham'. The broadsheet went on to tell how 'MPs Say Tabloids Are to Blame for Football Violence'. Whether blaming the press is an adequate explanation for the violence and disturbances however is questionable. What is evident though is that the crudely nationalistic rhetoric of the tabloids in particular generated an overconfidence and complacency across sections of the nation. This may well have raised public expectations that England not only could, but indeed was, destined to win the championship. Germany of course stopped that yet again and the proverbial 'bubble' burst with frustration and petty-minded violence being one apparent consequence. In this sense the media plays a role in reflecting, as well as reinforcing, these hang-ups regarding Englishness more broadly.

A nation that can only look for the short-comings of others and dwell on past hostilities or scores to settle from anywhere other than the football field, suggests a nation that is not at ease with itself, which is struggling to maintain a very fragile and threatened sense of its national identity. Commenting on the aftermath of England's defeat, *The Guardian*'s Matthew Engel made some pertinent observations to this effect: 'Maybe Scotland, Ireland and Wales can take defeat with more unanimous good grace. But these are countries with greater social cohesion. The blame [for the disorder] should not be heaped on to football. In a country as large, as diverse and as generally out of sorts with itself as England, it was probably impossible for a balloon that grew as big as this one did, to have been pricked with a smaller bang.'

Yet there is so much to be proud of and positive about in our nation, our football and our team today. That is not to forget our past. But we must live in the present and be forward- rather than backward-looking. We should celebrate the values and achievements of this multi-cultural, multi-racial English nation.

We have one of the best football leagues in the world. We attract some of the best players in the world. Indeed some of those players are home-grown. Isn't it about time we loved Ingerland for what we are today, instead of harking back, in insecurity, to past glories?

Acknowledgements and thanks go to Joseph Maguire and Cath Possamai; personal thanks go to David Stead, Ian Henry and Jason Tuck for their support and encouragement; thanks also to my family and friends who discussed ideas for this chapter. Lastly, my deepest gratitude to Mark James.

No Surrender to What?

Dominik Diamond

Winds of the World, give answer! They are whimpering to and fro –
And what should they know of England who only England know? –
The poor little street-bred people that vapour and fume and brag.
Rudyard Kipling, The English Flag (1892)

It is often said that there is nothing a foreign pub owner looks forward to more than a bunch of Scottish football fans, and nothing he dreads more than a bunch of English ones. Those draped in Saltires will bring benevolence, bonhomie and bucks while those bedecked in the flag of St George will arrive with aggression, arrogance and agitation. I'm not going to debate the truth of those sentences – it's incontrovertible.

In the lead up to France '98 I made a documentary for Radio 5 Live called *A Drowning of Sorrows*. The programme set out to explain why Scottish fans spend money they can ill afford travelling to far flung countries to watch a team that continually breaks their hearts. The experiences I had in making this – trawling up and down the country talking to the Tartan Army – added to one unforgettable Wembley encounter with the English equivalent – defines and establishes the differences between the two fan cultures.

For signed up members of the Tartan Army, the experience is far more important than the result – their famous chant being 'We'll support you evermore. Fuck the score'. One of the guys I interviewed in that summer of 1998 spoke of going to Utrecht for a friendly in 1994. Scotland were duly beaten 3–1 and afterwards the fans were kept locked in for the habitual hour or so. Some music was being piped in over the tannoy so the Scottish fans started dancing. An English guy, who was there expressed amazement and said: 'What do you guys do if you win?' to which Jim replied: 'Don't ask me I can't remember.' The same guy met an Estonian woman at the infamous game in Tallinn that never happened and is now married to her. Presumably he was so excited that he didn't witness defeat – he wanted a unique way to celebrate.

Scotland fans have a genuine desire to immerse themselves in the culture they are visiting – rather than the English fans' desire to import their own culture and then rigorously defend it. Marrying someone from the country you're playing against is a bit extreme, especially if the bastards got a 0–0 draw against us from the re-arranged game in Monaco.

Scottish fans' immersion in foreign culture takes many forms – from the volumes of alcohol bought for the hosts to actions which have much longer-lasting consequences than the next day's hangover. Ian Black, author of the excellent book *Tales of the Tartan Army*, told a brilliant example of this to me. For the 1986 World Cup his gang were in Nezahualcoyotl in Mexico, hereafter referred to as Neza. It is a phenomenally poor place and during the World Cup the locals had been given a couple of tickets each by the Mexican government. It was the day of Scotland's first round clash with Denmark (why did I bother writing the words 'first round' there – it was the World Cup for God's sake – have we ever played in any other rounds?) One of Ian's group, a woman called Anne, was approached by a young girl who was trying to give away her two tickets. Now these tickets were worth two weeks' wages to the Mexicans but they didn't even try to sell them – such was the love (and I don't think it's too strong a word to use here) they had for the Scottish tourists.

Anne lost the girl in the heaving throng but, instead of going to the game, spent the whole evening wandering around Neza trying to find her in the midst of a place where according to Ian there were 'shacks made out of tins and bits of stones. No electricity, no sanitation. Shops that were people's one-roomed houses where they'd built a half-door in front of their living-room. Inside there would be two shelves with a couple of packets of cigarettes and four packets of sweets – that was their living.'

The experience deeply affected Anne and so, as her section of the Tartan Army returned from yet another unlucky loss (a Preben Elkjaer shot deflects off Willie Miller's shin and goes in off the post in one of those rare 'not actually Jim Leighton's fault' scenarios), she organised a collection of the spare cash that her group had in their pockets and even got the Danish fans to cough some up as well. They were able to hand over a tidy sum to their newfound friends in Neza. I know there's the argument that spontaneous donations of this ilk are like trying to stick a Band-Aid over a gunshot wound but, as a result of this experience, Anne's life now revolves around helping the less fortunate.

Before this picture of Scottish fans and their reception worldwide becomes too positive it's worth pointing out that not every country rushes to elect the Tartan Army as 'Kings of Niceness'. But even when there is confrontation, the Tartan Army's first response is to diffuse the situation rather than help it aggressively along to an ugly boiling point. Another Scottish stalwart, Kevin Donnelly, once told me of a time when they were in Latvia, safely ensconced in an Irish bar in Riga during the 1998 World Cup qualifying campaign. A bunch of Latvian nationalists marched out of the night and stood outside the bar with flags aloft and challenged the Scots to a fight. With 99 countries out of 100 the sky would have rained bottles within seconds. However the Tartan Army counted how many there were – nineteen or twenty according to Kevin. They then bought each of them a pint and walked outside. To the amazement of the Latvians the Scottish fans gently lifted the Latvian flags from their bunched fists, replaced them with pints of lager and beckoned them to drink. After toasting their health, the Tartan Army retrieved the glasses and went back inside, leaving the Latvians with nothing else to do than wander home, their aggression punctured by spontaneous, witty generosity.

Maybe it's the kilt – how threatening can a man in a skirt possibly be?

There's always a fair few England fans who churn out the old chestnut about acts of violence perpetrated by English fans being committed by a 'mindless minority'. The Tartan Army takes the line that their reputation is only as good as the lowest common denominator, it's their responsibility to ensure it is not sullied and so they strive to prevent the 'mindless minority' taking root. In effect, they are a band of fans who are self-policing. If any Scottish fans are involved in behaviour that is seen in any way to be, shall we say, anti-social to the host country – they are dealt with there and then. It would be interesting to see what would happen if the 'innocent majority' of English fans decided to take the 'mindless minority' in hand next time it kicked off on some foreign field. I'll give you a clue – which group would have the strength in numbers?

It is true that the troubles English fans have been involved in have strengthened Scottish fans' resolve in being gracious football followers, so it came to pass that as I was finishing interviewing these legions of cuddly Scottish supporters, I had an excellent opportunity to compare and contrast when I went to see England play Saudi Arabia in one of their World Cup warm-up games at Wembley.

Saturday, 23 May 1998 was a very important day for British people, not because England were playing hosts to Saudi Arabia, but because as we awoke we were greeted with the news that in the first all-Ireland vote for over eighty years the country had voted to back the Stormont Good Friday peace agreement. I know in retrospect there were still numerous mountains to climb but this was the first time in my lifetime when it felt that there would be peace in Northern Ireland. The politicians had debated and now the people had voted and both groups, on both sides of this bloody divide were in concordance. Hundreds of deaths, decades of hatred, millions of pounds of tax payers' money – and it finally looked like it was ending. What a day to celebrate! Peace in Ireland, the World Cup around the corner and Wembley on a sunny May day – could it get any better?

The answer was no. I turned the corner to walk up the main drag to Wembley and I saw them, like I have always done at the dozens of England games I've been to in the last few years. A bunch of ten blokes, shorn of hair and wild of eye, fixing any passers-by that were not bedecked in the cross of St George and belting out the popular anthem without which no England game is complete: 'No surrender, no surrender, no surrender to the IRA'.

Saudi fans were walking by, clearly terrified, but also confused. What do the IRA have to do with Saudi Arabia? Is it an acronym for the surnames of Saudi Arabia's back three? Are there sections of the Republican militia who have swapped balaclavas for white headscarves? Is Dublin twinned with Riyadh? If not, why were they singing this? Who were they singing it to?

I was so angry, I just thought: 'You pricks! This is the one day where it looks like all this bigotry might end and you're standing there, sharing the same brain cell and taking all the efforts of people braver and smarter than you and pissing it up against the wall.' The worst thing about these people is they probably couldn't even find Ireland on a map. I saw other English fans just walk past. I saw policemen standing there doing nothing. Throughout the game the chant rang forth, and afterwards it escorted us homewards. Still the Saudi Arabians were bemused. Still I was angry.

Now I can understand English people hating the IRA and wanting to make their feelings known, but why bring it up at a friendly football match against a team from the Middle East? Why is this the second most popular chant I hear at Wembley (the first being 'Football's Coming Home' repeated over and over again – another lyric that makes precious little sense by the way).

Maybe it's obvious, maybe it's pretentious, but the answers lie in history and this is why a comparison with Scotland is revealing. England used to rule the world until various Commonwealth outposts decided they'd had enough exploitation and rose up to take their rightful place controlling their own destiny. From a geographical point of view the Empire now consists of two thirds of this island plus a few timeshares in the Costa del Sol. From a military point of view England's forces are used as a kind of Territorial Army for the USA and from a sporting point of view the Commonwealth Games, the Ashes, Rugby Union and countless others only seem to exist as an exercise in England's humiliation at the hands of the former criminal outpost of Australia.

But football is a bit different. England won the World Cup less than forty years ago. They got to the semis in the past decade and on their day, as long as they don't have a barking mad faith-healing religious zealot at the helm, they can beat anyone in the world. Football is the last bastion of the Empire. That's why the attitude from the headcase element of the fans is one of a rearguard defence. The words themselves 'No surrender' may be sung about the IRA but they could apply to any foreign band who threatens a small country that can't forget it once ruled an empire on which the sun never set.

With Scotland it's different. As a nation we have had the shit kicked out of us by more powerful neighbours from Day One. Our country's survival has depended upon treaty and wily negotiation. We have sent generations all over the world – to Australia, Canada, USA, the Far East – to integrate with rather than dominate foreign cultures, which is why whenever I go to America almost everyone I meet claims to be Scottish. Perhaps it's through decades of footballing disappointment but for the vast majority of Scottish football fans – it is only a game. This is why our songs and actions are non-confrontational. The most violently aggressive ditty being the re-wording of the hokey-cokey which celebrates a certain Argentian's eye for goal:

> You put your left hand in, your left hand out. In out. In out. You shake it all about.
> You do the Maradona and you turn around – and that's what it's all about.

Oh Diego Maradona. Oh Diego Maradona. Oh Diego Maradona.
And that's what it's all about.

And I was pleased to hear that one still being belted out at Wembley during my darkest day as a Scottish football fan. Euro' 96. Need I say more?

I just feel it's such a shame. I've lived in England for 15 years and love the country and the people so much I allowed my daughter to be born here. There is so much about England and its culture that I adore, it's just tragic that the crowds at football matches take it upon themselves to be the last line of defence against the dwindling of the Empire. 'No Surrender' may be struck up by a few thugs but it spreads like wildfire as soon as the team starts to underperform. Those who started the game against Saudi Arabia singing 'Rule Britannia' (which lyrically is only a small step from 'No Surrender', after all) turn to the more violent alternative – because with a dull 0–0 draw – every England fan has been served a reminder that Britannia no longer rules the six-yard box let alone the waves.

What pressure this puts on the national team! Year in, year out England have players Scottish managers can only dream of – yet a defensive attitude pervades them. They are driven by a desperate fear of failure, made to feel that they are not just representing a country but an entire history. As a result they play with terror rather than arrogance urging them on. As a result the team loses, the defiance becomes even more hate-filled and the spiral continues downward. The more the fans chant 'No surrender' – the more the team does precisely that.

The fee for this article has been donated to The Omagh Fund Line, set up to help the survivors of the Omagh bombing. They can be contacted on 01662 259 575.

Don't Cry for Football, Argentina

Marcela Mora y Araujo

'You can change your wife or your girlfriend but you can't change your club,' they say in Argentina. And football celebrities will list the loves of their lives thus: 'Football, my wife and my children.' Ex-goalkeeper now turned politician Hugo Gatti explains it convincingly: 'Before I met my wife, I had football.' A rationale echoed by most Argentines, from architects to street-sweepers, presidents to thieves. Middle-aged men in Argentina will often reminisce: 'When I was a boy, football was everything.'

During the 1950s, school lessons were interrupted and all the children were led out onto the school yard where giant loudspeakers had been set up; Argentina's international game was to be broadcast live on the radio. The school yard was the area reserved for homages to national war heroes on Independence Day. But Argentina playing football was tantamount to that. Football was everything. Still is.

'Nobody, apart from the British, have been playing the game longer, and only a few have ever played it better, than the Argentines,' wrote Guy Oliver in *The Guinness Record of World Soccer*, adding that 'a championship was played in Argentina in 1891, a full five years before anywhere in mainland Europe.' Whereas in Britain football is just one of the many sports, games and traditions that go back a long way, what you have to remember about the American continent – North and South – is that most cultural references are relatively new. To talk of something that has been going on for over a hundred years is to talk, quite literally, of history and tradition. Although there are claims that ancient Indian tribes in Central America played a game resembling football (some anthropologists have claimed they used skulls for a ball) it seems clear in the case of Argentina, Brazil and Uruguay – the countries which have established themselves as powerful players on the world stage – that football arrived at the end of last century with the English.

The history of football in Argentina is as old as anything gets. Furthermore, no other sport has come anywhere near it in terms of popularity, development as an industry, and excellence. The fact that historically Argentina has achieved a position in world football which places it among the Four Big Nations – at least in World Cup terms – only helps to feed the fantasy. In most senses a developing country, Argentines know that football is the one area in which they cannot be regarded as such. In football, Argentina is a first-world country, up there with the best.

Argentina was appointed by FIFA to host the 1978 World Cup finals shortly before a military government took control of the country. They soon saw how this would provide them with an excellent opportunity to show the world an Argentina which would not reflect the atrocities the *junta* was responsible for. Some of the organised left-wing activists opposing the dictatorship lobbied for a boycott of the World Cup, but most of them agreed to allow it to happen. 'It was harder for the men,' says Graciela Daleo, a member of the People's Revolutionary Party, ERP, who took up violence as a form of political resistance and spent the World Cup in a military-run concentration camp where she was forced to watch the games as part of a rehabilitation plan. 'I thought we should have boycotted the tournament but it is such a sensitive issue. It has to do with the still unresolved problem of how to strike the right balance between supporting something which is genuinely a popular sentiment, like football, and how to always voice political opposition, even through sport. You run the risk, as happened to me, that even within the popular movements I was snubbed with the remark "your problem is that you're an intellectual and you don't like football".'

In the end, a truce was settled. Little is known of the exact way in which this negotiation between organised groups such as the ERP and the military was conducted, but it has become a relatively well-known fact that some sort of tacit agreement had been reached which meant certain guerrilla-type activities were suspended for the duration of the championship. Every national team participating had military guards with them at all times and the military state that was Argentina wasn't suspended or relaxed in anyway. But it's understood that in as much as the ERP and other active groups could discuss policy – although there were voices of dissent such as Daleo's – a conscious decision was taken to allow the World Cup to take place in Argentina, and Argentina won the Championship that year.

'At least we had peace for one month,' says Julio Grondona, president of the Argentine Football Federation and First Vice-President of FIFA. He adds that if the military had known Argentina were going to win, they would have taken over the entire running of the tournament. As it was, the military let Cesar Luis Menotti, the national manager, and his squad work freely. Dutch journalists visiting the country, no doubt hoping Holland might take the title, can now claim the morally more impressive achievement of being the first of the world's media to air the views of the Mothers of the Disappeared. These women marched outside the presidential house, known as the Pink House, every Thursday, demanding information about their missing children, but the Argentine media, out of complicity with the regime or simply out of fear, had not featured them at all.

The World Cup opened the country up to the rest of the world, including Amnesty International supporters who also campaigned for a boycott of the tournament, and the impossibility of diverting popular attention from football has since become a point of scrutiny, and even criticism. 'All I can tell you is that people were celebrating on the streets for days', says Menotti, who has no time for journalists who 'now want to jump on the bandwagon of democracy and human rights'. Menotti has a reputation for being a left-wing intellectual, and back in the late seventies his long hair and chain-smoking touchline instructions looked the part to a tee. His football philosophy is that the game is 'entertainment', because it has to do with 'what man choses to do in his free time'. But it is understood that in 1978 he protected his players from the political scenario, with football the only topic on the agenda. For this, both he and his squad have since come under much criticism, and in spite of the fine football they displayed the 1978 World Cup has remained somehow stained.

When Argentina won the championship again in 1986, it was unarguably thanks to the on-the-pitch prowess of a young man whom a Dutchman once described to me as having performed 'the only miracle of the twentieth century'. Diego Maradona, a little boy from the slum so uniquely magnificent at 'playing ball' that he was able to use his shoulder-blades and inner shins with the same dexterity with which most mortals can only use their right hand to scribble their own signature. In his 20 years as a professional football player he became the symbol of Argentine football – Argentines could now not only claim to be among the world's best, they could also lay claim to ownership of the God of football himself.

The 1986 World Cup victory, perhaps even more so than that of 1978, filled every member of the Argentine Republic with a unique sense of pride and achievement. Maradona, not surprisingly, crowned his already remarkable popularity with the fulfilment of his own boyhood dream which was at the same time the dream of the nation. His first goal against England, infamously scored with the aid of his hand, was not regarded as the cheating, devious, unacceptably despicable act the English – on the whole – consider it to have been. It became just another manifestation of the national cheekiness known as *viveza criolla* – creole smart-ass. The rules of Association Football are basically 'anything goes as long as the ref doesn't see it' and nowhere is this more overtly the case than in the Argentine rule-of-thumb book. As far as the country is concerned, his second goal more than made up for the first. As Jorge Valdano, Maradona's team-mate in that squad, puts it: 'In a kick around in the park, that goal would have counted as two.'

The notion that a particularly good goal can count as two is easily comprehensible by any Argentine; no one would expect it in a proper game, but everyone would appreciate the sentiment. Transposing what would be regarded as valid in an informal park game, validating the makeshift rules of the games played on the *potrero* – the vacant lot as it has mostly been translated – that's the essence of the Argentine mentality, shared by players as well as fans. It is worth noting that a substantial number of Argentine footballers started their relationship with the ball in their early years, most of them coming from origins which are far humbler than their English equivalent. With the possible exception of Gabriel Batistuta (who didn't like football very much and grew up within a traditional lower middle-class family) and Juan Veron (whose father was a well-known footballer, and later manager) the squad representing Argentina in the World Cup in France 1998 had its proportionate share of players who came from typically third-world small towns, extremely low-income families, with limited educational opportunities. Of the squad that went to represent the country at the Copa America 1999, Gustavo Lopez used to be a street vendor with his father; Boca's sensational defender Samuel, was abandoned as a new-born baby and later adopted.

Every national squad has had more of the poor than of Batistuta's type in the teams. In some regions of Argentina the poverty level is well below what in modern day Europe would be considered extreme: Jujuy, for example, where Ariel Ortega grew up until he was spotted by a tout and taken to River Plate in the capital, Buenos Aires. Or Misiones, home to Pedro Monzón, defender in Italy '90 (he was the first player to be sent off during a World Cup final, for allegedly having fouled Germany's Klinsmann), until he took off alone to Buenos Aires, barely 13, to sell melons in the streets. Monzón would go to watch the training at the club he supported – his father too – Independiente, waiting for trials to come up so he could try his luck. Eventually, he was picked for a junior team, and he was given a mattress to throw on the dressing-room floor every night after training, together with the dozens of other little boys from 'the interior' – which is how Buenos Aires likes to think of the rest of the country – who, had they not been fortunate enough to be taken under the club's wing, would more than likely be begging in the streets, sleeping rough.

Monzón's story is not an exception. An average player, he made a lot of money for a brief time, and blew it all before he had managed to make any plans for when the playing was over. There are thousands of professional footballers in Argentina, and less than hundreds making more than a few pennies. Most of them lack any sort of decent education and if they weren't professional footballers – or boxers – they would probably be having a stab at the only other way out of the slum: crime. But nobody represents the potential upward mobility provided by football to the poorer, most marginal sectors of the population more clearly than Diego Maradona.

Even today, as football as an industry catches up with the European top leagues, and clubs become more impressive in the range of VIP and corporate hospitality they can offer, one of the most immediately striking differences between football in Argentina and football in England is the demographics of the crowd. In Argentina, football is very much the opium of the people. And the people are, on the whole, poorer.

Argentine club fan culture is as old as the game itself. In the 1920s and 1930s, although men wore suits and ties to go to the stadia, they were already organised into groups. Some were more fanatical than others, clearly identifiable as stronger or more predominant. Confrontations between rival clubs' supporters were commonplace right up to the end of the seventies. But these confrontations, although often violent, were characterised by a folkloric, romantic notion. Fights were with fists, rather than knives or guns. Around this time organised activities outside football started to take place, most notably fundraising in order to buy enormous flags, known in terrace terminology as 'cloths', and even to cover travel costs for away games. On the terraces, there was always a group which directed and orchestrated everything: the display of flags, the chants, the whistling and swearing against target players and, of course, the manager if deemed to be doing something wrong; even the silences were 'ordered'. The organised groups gradually became known as *Barra Brava* – the 'tough gang' – and their actions reached a climax of uncontrollable violence in the late 1960s.

But the real force of the *Barra Brava* phenomenon for society as a whole came when politicians started to cash in on them; they both soon realised that they could become a powerful partnership. The *Barras* would charge money for marching on to the terraces banging their 'bombos' – big drums – and with the same clockwork precision with which they unfolded club banners in the stadium, they would now display and chant messages of support for a particular party, group, or politician. In this way, the gangs begun to be hired by different groups to appear also at political rallies, go on demonstrations and so on. Although some clubs have traditional affiliations to some political parties – Boca Juniors is supposed to be a 'Peronist' club, for example – gang members proved to be flexible; as flexible as the pay required.

During the 1970s, after the military coup, street violence was dramatically reduced in the country by the brutal and oppressive presence of the police state. Tanks in the streets and the very real fear of civilians kept all sorts of organised activitites underground and this was naturally reflected in the football scene. Perhaps this is one of the reasons why the 1978 World Cup was so smooth and incident free. The *Barra Bravas* were nowhere to be seen, other than perhaps orchestrating the now famous showers of small bits of paper. But with the return of democracy, ironically, came the return of the organised activities of hardcore football supporters. In the early eighties, three extremely violent deaths took place in football stadia.

The most tragic and well known of these inspired a hit rock song called 'The Lost Bengal'. The gangs had started a trend of firing Bengal flares up into the air. They bought them cheap on the black market because they were past their expiry dates and when one of them practically killed a player because it was deflected and lost its course they realised the full potential of their weapon. They fired them against the terraces opposite. It was the first match he went to, the young man who got killed. His only one as it turned out. Another sadly famous killing was when 'El Negro' Thomson, then leader of second division Quilmes' *Barra*, killed a Boca fan. Thomson was arrested and later died in prison, but word is the five who were involved in the lost Bengal incident, although known to the police and briefly taken into custody, were released shortly afterwards. Many people believe the *Barras* often act with police complicity, or at least, protection.

Even now, football related violence has an unacceptable yearly death toll.

One football-related death is unacceptable, obviously, but although Argentina never experienced a tragedy on the scale of Hillsborough, lack of adequate security at the stadia and increasing social unrest and economic hardship is proving a dangerous combination.

Even so, it is worth pointing out that, not unlike England and the demographics of its fans at any given stadium, during a game of football the bulk of the thousands of supporters attending week in week out are not organised thugs. They follow the chanting, sure, but in relative terms the truly violent element in any given match never exceeds a few dozen amidst crowds which average several tens of thousands. Whatever the core leaders sing, everyone follows suit without thinking analytically about the content. The collective euphoria and elation in such crowds is contagious. Several thousand voices can very well sing that they will kill a rival fan without any fear of the police. But several thousand would not and do not actually do it.

What is the case, however, is that the louder, tougher, ring-leading core club supporters are more often than not the most likely to organise mass attendances at away games as well as international trips to support the country, even if they always – always – display their club colours and stick together, bonded by their club first, their country second.

As Argentina's squad miraculously progressed through the finals in Italy 1990, someone congratulated the man known to be the most ardent football supporter in a business meeting. 'Why are you congratulating me?' the man asked. 'Because Argentina have beaten Brazil,' came the reply. 'What do I care about Argentina?' he said angrily, 'I'm a Racing Club fan'. The same man then told the tale of how he learnt as a child what it meant to be a true supporter, loyal to one club above everything else. He used to play in a little-league with kids from the neighbourhood and the best player of them all was a rugged boy known for his allegiance to Tigre, a third division team from the outskirts of Buenos Aires. Everyone admired this skilful little devil who in true Latin style could do what he wanted with a ball. One day, the businessman tried to befriend him and said: 'I know Tigre is your club, but in the first division, who do you support?' The lesson he never forgot was the loyal fan's sincerest answer: a right hook bang in the middle of his face. Knocked out and with a black eye that took ages to go away, he had received the true mark of devoted fandom.

Some social historians and anthropologists believe it is the rich mixture of immigrant descendants which gives Argentina's people the bizarre lack of sense of identity which is then overcompensated for by excessively deep affiliation to a club. Others use the same argument to explain the fervour with which the national team is followed. In actual fact, football clubs as institutions of a locality play a more important role in people's everyday lives than following the national team. Football clubs were started in each neighbourhood as genuine clubs, with members who joined up to enjoy the facilities. Most of them still have swimming pools, gyms and athletics facilities with a range of other sporting activities from basketball to fencing. Some have libraries, childcare centres and even schools. They provide an important site for activities in their local communities, football only being one of the many. Clearly, 'new' societies may include more people actively seeking a sense of belonging, a need to be a part of something bigger than themselves; unlike societies with more established social strata.

Of course there's no denying also that Argentina becomes elated as the national team succeeds internationally, almost regardless of the particular competition. Everyone is behind Argentina whether they're playing a friendly international against the United States or whether the under-21s qualify for their World Cup. Perhaps it's the memory of a national sense of happiness enhanced in 1978, when the entire nation danced in the streets for days, or perhaps it's been going on for longer: the first World Cup, which was hosted in Uruguay in 1930, offered Argentine fans the opportunity to travel abroad to watch their team. They were shipped over in boatloads, their cheers and chants having become one of the clearer memories of the only surviving player from that final, Francisco Varallo.

Occasionally, even rival club gangs would do things in unison, both at home and away. Most notably during the Falklands/Malvinas war in every terrace in the land similar banners were flown high – some anti-British, most just of support, encouragement and gratitude for the young Argentine conscripts who were rightly perceived as the victims in the conflict. All the *Barra Bravas* raised money for the soldiers and the veterans associations, regardless of club. On 2 April every year ex-veterans are still invited by the *Barras* to parade in the clubs. Personal tragedies afflicting great personalities have had a similar effect. When the 1978 national captain and 1998 national manager Daniel Passarella's son died in a car accident, even the Boca gang expressed their support: Passarella had not only been a hero when a player for River Plate, Boca's arch-rivals, he also managed them to five consecutive championship titles before taking over as national coach. Similarly, when the legendary racing driver Juan Manuel Fangio was in agony with a fatal disease, all the clubs' core gangs raised money and sent messages of support.

But the extent to which rival clubs' gangs unite when following the national side abroad is less clear, with contradictory testimonies telling different tales. For example, Mexico 1986 was the first big outing for these gangs – there are many wild rumours as to how they afforded the long trip, particularly as Argentina was in deep economic crisis at the time, with hyper-inflation stifling the country. Some claim that then national manager Carlos Bilardo contributed to their trip and there is also a rumour that Maradona paid for the Doce, Boca's *Barra Brava* – known as The Twelve to symbolise that the supporters constitute the twelfth member of the team – to get to Mexico. This is often denied, particularly by the then leader of The Twelve, a man known as the Grandfather. When I asked him about this once he accused me of falling into the trap laid out by certain sectors of the media, interested only in labelling football supporters as thugs, criminals, and 'little black heads' – the derogatory term used to refer to the darker-haired, darker-skinned, working-class people. 'We raise the money. A guy with a job can afford to save a little and take a holiday, can't he?' he said matter-of-factly, adding that Argentine suporters get less help in financial terms than any other fans in the world. 'In Brazil, the club will take buses full of supporters around the world,' he added, as if to point out that even in Brazil there is a certain respectability attached to being a football supporter which is recognised by the institutions. But the seemingly contradictory fact remains that Argentina is probably the one place in the world where the importance of the contribution the fans can make to the outcome of a game is widely recognised. Although the Grandfather denied it at the time of our conversation, it is widely assumed that clubs did make contributions for fans to be present at away games, and that fans would stop at nothing when raising funds for such trips, knocking on the doors of players, celebrities and politicians alike. Maybe what the Grandfather meant was that there was not (nor is) any organised supporters association which enables fans to purchase tickets and trips through official channels; everything has always been done in a black-market, sleazy, sort of way. 'Get us a few hundred tickets, or dollars or whatever, and we'll bring a hundred strong crowd to your trade union meeting, or your campaign, or your whatever' type of dealings.

It was during the 1986 tournament that one of the most famous crowd confrontations at international level took place, when the Argentine *Barra Bravas* faced the English hooligans after England versus Argentina. Rumour has it that Boca's Grandfather came very close to having his head severely kicked in by a group of English fans outside the Azteca stadium in Mexico, when the leader of the River gang came to his rescue. The legend says that since that day a huge respect grew between the two rival leaders, although this didn't prevent them from continuing their combats and encouraging hatred of each other for evermore once they were both back home. The counter-rumour is that the River Barra never even went to Mexico, although this wouldn't necessarily mean the leader wasn't there. Confused? You will be. The history of these groups has not been well documented, and newspaper reports are both contradictory and at each point in history heavily weighted by the political allegiances of each paper and the socio-political climate of the day.

At any rate, adversaries who respect each other are perhaps more common than might appear at first sight. Argentines who took part in this legendary incident, where Union Jacks were taken back home and religiously burnt during games for years to come, still talk of the 'hooligans' from England with enormous respect. 'We met the hooligans in Mexico 1986', they would boast years later, 'a different category of fan altogether.' Perhaps ironically, the so-called 'hardcore' organised fans speak of their English counterparts with similar respect to that shown by Argentine soldiers who returned home from the Falklands for the English soldiers. 'Nobody hates war more than a soldier,' a war veteran who was a regular at the terraces told me once, before adding, 'all soldiers speak the same language.'

Argentina is after all a country where military service was, at the time of the Falklands/Malvinas war, compulsory, and where most of the young men sent to fight were recruited from the poorer provinces. Many of them had little adequate military training. The corrupt military running the country ran the war in similarly corrupt and devious ways and for many of these young men the best thing that could happen was to be captured by the British which meant that even as prisoners of war they would at least be fed and clothed and kept warm.

During the 1982 World Cup in Spain, *Clarin*, Argentina's biggest circulation newspaper, devoted equal space on their front page to the progression of the conflict in the South Atlantic and to the developments in the finals. Perhaps precisely because there was plenty going on elsewhere, perhaps simply because Argentina did not do so well and returned home early on in the finals, the *Barras'* presence in Spain, if any, went unremarked by all. Many of the fans who turned up at the games were residents in that country, a substantial number of them political exiles who have since echoed the profound emotional contradiction awakened by the boys in the blue and white strip: perhaps some of the fans were those same freedom-fighters who had an influence one way or another in 1978. Other than Maradona's goal against Belgium, there isn't much about 1982 that remains treasured in Argentina's collective psyche.

By 1986, the war was meant to be long over and both countries had instructed their players not to confuse football with politics. The war was the great unmentionable in the build up to the game between both countries, and yet, inevitably, it was the big peg the media latched onto. But it was not until recently, May 1999, that Diego Maradona revealed in an interview with *Rolling Stone* magazine in Buenos Aires that when he walked out of the tunnel onto the pitch that day he was thinking of the boys who had died back in '82.

> The England thing, in Mexico '86, was more than anything about defeating a country, not a football team. We said, before the game, that football had nothing to do with the Malvinas war, but intimately we knew a lot of Argentinian lads had died there, that they killed them like little birds . . . It was a lie that you shouldn't mix things, it was a lie. Because unconsciously it was something present in all our minds. We blamed the players for everything that happened . . . Yes, I know it sounds crazy, but that's how we felt and it was stronger than us. We were defending our flag, our boys, that's the truth. And my goal . . . my goal had a significance . . . Both of them actually. The first one was like pickpocketing an Englishman and the second one . . . covered everything up.

Of course those boys who were sent to die or be maimed in the South Atlantic were, practically without exception, of the exact same social origin as Diego Maradona. Of the exact same social origin, also, as the majority of the core of football supporters labelled as *Barra Bravas*.

An Argentine rock band had a hit record with their song 'Marado' – pronounced with an accent on the final 'o' echoing the sound of the terraces chanting his name, when the final 'na' becomes an almost silent whisper. The song describes a being 'born out of a dream' who manages to 'defeat Her Majesty's troops, as well as the rich Italians from the North' and not only this but 'with no other weapon to hand than a ten on his strip'. The main point being that on the football pitch, led by Maradona, Argentina was victorious. The war, on the other hand, was lost.

Encounters between both countries have always been memorable, and the loaded rivalry between them, in terms of football at least, goes back way before the 1982 conflict in the South Atlantic. 'The English have given us Borges's literature and football,' says Juan Sasturain, one of Argentina's most prestigious football writers, 'perhaps that's why the most important moments in our country's football history have happened in games against the English.' Ironically Borges, regarded as one of the greatest writers of the century, hated football. A devout Anglophile, it is widely believed he had only one thing against the English: 'The English have also done great harm to the world,' he is often quoted as saying, 'they gave us football.'

One of the most infamous incidents in this love–hate affair was the Rattin incident in 1966. That was the year Sir Alf Ramsey called the Argentines animals. Argentina's captain, Rattin, was sent off by the ref but he insisted on taking an awfully long time to leave the pitch – claiming he didn't understand what was being said to him. Ken Aspden, then head of referees, was inspired to invent the yellow and red card system to avoid similar delays during international games. These went into effect in 1970.

Even before the sixties, in 1953, another Argentine player with the number ten on his back, Ernesto Grillo, scored a goal against England which has become known as 'the impossible goal' because of the awkward angle from which he managed to do it. The English goalie, Ditchburn, was just a stunned spectator and Grillo entered the Argentine history books forever.

Encounters against England awaken something in the Argentine national psyche which no other rival can reach. Geographically closer competitors, such as Brazil, spark a certain kind of hatred, but not in the same way. Beating Brazil, on the whole a fairly regular achievement, does not carry the same special meaning as beating England. But then again, other than in World Cup finals, games against South American opposition are not rated so highly. Fan attendance at championships such as the Copa America tends to be low and the *Barra Bravas* rarely go at all. Perhaps this is due to a certain type of snobbery Argentines are often accused of: a strong identification with Europeans and a sense that other Latin American countries are rated less as opposition. Proper supporter fanaticism is at its best, in terms of the national team, at World Cup time.

Between 1986 and 1990 the scene had already changed quite radically. Maradona publicly refused to help the fans who had scraped enough money for the air fare to Italy only to find once they got there they couldn't afford Rome hotels. Italy became littered with 'little black heads' sleeping in the streets and generally causing havoc and the press reported looting, wild drinking, and mayhem among the contingent of supporters. Many of the *Barra Bravas* who were there have since told of tabloid reporters offering them thousands of dollars to pose in front of broken windows and smashed glass with bricks in their hands. There were no incidents among Argentines and English fans reported however, nor any incidents among rival Argentine club fans. It is likely that, as is the case with violent outbursts at club level back home, only a minority of the fans in Italy were in dire straits, the majority of them being the wealthier, better behaved supporters who stayed out of the limelight.

This crowd is just as fanatically football crazy as the *Barra Bravas*. They have the strips and the banners and they chant the tuneful, sweet sounding chants which are, in fact, mostly obscenities about the opponent's mother (and sister!) being a whore – and how the rivals should cover their arseholes because 'we are going to bugger them' – all of this sung in beautiful harmony, like a crazy lullaby. The songs, which often borrow the tunes from more famous versions of themselves, can vary from the loving 'Bring Joy to My Heart', or 'Argentina, Is a Sentiment, I Can't Stop', to the more controversially worded 'I Will Follow You Everywhere You Go, Without Fear of the Police', and the more specifically targeted 'That's Not a Goalkeeper, that's a Whore from a Cabaret'.

On the stands these supporters are indistinguishable from the *Barra Bravas*. Back home, they might stand regularly by the hardcore fans, know some of them by name, even now and again get into a slight scrap if pushed at the wrong moment. At these international venues too, they may well go and stand as near as possible to the flag-holding élite, knowing all the standard songs by heart since childhood. But their defining characteristic is that they are able to contain their passion, they understand that hassle with the foreign police should be avoided, they do not pickpocket, they are capable of self-control. After the game, they go their own way and don't hang out in the town streets looking or waiting for trouble. One other factor that may be hugely relevant here is that whereas the English are renowned for losing their heads when face to face with cheap beer and hot sunshine, Argentinians do not drink that much, and are well acclimatised to the heat. In Argentina, cocaine is a big problem on the terraces because it is actually cheaper than beer. Many are of the belief that the problem of violence is in fact a natural consequence of the wider problem of cheap and easily obtainable drugs such as cocaine, as well as guns. But in Europe, where the Argentine fans lack the contacts and it is much harder to bring their own drugs and guns through customs, they go to the games relatively sober and unarmed. Only the very élite jet set can get hold of cocaine and they are usually seated elsewhere in the stadium.

In 1994 the CIA and the FBI had been issued lists by every participating country's police force and FA with hundreds of names of those who were to be denied entry visas to the USA. The faces of the football supporters which reached the TV screens round the world were mainly those of clean-looking folk with Valderrama wigs and bags of popcorn, and it is understood that the Organising Committee wanted it that way. Aware that football-related violence was an issue in many countries, rather than opt for an Interpol-type operation to eradicate violence from the stadia, the Americans – who have no equivalent problem in sport, just ghetto gang warfare – thought it would be easier to block access into the country altogether.

In Argentina's particular case, some of the most notorious *Barra Bravas* were in prison at the time of the World Cup, awaiting trial for a post-match ambush which claimed two lives and shook the nation. Even those who hadn't been arrested, or were known to the police and had had their names passed on to US immigration, found it difficult to afford the trip, with ticket prices and hotel accommodation targeted at America's middle-class events consumer – altogether a different layer of the market. Whereas Spain 1982 had also been expensive, Spain boasted a more substantial Argentine residency – also, the World Cup had coincided with the end of the military dictatorship's stint in power, the surrender in the South Atlantic marking the beginning of General Galtieri's demise. The currency was weak, the domestic situation was in turmoil, and the World Cup actually had to share centre-stage with other more martial matters. Mexico in 1986 was a different proposition altogether; Argentina by then had had almost four years of democracy and an economic plan which stabilised the currency with regard to the US dollar. Mexico on the other hand was undergoing a tough economic situation, which was not aided by the shattering earthquake that hit the country in 1985; an exchange rate which was favourable to holders of Argentine rather than Mexican *pesos* meant the trip was not so beyond the budgets of a substantial number of Argentine fans. Add to this the fact that the *Barras* got some financial aid from the football establishment – players, directors, who knows exactly who paid for what – and it becomes easier to see why by the time they reached Italy in 1990 a lot of them were sleeping rough and shoplifting their *panini* sandwiches as the price of away travel went higher and higher.

The US did not want a repeat of this – from Argentine or any other fans – and the entire event, which gained record viewing figures, sponsorship and billboard advertising deals, ticket and merchandising sales, was altogether a different type of proposition. Argentine journalists covering the event complained about the players who during interviews would change their baseball caps every two minutes to display as varied a range of logos as they had signed contracts. The football fans suffered the blow of Maradona's ephedrine-related demise and sank quietly away: it was a day of national mourning in the streets of Argentina, after which the World Cup continued without their presence.

France 1998 saw the total absence of any *Barra Brava*. A few months before, a national scandal broke out when several hundred of the River Plate *Barra* demanded paid trips to France from the club president. Their wish was denied, and the fans boycotted the games at River, leaving an enormous empty space in the middle of the stands which other fans, out of respect, refused to occupy. The club presidents of most of the big clubs got together and an extraordinary FA meeting was called with a view to putting an end to 'the extortionate practices' of the *Barras*. In the end, no financial help was offered for known organised fans to travel, and once in France the noise which led the chants came from the familiar drum of an old man known as Tula, a drummer for hire who is now well into his sixties. More than ever before the bulk of the Argentine supporters consisted of well-to-do middle-class folk, more often than not on a corporate package, many ripped off by the ghost ticket scandals, and a handful of kids from small towns who had saved up for the trip to commemorate finishing high school. It is traditional in Argentina for the whole class to take a trip together at the end of high school, something which is financed by organised activities throughout school such as draws, raffles and parties. The media hype expecting trouble was there, and at one point there were even Reuters wires claiming that 'thousands' of Argentina fans were heading towards Marseilles to meet the hooligans. But as some Argentines in Toulouse for their game against Japan put it on the night, why would any Argentine in France go to Marseilles on that day, of all days?

Even in St Etienne, the night before the second round match, it became very clear that whatever bone Argentines and English had to pick with each other, it would be done on the pitch rather than off it. For those who hadn't been to a town where England played – which was most of the Argentine fans – the Kubrick-like set up of the town was unimaginably bizarre. In fear that a repeat of Marseilles would take place, thousands of security troops, both military and police, had been mobilised. In St Etienne, with the added spice of the opponents being Argies, the young *gendarmes* were eagerly ready for it 'going off'.

At 10.00 p.m. on the eve of the match, approaching the town centre was just like an excursion into a war zone. All the street lights were off and most of the bars closed. Rows and rows of military vehicles, huge long metal lorries, lined the streets and armed policemen stood on guard. They did not prevent anyone from entering the square but grinned somewhat perversely as they explained that you were doing so 'at your own risk'. In the dark, in the distance, it was possible to make out the silhouettes of young men running now and again, of stones and bottles being thrown randomly through the air. Every so often everyone would stand still, as if waiting for something to happen, wondering if it was their immediate neighbour who would 'set it off'. Then suddenly, a wild roar would set the crowd in motion, and everyone would stampede in this direction or the other, running away from an unknown threat, towards a more uncertain safety point. This went on for several hours with few serious incidents reported. There was a noticeable lack of Argentine fans in the crowd, some English, and many young French-Africans, many more policemen and several journalists, camera crews and tourists simply standing by, observing.

But for all the horror and bleak lack of fun of the eve, the day of the game itself was radiant. The sun was shining with gusto and although the police presence was still heavily felt, there was a tremendous atmosphere with both sets of fans buying each other beers and wishing 'may the best team win'. As they started to fill the stands, the real feeling of football had begun to take over everything. As was later much observed, this was the one game where the Mexican Wave didn't stand a chance: the English would clap three times in unison after chanting 'In-Ger-Land' in a war-like way. The Argentines, led by Tula's drum which did not stop beating once for the entire 120 minutes, sang melodically that football 'is a feeling we carry in our hearts, each time we love you more' and adding tunefully that those who didn't jump 'were English'.

Bonded by the essence of being 'Argentine', clad in blue and white and standing on the opposite end of the ground to the respected enemy with the painted faces, the fans hugged, kissed and cried together as the penalty shoot out determined that Argentina would go through to the next round, while the defeated English returned home. But within thirty minutes of the end of the game, most of the Argentines had cleared the town, speeding along the French highways in their hire cars towards the Mediterranean coast or rushing to the airport to catch the late flight back to Paris, where shopping along the Champs-Elysées awaited.

It may well be the case that the global shift in the target-market of football will lead to a dramatic change in the type of spectator that follows Argentina round the globe. Right now no one can imagine who, if anybody, will travel to Japan and Korea in 2002. But it is also becoming increasingly clear that having no live spectators and no passionate support is bad for the game.

Meanwhile, back in Argentina, the problem of sporadic football-related violence continues as the number one issue to be tackled on the agenda. Crime is on the increase anyway – with or without the fixtures list – so it is important for politicians to be seen to be doing something about this. At the same time, football continues to grow as an industry and stadium upgrades, ticket price increases, and a more concerted security involvement on match days are now facts of life. The challenge – perhaps universal – is to try and strike a balance between lively, colourful, energetic enthusiasm for the game while making it feasible for nice middle-class families to go to matches with the prospect of returning home safely afterwards.

Football, and the loyalties of its supporters, have been such a distinct factor in the shaping of Argentine popular behaviour, its perception by the media and the people, its role in illustrating issues of policing, justice, even political attitudes, that it is impossible to imagine this presence will decrease now, with football reaching an unprecedented peak of popularity and little evidence that it's going to stop.

One thing is clear. If the poorer, more deprived sectors of the population who have only football to cling onto as a source of hope and joy, a dream to take them out of the appalling conditions of real life, are priced out of the game, they are more likely than not to put their particular brand of expertise in organised violence to use elsewhere. A frightening spectacle, for sure. With or without the football.

You Send Me Bananas

Richie Moran

I actually gave up playing professional football because of the institutionalised, direct, indirect, overt and covert racism which exists in the game. I did not become a pro until I was 25 (having not played at all from the ages of 16 to 20), and spent many a cold afternoon on the terraces at the Millwall's old Den as a kid and Fratton Park when I moved to the Portsmouth area, (yes I know I could have cut out the middle man and just ripped my money up and thrown it down the drain but I'm after the sympathy vote here!).

As a kid I was fostered/adopted by a white family and not only spent time living with my natural mother in south-east London, but spent the vast majority of my secondary education and beyond in Gosport, Hampshire, where, after attending multi-cultural schools in Bermondsey and New Cross I was suddenly one of only three black kids at a school of 1,200. I still live in this area but have also lived in places as diverse as Tokyo, Tenerife, Birmingham as well as spending time in Leeds, Norwich, Amsterdam and travelling to many other places both in England and abroad. I can get by in Japanese, French and Spanish.

Having spent the vast majority of my on-pitch career in predominantly white leagues, I have experienced the whole range of racist behaviour from the older central-defender who resorted to racist abuse because he didn't like being given the run around by a younger player, to the loud mouths at semi-professional grounds where you can hear every comment.

I remember playing at Trowbridge for Gosport Borough in a cup game when a supporter shouted 'why don't you go back to Jamaica you black bastard!'

As we were 4–0 up at the time, I replied with a broad smile (which disguised the fact that I wanted to punch his lights out) that the reason was that I am actually Nigerian by origin and so therefore would be going several thousand miles out of my way! I have also on occasion at this level gone into the opposition's changing-room to confront a player who had been abusing me all game. Needless to say he did not show up at the bar for a post-match drink and a chat!

There is, however, a much greater underlying and even subtle (not a word associated much with football, I know) racism that eats away at you.

At other levels you can leave it behind as you are playing principally for fun, but when you are a pro and as part of your everyday life the casual use of racist invective in the dressing-room or training-ground is dismissed as banter, it has a direct effect – I mean there really are not too many jokes I have not heard about the size of my penis and how it is directly attributed to my skin colour.

The factor that I feel I should make clear is that I did not quit professional football because I could not take what was going on but because I DIDN'T HAVE TO.

I had certainly been the victim of racism, even from my own team-mates, whilst playing in Japan (the alacrity with which I picked up Japanese came as something of a surprise to them on more than one occasion). There was also a nasty incident in a hotel in Belgium where I had gone to see about signing for a team there (the Belgian player told me the hotel was double-booked. My French is good enough to understand the hotelier saying he was not having any blacks in his hotel).

England remains the country I was born in and have lived in for most of my life and the fact that I am reminded virtually every day of my life of my skin colour on a personal level somehow makes it seem more insidious. In the end, there were three incidents that made me decide I wasn't going to play any more.

The first major incident took place after I had been sent off (never touched him ref, honest) in a reserve-team game for Birmingham City at Halifax Town. Their assistant manager was Arthur Graham, the ex-Leeds, Man Utd and Scotland winger, who proceeded to follow me into the dressing-room and called me a black c**t among other pleasantries. Being still a little miffed about my unjust dismissal I decided that a discussion about the vagaries of racism was not on the agenda so I punched him. You can debate the rights and wrongs of my actions and I do not advocate violence as the solution to the problem but it felt good at the time.

On returning to Birmingham I was called into the office by our management team, Dave Mackay and Bobby Ferguson. After recounting what happened I was merely told that I should be able to take it. My argument that if Graham wanted to diss my ability (or lack of it) he was perfectly entitled to his opinion, but I didn't have to take abuse based on the colour of my skin, fell on deaf ears. They tried to sack me but couldn't, so fined me two weeks' wages and ostracised me thereafter.

Later on that same season when Lou Macari had taken over as manager, I was summoned to his office one day and asked why I had dreadlocks. My answer (not that I actually deemed an explanation necessary) that it was an affirmation of my African heritage was met with derision. I was told I had to cut them off as they were not appropriate for a professional footballer. My answer was that I could think of a certain Dutchman that this conversation would not be taking place with (I also threw in a few English players who looked like they'd never seen a comb). When I added (tongue firmly in cheek, of course) that as he had insulted my whole heritage, it was akin to me suggesting he had elocution lessons to get rid of his Scottish accent, I was asked (and none too politely either) to leave the office and I never played for Birmingham again.

This incident bears nasty similarities to the infamous Jason Lee case where after being taunted by Frank Skinner and David Baddiel and subsequently most opposition fans around the land about his so called dreadlock 'pineapple' haircut he eventually cut his hair off actually citing the abuse as a major factor. This comes from two 'comedians' (and believe me the inverted commas are intended) who should know better.

The final straw occurred at pre-season training at Torquay. I had already heard reference to the terms 'nigger' and 'spade' and when the assistant manager John Turner suggested a coons versus whites five-a-side you could say that I took umbrage. I confronted him and suggested that if he wanted to talk to me, being a sensitive soul I much preferred to be addressed as Richie than any of the aforementioned monikers. Satisfaction not being offered, I ventured the proposition that should he continue in this vein he was likely to be met with a very unfavourable reaction (or words to that effect). Never did sign for Torquay strangely enough!!!

One of the constant phrases which crops up when I relate these experiences (and on innumerable occasions prior to this) is that I should have 'risen above it'. All my life I have wanted someone to explain the meaning of this. As a rule I never practise levitation (particularly before a game).

A constant theme of discussion (or argument depending on the sobriety of the occasion) has been whether or not I should have quit. I have never subscribed to the theory that you can only effect change from within. I feel that the subsequent work I have done has had far more effect than if I had tried to voice my opinion from within the game, particularly as a player in the lower divisions. Anybody who has seen me play will bear testamony to the fact that I never changed a bloody thing through my efforts on the pitch.

It is my firm opinion that racism is actually ingrained in the national psyche of this country. After all do we not live in a country whose past is based on the subjugation of, and by, other races?

If you look at the whole history of this island and its infiltration by and assimilation of Vikings, Celts, Romans and Picts, Normans *et al,* not to mention its legacy of slavery and colonialism allied to the fact that the most supposedly English of families, the Windsors (formerly known as Saxe-Coburg-Gotha), has barely a drop of English blood in it, it has always been a constant source of amusement and amazement to me when I hear some of the vitriolic disparaging of other races with whom many of the perpetrators are inextricably linked.

Over the years I have been subject to some great phrases from people who have been horrified at being branded racist, such as 'it's OK, you're one of us', 'you're just as British as we are', 'you're OK, it's just the rest of 'em I don't like'. 'I'm not a racist, I don't mind blacks, I just hate Pakis', and my all-time favourite when remonstrating with some particularly vehement abusing of John Fashanu on his Wimbledon début at Portsmouth: 'it's OK mate, you're one of our niggers'.

The last World Cup was for me one of the best examples of black populations in this country coming out loud and proud to reclaim their ancestry. Jamaicans and Nigerians were in evidence everywhere on the streets of this country wearing national shirts with pride. Indeed I was swiftly brought down to earth with a bump as I had spent so much time bigging up Nigeria (genuinely believing they could win it) that I have never been allowed to forget the defeat by Denmark, although I have had great fun pointing out amongst the ifs and buts that England did go out in the same round.

With the level of patriotism, jingoism and nationalism raised by the Argentina game I wonder on a far more serious level what would have happened on the streets of London, Birmingham or Manchester, had that been Jamaica or Nigeria knocking England out in such, or indeed any, circumstances. I vividly remember watching a Nigerian game in a pub and being asked in a somewhat unfriendly tone why I was supporting Nigeria. My nomination for the 1998 statement of the bleeding-obvious award already having been assured, he asked where I was born – London – what passport I had – British – and leaned back in triumph. I very patiently explained that although this was the case, both my natural parents were Nigerian which made the blood in my veins 100 per cent Nigerian and I was entitled to support whoever I pleased. By the time I added (slightly less patiently) that Cliff Richard was born in India but it didn't make him Indian, victory for myself and the Super Eagles was assured. So Mr Tebbit don't be coming in my pub again.

Potentially far more threatening was being in a pub (you can see a pattern forming, can't you?) during Italia '90 for the England–Cameroon game. When it looked as if England were going to lose, the atmosphere became incredible. People whom I considered friends or at least acquaintances suddenly began to spew forth the most disgusting racist bile. I remember being so angry I was shaking (it was anger, honest) and being profoundly pissed off when Lineker netted the winner. What made it worse was that apart from one or two people who had not joined in, people actually wanted to talk to me afterwards as if nothing had happened. From a personal perspective it was incidents such as these and a thousand others I could fill these pages with, allied to the things I had learned over the years regarding black history that had long since turned me away from supporting England internationally, that made me follow Nigeria – the country of my heritage. But I don't care who black people choose to support. I was struck by the fact that during 'Euro '96' whenever the cameras panned onto the Wembley terraces there were significantly more than usual black and Asian people wearing England shirts. I had hoped that this might be the catalyst for a new direction in racial awareness. The fact that players such as Emile Heskey, Sol Campbell and Rio Ferdinand all wear their shirts with such pride should send a message to those black fans who wish to support England. As far as I'm concerned black people can support whoever they choose.

Paul Mackenzie, a black journalist, wrote what I considered a very offensive article in the *New Nation* just prior to the last World Cup, saying that Jamaicans in this country should not be supporting Jamaica but should support England. It makes me profoundly angry when I hear what I consider to be apologist arguments from high-profile black people in the media.

Robbie Earle in *The Observer* equated racial abuse with the donkey chants hurled at Tony Adams and the taunts referring to Paul Gascoigne's weight. I find that Robbie's words lacked the perception of his midfield running. Whilst these slurs are enormously unpleasant they can NEVER be equated with racial abuse. In the same article Earle also stated that he regards such abuse as a backhanded compliment meaning he must be playing well. It's strange but I always missed the complimentary aspect of terms like 'nigger', 'coon', 'black bastard', but perhaps I'm just funny like that.

Likewise Garth Crooks and his leap to the defence of John Motson over his comments about games becoming more difficult to commentate on as most teams now have several black players who look the same. Crooks was very quick to point out that dear old Motty doesn't have a racist bone in his body but what Motson said was at best crass and insensitive and at worst overtly racist. I find it incredible that Motson could say that black players were not offended. Although, as usual, the leading black players were conspicuous by their silence.

The same Garth Crooks again leapt to the defence of Peter Schmeichel in that now notorious incident involving Ian Wright. Crooks stated in the *New Nation* that he was prepared to accept that Schmeichel may have said something in the heat of the moment, but he is the world's best keeper and handles the media like a superb pro. So naturally that makes it OK to allegedly call Wright a dirty black bastard. In my opinion Wright is just as culpable – here is a man not exactly known for his reticence: I would say he was more than just a little bit miffed by what Schmeichel did or didn't say, but lo and behold, all of a sudden Ian Wright is saying that it is not his duty to get a fellow professional into trouble. The FA breathe a huge sigh of relief because they don't have to be seen to be punishing one of the most well-known players from the most well-known team. Perhaps before Wright did his 'One-to-One' advert with Martin Luther King he might just have considered that King actually had the courage of his convictions and did not say it was not his duty to lead the Civil Rights Movement. (Mind you, MLK probably didn't have a lucrative chat-show contract to worry about either.)

I find it increasingly disturbing and more than a touch ironic that there is a new standard phrase being trotted out that 'if it had been a black player being abused in such a way something would have been done about it'. Over the years players such as Arthur Wharton, Walter Tull, Albert Johanneson, Clyde Best, Cyrille Regis, Laurie Cunningham, Brendan Batson, Viv Anderson and all the current stars have taken the most virulent abuse, yet it was still the violent reaction of a white Frenchman that actually sparked a proper debate about racism in football in this country. Football being merely a microcosm of society as a whole, maybe we should think through why it took the tragic and senseless murder of an innocent black teenager at a bus stop in south-east London to actually begin to force the indigenous population to take a serious look at just how racist it and its institutions are.

Over the past few seasons there have been the alleged incidents involving Bobby Gould and Nathan Blake (Blake actually having the courage of his convictions and refusing to play for Wales for a period). Gould was later quoted as saying: 'All I said was why didn't someone pick the big black bastard up.' There was the incident between Paul Hall of Portsmouth and Eddie McGoldrick of Manchester City, (McGoldrick apparently sent Hall a fax of apology after allegedly calling him a black c***, well fax you too, Eddie). Aston Villa's Stan Collymore was outraged and allegedly confronted Liverpool's Steve Harkness over racist remarks made during a game. Former Everton and Wales captain Kevin Ratcliffe was found guilty at an industrial tribunal of racially abusing black trainee James Hussaney whilst manager of Chester City. Ratcliffe admitted he had abused Hussaney for the heinous crime of failing to change the studs in the team's boots before a game. Hussaney was subsequently released by the club, something that Ratcliffe attributed to the fact that he had neither the technical ability or mental strength to be kept on. This, of course, renders virtually irrelevant the fact that Ratcliffe's chairman, Mark Gutterman, had warned Hussaney's family not to take the matter further because if they did 'no other club would touch James with a barge pole'!!! The truth is he is almost certainly right.

Emile Heskey was the victim of abuse at Leeds, Ruud Gullit at Bolton. Perhaps someone should ask Andy Cole what happened to his parents when they went to watch him at Newcastle and if it had any bearing on his decision to leave, and allegedly Dion Dublin was none too pleased about remarks attributed to Coventry chairman, Bryan Richardson, about the size of Dion's manhood.

I read an interview with Andy Cole in a magazine where he stated that he thought that you were weak to give up because of racial abuse. What I actually consider to be weak and unforgivable is the acceptance of or apology for racism from leading black players in the game. There are now enough high-profile players in the international team and the premiership to make some sort of proper collective statement about ZERO TOLERANCE OF RACISM. There are also several TV personalities, for want of a better expression, who spring to mind who could give a far more positive image of black people instead of accentuating that grinning, singing, shuffling, all-sporting prowess, no-brains sterotype. You can add your own names to this. Where the players themselves are concerned it is equally important that players such as Shearer, Batty, Giggs and so on also need to show the same commitment as should Ferguson, Wenger and Graham.

The FA have mouthed many a worthy platitude and then, when a real chance emerges to actually translate actions into words, they fail miserably – see most of the cases mentioned earlier.

The whole issue of race is not merely a black/white thing. Can someone please tell me why there is such a dearth of Asian talent in the football leagues? I have asked people for an explanation and got some corkers in reply such as 'they're all interested in business', 'they only like cricket' or the classic 'they're not physically big enough to handle it'.

I have spoken with the manager of Bari FC, the Asian team, who after complaining about persistent racial attacks were actually kicked out of their own league and had to wait more than a year for the promised visit from the FA. *This kind of treatment is not acceptable.* I helped to coach a group mostly made up of Asian lads in Portsmouth a couple of years ago, and they were as talented as any young bunch of footballers I have seen.

The influx of foreign players into the Premiership seems to have given certain people leave to vent some of those endearing fancy-dan-foreigners-don't-like-it-up-'em theories. Messrs Redknapp, Bassett and Kinnear have all expressed some very disparaging views about foreign players and their mentalities. Whilst I do not in any way condone the actions of Paulo Di Canio, did not David Batty lay his hands on the referee with a fraction of the furore? Pierre Van Hooijdonk has acted disgracefully, but I can think of at least two other English Premiership players who have also thrown their toys out of the pram and been rewarded with multi-million-pound transfers.

For me one of the most disturbing aspects of this type of racism was engendered by the complaints that Eyal Berkovic made about anti-Semitic remarks following a game at Blackburn. Roy Hodgson, then being touted as a potential England manager, was quoted as describing such events as 'a storm in a tea-cup'. He then went on to say that: 'The real controversy of the game surrounded the sending off of Kevin Gallagher and not what people are alleged to have said'.

And what about the patronising drivel emanating from the mouth of Ron Atkinson? Atkinson when commenting on games involving African teams during the World Cup was almost colonial in his paternalism. There was a constant reference to the 'natural speed and skill of the Africans'. Bob Wilson, before the Argentina game, made a comment about the suspect Latin American temperament. Maybe Señor Beckham has by now realised the irony of this remark.

The Task Force's David Mellor appeared on the TV brimming with righteous indignation about the treatment of English fans in Rome in the World Cup qualifier. As Paul Hayward wrote in *The Guardian,* Mellor wasn't there when England fans gave Nazi salutes in the Caffe Greco nor was he there when English and Polish skinheads swapped Nazi insignia 25 miles from Auschwitz. Nor was he there when on the Paris Metro Arsenal fans rocked the carriage with a chant of 'if it wasn't for the English you'd be krauts'. Perhaps those self-same Arsenal fans would do well to remember that if it wasn't for the French and Dutch they'd still be boring, boring Arsenal. Maybe if Mellor had been an innocent bystander in Dublin, Stockholm, Marseilles and various other places trashed by England fans over the years, he may not have been quite so vociferous in his claims.

For affirmation of how deeply ingrained racism is into the English psyche look at certain parallels in two celebrated criminal justice cases. O.J. Simpson acquitted of murder, judged guilty by virtually all and sundry. Louise Woodward found guilty of manslaughter of a child, campaigned, toasted in champagne and adjudged innocent. Reverse those situations, ask yourself if

Louise Woodward had been black or Asian would she have elicited so much sympathy? Likewise if O.J.'s wife had been black would there have been so much fuss?

And what of Stephen Lawrence, whose tragic death has done more to make people examine their racism than most recent events? You would have to be made of stone to fail to be moved by the courage, dignity and persistence shown by his parents, Neville and Doreen. There is a real sense of anger towards the killers who are still walking free, the police who allowed him to die without even administering first aid, the treatment of Duayne Brooks, the blatant lies subsequently told by the senior police officers and the refusal of Sir Paul Condon to concede one inch that his police force is institutionally racist when every other institution in this country is.

But I do not recall one significant statement on the Stephen Lawrence case from a leading black player. Surely the black community would give massive respect to any of the leading black players who would actually speak openly about this anger and pain.

Football is the most popular game in the world. But in this country, less than one per cent of black and Asian people feel safe enough to attend football matches. Then think about the deaths in police custody of Shiji Lapite, Ibrahim Sey, Brian Douglas, Wayne Douglas, Colin Roach and Clinton McCurbin. Remember these racial murders since 1991: Rolan Adams, Panchadcharam Sahitharan, Navid Sadiq, Mohammed Sarwar, Siddik Dada, Donald Palmer, Rohit Duggal, Ruhullah Aramesh, Ashiq Hussain, Khoaz Aziz Miah, Sher Singh Sagoo, Fiaz Mirsa, Saied Ahmed, Ali Ibrahim, Donna O'Dwyer, Mohan Singh Kullar, Mushtaqg Hussain, Liam Harrison, John Reid (a white man beaten to death for having a black wife), Michael Menson, Manish Patel, Lakhvinder 'Ricky' Reel, Imran Khan, Farnhan Mohamoud Mire, Sheldon Anton Bobb. In the words of the Manic Street Preachers, *If you tolerate this your children will be next.*

Dedicated to Kofi Joe Moran – my hero, and Anni Bury – my soulmate

Vorsprung Durch Identikit

Claus Melchior

In the 40th minute of the 1998 World Cup quarter-final match between Germany and Croatia, the German full-back Christian Wörns was sent off. The score at that time was 0–0, but after this incident the German defence could no longer contain Davor Suker and his team-mates, and Germany crashed out of the competition to a resounding 0–3 defeat.

After two frighteningly bad performances in friendlies in September 1998 the German national coach Berti Vogts resigned. His successor, Erich Ribbeck, celebrated his début with a 0–1 loss to Turkey to a Euro 2000 qualifier.

And things got worse; on 6 February 1999 Germany again lost 0–3, this time in Florida against a USA team that had hardly scored a goal in its recent matches. 'That's enough,' read the headline in *Kicker*, Germany's foremost football magazine.

The end of a love affair? Football in Germany is booming like almost everywhere else in Europe, but the national team, the focus of most people's interest in the game, seems to be in terminal decline.

The love affair had begun with the 1954 World Cup final in Berne, when a West German team, coached by Sepp Herberger and led by midfielder Fritz Walter, came back from two goals down to overcome the clear favourites Hungary 3–2, becoming the biggest outsiders ever to win the World Cup. In 1954 the 'economic miracle' was well under way and became the most important factor in West Germany's acceptance of parliamentary democracy and European integration. But the emotional impact of the World Cup victory on the German people's attempt to come to terms with themselves and their new state, after the misery of the war and the immediate post-war period, should not be underestimated. Rainer Werner Fassbinder depicts this period in his film *The Marriage of Maria Braun* and quite fittingly the film ends on the day of the World Cup final with the repeated shout of the German radio commentator: 'Germany are world champions! Germany are world champions!'

Of course there had been a national team in the first half of the century. It played its first official matches in 1908, but only after the First World War did football gain a mass following in Germany, crowds of over 10,000 becoming a regular occurrence at football grounds. Nevertheless, football in Germany remained strictly an amateur sport, and when the Nazis came to power they thwarted the developing moves towards professionalism.

International matches were considered important as an indicator of the strength of German football, but since the players were competing in amateur regional leagues which clearly could not provide the level of play a professional national league would have demanded, the national team came up with very mixed results. In 1930 they managed a very respectable 3–3 draw in their first meeting with an English national team made up of professional players, only to lose 5–0 and 6–0 against the Austrian *Wunderteam* a year later. The sporadic successes of the team were in part due to the fact that it was picked by a commission set up by the German Football Federation (DFB) whose members did not see their job as selecting the strongest team but to ensure that each of their home regions were properly represented, regardless of the quality of the players.

After 1933 the Nazis soon began to make political use of the national team, spurred on by Germany's surprising third-place finish in the 1934 World Cup in Italy. The number of international friendlies was increased, mainly because during the build-up to the 1936 Berlin Olympic Games the government wanted to present the image of a peace-loving Germany that competed honourably on the playing fields. In propaganda terms the Berlin Olympics may have been a success for the Nazi regime, but the football team did not contribute to this success. It lost 0–2 to Norway in the first round of the knock-out competition, much to the dismay of Adolf Hitler, who visited his first and supposedly only football match on this occasion and left long before the final whistle. To make matters worse from the *Führer's* point of view, both of Norway's goals were scored by a player named Isakson who may not have been a Jew, but whose name certainly sounded Jewish enough.

The 1938 World Cup in France took place shortly after the '*Anschluss*' of Austria to the German Reich and the Nazi government demanded a team comprising German and Austrian players in equal parts to demonstrate the new unity. But Germans and Austrians were used to different styles of football and did not play well together. Consequently the team again was knocked out in the first round, this time by Switzerland.

After the start of the Second World War the Nazis still arranged a large number of international matches, mainly to create an impression of normality in times of war. Of course, the team was expected to win all of those games in a demonstration of German superiority. This was asking a bit much of players who often had only just made it back from fighting in order to play, and after a 2–3 loss against Sweden in September 1942 in Berlin, a foreign office official noted that 100,000 people had left the stadium in a sombre mood and seemed to be more affected by the loss of a football match than by any news of successful ventures on the Eastern front. Football as propaganda was not working any more, and not long afterwards Joseph Goebbels put an end to the activities of the national football team.

Such direct meddling of the government in the affairs of the national team ceased after the Second World War, but any relationship between a nation and its football team immediately raises the spectre of nationalism, and in the case of Germany that is a rather dark spectre indeed. The general feeling after the 1954 World Cup was expressed by the slogan '*Wir sind wieder wer*' ('We are somebody again'). Taking the ability to beat a few other countries at football as a yardstick for the status of a nation is of course decidedly unwise, but it's preferable to using the capability to invade Poland as a measurement. There may have been a bit of national hysteria at the return of the 'heroes of Berne', but eventually it proved harmless.

The reaction to Germany's elimination from the 1958 World Cup by the hosts Sweden in the semi-finals was anything but harmless. A German player had retaliated and was sent off after having been fouled by Swedish star Kurt Hamrin. Unlike the players, the German public blamed his loss on the fanatical atmosphere created by the Swedish crowd in Gothenburg's Ullevi Stadium. In the months after the tournament some filling stations in Northern Germany refused to serve cars with Swedish licence plates, a number of establishments on Hamburg's Reeperbahn declared themselves off-limits for Swedes, and holidaymakers from Sweden had to fear for the safety of their car tyres. 'Never since the battle of Fehrbellin [which took place in 1675] has the relationship between Germans and Swedes been as hostile as after this football match,' writes Gerd Krämer in his history of the German national team.

None of the other subsequent early exits at an international tournament caused such an emotional uproar. And the defeat in the 1966 World Cup final was accepted in a much more sporting manner, although of course the circumstances around Geoff Hurst's decisive goal are well-remembered even more than thirty years later. As opposed to 1958, Hurst's third goal, allowed by a Swiss referee after conferring with a Russian linesman, certainly had no impact whatsoever on German relations with Switzerland, the Soviet Union or England.

Public reaction to Germany's second world championship in 1974 was much less emotional than 20 years earlier. With the tournament taking place in Germany, the title had been expected and came almost as an anticlimax – and Holland had clearly been the better team on the road to the final. The comparatively muted reaction can also be seen as an indication of a much more settled and businesslike West Germany, which had found a place in the European community and put its relationship with East Germany and eastern Europe on a new basis through Chancellor Willy Brandt's *Ostpolitik*.

The 1990 World Cup win came at a much more turbulent time in German history, between the fall of the Berlin Wall in November 1989 and eventual reunification in October 1990. The national team had lost some of its popularity after it had taken the concept of 'boring, boring Deutschland' to new lows at the 1982 and 1986 World Cups. National coach Franz Beckenbauer certainly got it pompously wrong after the final when he said he felt sorry for the rest of the world because a German team soon to be strengthened further by the addition of players from East Germany would prove to be unbeatable for years to come – Denmark in 1992, Bulgaria in 1994 and Croatia in 1998 did not agree with the Kaiser's predictions. There were celebrations in the streets, but there was nothing to distinguish them from similar celebrations in other countries when they were lucky enough to win the ultimate prize in world football. In 1954 the after-effects of the war were still acutely felt and the World Cup win, in the words of the German writer Dirk Schümer, 'unpredictably became the foundation of a national identity'. In 1990 people in West Germany could look back on a long period of economic success and prosperity and the country was among the beneficiaries of the end of the Cold War. Winning a major football championship was nice but not unique, and football was no longer needed as a catalyst in developing a national identity. East Germans also celebrated the 1990 title, but at that time it was by no means obvious how large the gap between East and West Germans, created by 40 years of different experiences, had become. Almost ten years after the fall of the Berlin Wall this gap has not been noticeably diminished, and even Germany winning the World Cup in 1994 or 1998 would in all likelihood not have had a major effect on this situation.

Although the German public on the whole has hardly been given to nationalist excesses in connection with football tournaments, the whole concept of following the national team has increasingly come under attack in recent years: 'Why the national team – why follow this advertisement for the idea of nationalism in times of open borders, globalisation, anti-national spirit?' asked the journalist Bernd Müllender in a book published before the 1998 World Cup, and at the same time his colleague Christoph Biermann suggested that since Juventus was probably a better team than the one that would eventually win the title, wouldn't we be better off supporting a team like Juve than *any* national team? This is a rather eurocentric 'post-nationalist' approach which probably would not go down too well with fans in Jamaica who found so much joy in their country qualifying for France. The answer to this question probably is that people actually rather like the unpredictable and, for some, anachronistic elements that go with national teams. A 32-nation World Cup is still the largest football showcase in the world and its rarity in contrast to the regular cycle of the club season gives it a special aura. And with all the fast-paced changes in club football, with players hardly ever staying with one club for a long period, part of the attraction of following a national team is that players remain eligible for the same team all through their career, providing an element of continuity largely lacking in club football nowadays.

In spite of recent setbacks, interest in the national team among the German public remains huge. It is still considered the main indicator of the quality and international standing of German football and even unimportant friendlies draw high television ratings. The players are looked upon as 'ambassadors' for a Germany that tries to bury the ghosts of its past, and in a similar fashion fans travelling in support of the national team are also considered as ambassadors of some sort.

German fan culture has always been strongly influenced by what was current in England at the time. Since the sixties young Germans have been looking to London for new trends in music and pop culture and those who crossed the

Channel to take a closer look brought back many of the typical features of football fandom as well. Banners, scarves and replica shirts were all ideas picked up from England and introduced to German terraces.

Not surprisingly then, once reports about this new English phenomenon called 'hooliganism' had filtered through to Germany in the seventies it caught on too and violence at and around football matches became a common occurrence in Germany, though maybe on a smaller scale than in other European countries. By the nineties it looked as if the police had the problem more or less under control. But events during the 1998-99 season, especially a major battle at a third division match in Offenbach in May 1999 which ended with more than a hundred injured persons and the police firing warning shots, indicated that the problem may be resurfacing. There have also been a number of outbreaks of violence at games in eastern Germany, some of them racially motivated. All of these incidents occurred at lower division matches, but at the 1999 German Cup final in Berlin fans of the opposing teams arranged a battle which ended in 141 arrests.

In parallel to the increasing amount of football-related violence, the one indigenous element of German fan culture began to develop, the so-called *Fanfreundschaften* (fan friendships). Nobody is quite sure when and how this curious phenomenon started, but at some time around the beginning of the '80s, fans of the two traditional pre-war powerhouses, FC Nürnberg and Schalke 04, discovered a common bond and began celebrating meetings of the two clubs with large post-game get-togethers. Similar friendships between the fans of other clubs developed and nowadays the fans of most clubs have not only traditional rivals but also one or two clubs with which they have formed some sort of alliance. These friendships bring a rather polygamous element into a very difficult and serious relationship that should be strictly monogamous, which is why not all fans are too keen on them, but it cannot be ruled out that fan friendships have played a role in curbing fan violence.

Besides violence, racism on the terraces became a major problem for German football in the eighties and for a while far-right political groups considered football grounds a fertile recruiting area for new members. In the years before the Bosman ruling, the number of black players in German football, against whom racist abuse could be directed, was rather limited. Due to the fact that Germany lost all its colonies in the Versailles peace treaty after the First World War there never was any significant immigration from Africa or Asia into Germany and consequently the percentage of people of African or Asian descent living in Germany is much lower than in Britain or France. In the seventies two players whose fathers had been black GIs stationed in Germany after the Second World War made their début in the Bundesliga and both of them briefly did play for the national team though neither of them took part in a major tournament. One of them, William 'Jimmy' Hartwig, has claimed that he would have been selected more often were it not for the colour of his skin.

The majority of foreigners playing in the Bundesliga came from Yugoslavia and Scandinavia, although two players from Asia, Yasuhiko Okudera (Japan) and Bum-kun Cha (Korea) had successful careers in the late seventies and early eighties and were quite popular with fans. Only in the late eighties did clubs begin to sign players from Africa and the best of them, Tony Yeboah and Jay Jay Okocha, became at least as popular as the Asians, Yeboah even commanding his own fan club called 'Yeboah's Witnesses' at Eintracht Frankfurt. Nevertheless even the best-liked African players had to deal with constant taunts and monkey noises from the stands.

To curb racism and in response to the problem of violence and the rampant commercialism that was beginning to take hold in football, fans, again strongly influenced by events in England, began to develop strategies to reclaim the game. Consequently Germany now has quite a healthy fanzine scene and a number of fan organisations which have taken up the fight against racism. Ticket prices in Germany are still reasonable compared to England and most stadia have not yet been fully turned into all-seater arenas. Violence became much less of a problem, and the membership drives of the far-right proved mostly unsuccessful. Recent reports in various fanzines, though, suggest that the neo-Nazis have again increased their activities on the terraces, and the fact that fans have resisted organised fascism does not mean that a large number of them do not hold partially or exclusively fascist political views.

Even though the lack of black players in the German national side can be explained historically, this explanation does not account for the fact that in spite of widespread immigration into Germany from a number of Mediterranean countries, especially Turkey, since the sixties, hardly any players of immigrant origin have appeared in the national team. This is rather surprising given that there is such a strong historical example for the successful integration of a major group of foreign immigrants into German society. In the nineteenth century a large number of workers from Poland came to Germany to work in the mines and steel industry of the Ruhr valley. Many of them came from areas of Poland which at that time were part of Prussia, and this automatically gave them German citizenship. Nevertheless they were considered foreigners and suffered the common problems of immigrant communities. But a large number of them or their children were pretty good at football and this played a major role in their eventual integration. The great Schalke 04 teams that won six German championships between 1934 and 1942 were full of players with Polish names, many of whom also played for Germany. Well into the sixties, teams from that part of Germany, besides Schalke, especially Borussia Dortmund, fielded players with names that hinted at a Polish heritage.

Why then do so few German players with Italian, Yugoslav or Turkish names feature in the Bundesliga and hardly any in the national team? The youth teams of German clubs are full of second generation immigrants, but since German law does not automatically grant German citizenship to children born on German soil these youngsters usually still carry their parents' nationality. Most of them could easily apply for German citizenship and would be granted a German passport. But this would entail giving up their original nationality which is rarely done and rather frowned upon, by their own, and especially among the Turkish, community. A revised citizenship law introduced by the coalition government formed by Social Democrats and Greens marks at least a half-hearted step towards allowing dual nationality. With the new law now in effect, the German federation might take some action trying to convince players from immigrant families to play for German national youth teams, thus becoming eligible for the national team later on. Up to now many talented players have chosen to play in UEFA tournaments for the national youth teams of their country of origin which automatically makes them ineligible for any German national team for the rest of their career. Racism or xenophobia among football fans is much less to blame for this situation than the lack of effort on behalf of the German federation in recruiting these players for the national youth teams. It is also an indication that immigrant children do not feel very much at home in Germany.

For the time being Maurizio Gaudino and Fredi Bobic remain the most famous immigrant children who were picked for the national team. Gaudino's family comes from Italy and he may be remembered in England for a brief stint with Manchester City; Bobic is of Slovenian-Croatian heritage, though his accent is pure Stuttgart – he played in three matches during Euro '96 before leaving the tournament with an injury. One of their successors may be defender Mustafa Dogan who currently plays for Fenerbahce but has a German passport. A German national team reflecting the actual composition of German society in all likelihood would not only improve the quality of German football; it might also have welcome repercussions on the relationship between Germans and the immigrant minorities in the country.

Would Germans support such a 'multi-cultural' national team? A majority of the general public probably would, but the national team would still be dogged by a hooligan element among its followers which since the late eighties repeatedly has used German international matches as a stage for violent exploits. The political orientation of this group was clearly demonstrated at a match between Poland and Germany in September 1996 in Zabrze when a contingent of German 'fans' carried banners and shouted slogans with distinctly anti-semitic messages, clearly aware of the effect such demonstrations would have on the German public, which reacted with proper but also rather helpless indignation.

During the 1990 World Cup, German supporters rioted in Milan on the day of the match between Germany and Yugoslavia. Eight years later, again on the day of a match between these two countries, the French town of Lens became the site of another violent performance by German hooligans. Long before the beginning of the World Cup in France people familiar with the German hooligan scene had predicted trouble at at least one of the three group matches. On Sunday, 21 June, about 600-700 German hooligans, quite a lot of them well known to German authorities, gathered in Lens. Like many other fans they had not been able to obtain match tickets and roamed the streets before, during and after the match. Not once, though, did these people get together and act collectively as a mob. There was no major battle at Lens. Only a smaller group of about 250 briefly got into a scuffle with the police, who quickly gained the upper hand. People ran from the police and a few people, who apparently did not know each other, ended up in a little alley where they encountered French policeman Daniel Nivel and two colleagues who were guarding a police car. The other two managed to escape but Nivel was caught, severely kicked and beaten. He spent weeks in a coma and suffered injuries from which he will never fully recover.

The fact that for the second time in eight years a World Cup match between Germany and Yugoslavia was accompanied by outbreaks of violence might be taken as an indication of a serious rivalry between the two countries. But although Germany has played more matches against Yugoslavia than any other country in international competitions, fans in Germany do not really consider matches against Yugoslavia in terms of a rivalry.

As opposed to Holland. As far as football is concerned, the beginning of this rivalry can be dated at Holland's 2–1 win at Hamburg in the Euro 1988 semi-finals. Why 1988 and not 1974, when the two countries met in the World Cup final? For Holland finally to beat Germany in an important game, on German soil no less, seemed to function as a long awaited exorcism of the ghosts of German occupation during the Second World War. On the other hand, quite suddenly it was brought home to many Germans that they were not really well-liked in this small neighbouring country and they resented the fact of being reminded of past wrongs in such a way. Emotions also ran high in Germany because after the game Ronald Koeman had used a German team jersey he had obtained in a swap with Olaf Thon to symbolically wipe his behind with.

Later in the evening there was violence in the city of Hamburg in which German neo-Nazis took a major part, and clashes between fans accompanied the two World Cup qualifiers the teams had to play in 1988 and 1989. After the match at the 1990 World Cup, during which Frank Rijkard had spat at Rudi Völler, who was then inexplicably sent off, together with Rijkard, skirmishes between Germans and Dutch broke out in several towns along the border, and before another match at Euro 1992 German fans rioted in Gothenburg. During a European Cup match in 1994 in Rotterdam between Feyenoord and Werder Bremen, Feyenoord fans were on the verge of attacking the Werder bench.

As an antidote to this history of violence, in 1996 the Dutch and the German Federation decided to cooperate in the organisation of a friendly match between the two countries which was supposed to demonstrate that German and Dutch fans actually could get along. Strangely enough it was decided to stage the match in Rotterdam, the site of the worst previous riots in 1989. Things did not go according to plan and the city of Rotterdam again became the scene of a violent battle between Dutch and German hooligans. The meeting between the two teams in November 1998 at last took place under less violent circumstances, helped perhaps by the result, a 1–1 draw.

The historical background to the soccer rivalry between Holland and Germany is important, but it may not be enough to explain why it has turned so violent. Denmark has also been occupied by German forces, Denmark has twice – 1986 and 1992 – beaten Germany in international tournaments, and Danish fans expressed quite a bit of joy at our expense – *Schadenfreude* – after their team had beaten Germany in the final of Euro 1992, and who can blame them. Nevertheless, club matches between the two countries so far have been free from violence and riots at meetings of the national teams non-existent. This is probably due to the simple fact that there is no hooliganism of any significant extent in Denmark. Dutch hooligans on the other hand have a reputation of being among the hardest in Europe. This alone makes it a question of honour for German hooligans to take up the fight whenever the opportunity arises. Another reason why the rivalry has become so pronounced is that in most meetings between the countries, Holland has usually fielded the more spectacular players and played a more attractive brand of football. This has allowed the Dutch to claim victories against Germany not just as victories for Holland but as victories for football in general. No team in the last 12 years has exposed the shortcomings of German football as consistently as the Dutch national side.

Apart from Holland, no other rivalry involving Germany has reached a similar intensity. Austrians, again for historical reasons, relish victories over Germany in a fashion similar to the Dutch, as when they beat Germany in 1978 in Argentina. But the two teams also did collaborate to preserve a result that suited both of them in order to eliminate Algeria in 1982, and on the whole Austria only rarely has a team good enough to pose a serious threat to Germany which, at least for Germans, takes some sting out of the rivalry.

Historically, on the continent France would pose a natural rival for Germany, but the teams have only met twice in international competition, both times in the eighties, not often enough to provide the basis for an intense rivalry. Italy and Germany, on the other hand, have played each other quite regularly, with Italy winning the two most important matches in 1970 and 1982. In the early seventies Italian players acquired a bad reputation in Germany, mainly due to a 7–1 win by Borussia Mönchengladbach against Internazionale which Borussia had to forfeit when UEFA ordered a replay because Inter player Boninsegna supposedly had been hit by a can. Most German fans assumed that he was faking it. Dirty play, diving and faking injuries came to be considered as typical for Italian players after this incident. But their German colleagues proved to be willing students, and to this day German fans have not realised that these accusations nowadays can be levelled at German players with much more justification. Nevertheless, neither German nor Italian fans seem to be much interested in sustaining a serious football rivalry between the two countries.

This leaves the old rivalry between Germany and England which dates back to 1966 or two world wars, depending which way you look at it. Before 1966 the two countries had never met at a World Cup and Germany at that time had never even won an international friendly against England – the first German win only came in 1968 at Hanover. For most of the century up to 1966, in football matters Germany actually looked up to England as the great teacher. Coaches from England had been instrumental in improving the level of play in

Germany before the First World War and again in the 1920s. Visits from English teams, especially professional teams, were considered the highlight of the season, though most of these games ended in rather lopsided victories for the visitors.

Certainly a lot of German football fans were, and still are, anglophiles and that did not change because of the 1966 final. There was some dismay about the 'third goal', but there was also pride in the performance of the German team and the way it carried itself in defeat, combined with a lot of respect and admiration for the English team and players like Bobby Charlton, Bobby Moore, Gordon Banks and Geoff Hurst, who were considered deserving world champions. Today English players are still widely considered as model professionals – honest and always giving their best – as opposed to the Italian tricksters.

The German team that came from behind to beat England in Leon in 1970 still featured six players who had played at Wembley in 1966, and there certainly was an element of sweet revenge in Germany's 3–2 victory for players and fans alike. And things got even better with the first win of a German team at Wembley in 1972. That 3–1 victory in the quarter-finals of the 1972 European championships is widely considered as the birth of the greatest German national team ever which went on to win that particular tournament and the 1974 World Cup. With the knowledge of these successes, 1966 began to be perceived as the beginning of an era in which Germany became a regular contender in important international competitions.

After 1972 the rivalry with England lost much of its edge from a German point of view. By now it had been established that Germany actually could beat England and the difficulties England experienced during the seventies and eighties in qualifying for major tournaments led to a decisive lack of encounters between the two teams in games that actually mattered.

Still, when Kevin Keegan came from Liverpool to play in Hamburg – just like the Beatles before him – it was noted with some pride that for the first time an English star player had decided to join a Bundesliga club. After a difficult first season Keegan established himself as a major attraction. He probably still is the most popular English football player ever in Germany. With his club Keegan lost the 1980 Champions' Cup final against Nottingham Forest, not an uncommon occurrence, since between 1977 and 1982 the German League champions were beaten by teams from England either in the semi-finals or the finals of the European Cup six consecutive times.

This series certainly did not diminish the respect German fans continued to harbour for English club teams that were clearly not affected by the decline of the English national team. The difficulties German clubs experienced against English sides in European competition were blamed on similarities in the approach to football in England and Germany, teams from both countries preferring a more physical game as opposed to the technically superior game played in Italy or Spain. This assumption neglected the obvious fact that tactically the German and English approaches differed widely, since Germany had imported the Italian invention of the *libero* in the sixties which never really found favour in Britain. Drawing a team from England was considered unfortunate, though the years from 1974 to 1983 were actually the most successful era for German clubs in Europe. They did rather well in the UEFA Cup and always reached at least the semi-finals of the Champions' Cup.

But in spite of the continued success of English clubs, by 1985 the reputation of English football and its fans in Germany had clearly suffered from repeated reports of hooligan violence. Heysel may have marked the low point, but four years later Hillsborough was widely misreported in Germany as another outbreak of fan violence. In spite of the fact that Euro '96 went by without any fan trouble, the perception of English supporters as violent troublemakers has not really changed. This is rather convenient, since it allows the German public to ignore the transgressions of German fans by pointing the finger at the excesses of those from across the Channel.

Nevertheless, German football fans in the nineties still remain anglophiles. Many of them would still name England as their strongest rival after Holland, but this is considered much more of a friendly rivalry, founded on respect. Many German fans probably would much prefer going out of tournaments against England or another great football nation like Italy instead of losing to the likes of Bulgaria or Croatia. And the same applies to club football. Going out against Man Utd or Liverpool – probably still the most popular English team among German fans – is always more honourable than going out against Bröndby or Rapid Vienna.

The latest manifestation of the rivalry was of course the 1999 Champions' League final between Man Utd and Bayern Munich. The build-up to the match provided an interesting twist as it became quite clear that fans in both countries did not automatically support the team from their own country. At least until the end of the sixties most German fans in a similar situation would have supported any German team regardless. This began to change in the seventies when Bayern established their dominance. Their success brought them a wide fan-base all over Germany, but their arrogance and often boring football also created widespread antipathy. Hardly any German football fan is indifferent towards Bayern, you either love them or hate them. Nowadays for most serious fans whether they like or dislike a club is much more important than mere nationality, especially when the German representative is Bayern.

The situation in England is clearly rather similar. How else could it be explained that on the day before the match English writer Kevin Sampson had an article published in Munich's *Süddeutsche Zeitung* newspaper in which under the headline 'Down with Manchester!' he expressed his dislike for United and especially its fans and more or less begged Bayern to teach them a lesson. Many German fans would have totally agreed with the sentiments of the article had the names of the two clubs been exchanged and the whole thing been published in *The Guardian*.

After the match there was an attempt by the German media to interpret the result as some sort of national catastrophe. 'Why Is the Football God So Cruel to Us?' headlined *Bild*, Germany's equivalent to *The Sun*. But most German

Bayern haters remained steadfast in their aversion to the club, and even in the city of Munich supporters of Bayern's local rivals, Munich 1860, rejoiced – just as Manchester City fans would have at a United defeat. Bayern fans meanwhile were devastated by the circumstances of the loss, not by the fact that it occurred against a team from England. Not even *Bild* would have claimed that.

After that match there may have been a feeling in England that the Germans, having been 'three minutes from eternity' as Mario Basler put it afterwards, finally got a dose of their own medicine. This probably stems from the fact that the last two times the national sides met in international competition Germany both times won on penalties. Going out on penalties must increase the feeling of having been oh-so-close but being denied the ultimate prize. If you go on to win that prize the previous games do not retain the same significance they continue to have for the losing side.

Italy actually have suffered an even bitterer fate than England, having been eliminated from the last three World Cups on penalties. Germany, on the other hand, usually seems to end up the winner once it comes to a shoot-out, but German fans still remember the final of the 1976 European Championships when Germany lost to Czechoslovakia because Uli Hoeness sent the decisive penalty into the Belgrade evening sky. Penalty shoot-outs may seem like a lottery to some, but at least they give players an opportunity to make their own luck. In the quarter-finals of the 1964–65 European Cup, German champions Cologne played Liverpool to three draws – this was the time before the away-goals rule and substitutes and Cologne defender Wolfgang Weber played the second half and thirty minutes of extra time of the third match with a broken leg – only for Cologne to eventually lose through the toss of a coin. Compared to this, penalties are much less of a lottery. This is not to say that German success in penalty shoot-outs is due to some inherent capability to stay cool, calm and collected in such situations. These situations cannot be practised and in the end the result usually comes down to a matter of inches either way. To lose in this manner is awfully disappointing, even more so if you do not have a number of recent successes to fall back on, but surely no nation should be considered better or worse because a football player missed a penalty kick.

To delve deep into football history one last time, at least one English team has come up a winner against a German side in a shoot-out. In the 1970–71 Champions Cup, Everton did win on penalties against Borussia Mönchengladbach! I do not recall who converted the decisive penalty. Probably a Scotsman.

Look at the State of Us

Pete Davies

Just after he'd passed his ninth birthday, my son took part in his first competitive game of football. The match took place on a Sunday morning in January; the scene was a chilly, windswept hillside a couple of miles east of Huddersfield. At half-time, Joe got to pull on his shirt for the Lepton Highlanders' under-10 side – and I wouldn't want to overdo it here, but I'd have thought this would hold a certain resonance for any father. You'd naturally hope for it to be a pleasant and a memorable moment, another little way-station marked off in your lives.

Before the game, however, there'd been a certain wariness in the air as to how that day's opposition might conduct themselves; during the match at their place some weeks previously their language had, by all accounts, been gobsmackingly foul. As it turned out, the anticipated torrent of juvenile cursing didn't materialise – not within my hearing, anyway – and with the exception of one very brief flare-up, the game seemed to pass off without any sour incident. True, we lost – the opposition had several good, strong players, while Lepton had a defence apparently incapable of clearing a ball further than the 18-yard line – so a 3–8 scoreline was fair enough, and there it was. Joe ran about, he had the odd kick of the ball, and another small but happy rite of passage seemed comfortably achieved.

When the game finished, I then noticed Lepton's best player leaving the field striving manfully to bite back tears. The only black lad on the park, he was a short, stocky, quick little kid named Devon, who'd played up front and showed enough touch and pace to zip past several defenders more often than they'd have liked. In the closing moments of the game, it now transpired, one of these defenders had therefore taken it upon himself to give this child a good kicking – then he'd turned to his mate and said grimly, 'Got the black bastard.'

The jaw drops. You stare at these children and think, 'Dear God – you're nine years old.' But it wasn't hard to see where that attitude was coming from, looking at a few of the parents on the touchline; in the harshness of their voices and manner, in the bizarre, bleak, soulless intensity they'd invested in a game of children's football, there lurked the seeds that have flowered for three decades into glass-smashing, stone-lobbing, blood-drawing rucks down the streets of one European city after another.

Will it ever go away? Dysfunctional racist berks thumping foreigners are as much an element of Englishness as the Queen on the banknotes or the stick of rock from Blackpool. New Labour have long since spoken of needing two terms to start properly reversing the social dislocations of the Thatcher-Major years, but the vein of ugliness that mars our national life runs deep, deeper certainly than can ever glibly be attributed to that string of Tory governments. You'd have to measure time in generations, not in parliamentary terms, if you wanted to dream that you could ever culture it out.

So with a third millennium beginning, how shiny and new are we really? Our national sport, we tell ourselves, is a game transformed, swamped in money, stuffed full with the exotic players of many nations. Our government, meanwhile, is New by self-definition, and busy about upheaving the constitution in the strutting pomp of its massive majority. Certainly, it does look sometimes as if we've changed, or at least as if we're changing – then you see a nine year old abused on a football pitch because he's black, and you see Bernie Ecclestone piling into Downing Street to keep the baccy ads on his racing cars after he bunged Labour a million, and you realise just how far we have to go before anything will truly be different at all.

Besides, part of the essence of England is that it doesn't really want to change. As one Labour campaigner put it to me six months before the '97 election, with a kind of weary nervousness: 'There are more Tories in England, in their gut feeling, than there are people who vote Labour. There just are.' Paradoxically, the statistics of the subsequent landslide confirmed this. Tony Blair didn't get to Downing Street on a flood of dramatically increased Labour votes; he got there because hundreds of thousands of Tory voters stayed at home.

This leaves the government in an oddly schizophrenic state of mind. It seems often to want to change the country by stealth; to change it, but not so much that it'll upset *The Sun* or the *Daily Mail* in the process. Similarly in football, it's OK having all these foreigners about, just so long as they take care regularly to reinforce our prejudices that foreigners, generally speaking, are diving whingers, bent as a fish-hook, and as often as not fairly bonkers with it. See Paolo di Canio tipping the ref on his backside, or Slaven Bilic getting Laurent Blanc sent off in the World Cup semi – and English players, of course, never ever do any such thing.

The only foreigners we really like are Scandinavians. They're cheap, they're solid, they're not given to extravagant displays of either skill or histrionics, and they speak English. They are, in the classic phrase – given extra poignancy since the advent of Euroland – sound as a pound. In fact, we can take them readily on board as a kind of honorary English, all but indistinguishable from the real thing. Who, after all, could sound or even be more nearly Mancunian than Peter Schmeichel? Who could ever forget the dulcet Scouse tones of Jan Molby? True, these folk do eat a lot of funny pickled fish and they think paying high taxes is OK – but you've got to give them a little leeway, right? They come from the Arctic Circle or somewhere, don't they?

We are, in short, a weird mix of tolerance and truculence – and in the end, I confess that I'm left utterly baffled by the state of Englishness at the start of this new century. Is it polyglot Chelsea or anglophile Villa? Is it Tony Blair or William Hague? Is it savouring the latest Pacific Rim cuisine at Kiwi chef Peter Gordon's fancy Sugar Club or is it hankering after another hunk of John Bull's beef on the bone? Of course it's all these things and much more besides, stirred into a juicy pot of many flavours – and nailing it down is like trying to dance on a floor made of paper.

The one thing I am sure of is that we're not a nation deserving of too much cynicism. In May 1996, when I began the 12 months during which I'd cover Labour's election campaign to its stunning conclusion for my book *This England*, I'll readily admit that I approached the task in a truly dark mood. To contemplate the fact that we'd been governed by the Conservatives for my entire adult life produced a kind of spiritual exhaustion, a helpless, enervated rage at the selfishness that seemed to have become the guiding principle of English society.

Looking back on the experience of that year now, however, it's good to be able to say that I emerged from it massively reassured. To be able to conclude that we're not actually such a bad lot after all felt positively exhilarating – and that emotion had nothing to do with the result of the vote, welcome though it was at the time. It had to do instead with the plain fact that in the course of the election campaign, and in all the time leading up to it, I'd met a great deal of simply very nice people. Some of them were even politicians – some of them were even Tory politicians – but generally, they were regular people on their doorsteps, at their pubs and their places of work and their childrens' schools. They weren't people who'll ever end up in the newspapers, which is probably the way they want it, but they were constantly a pleasure to be with.

They were the English – moderately decent and diligent, not easily fooled, slow to anger but quick to deride pretension, perhaps not wildly imaginative but often given to a sharp, dry wit, and minded by and large to care about local matters a lot more than national or global ones. Unlike some other nations, they tend not to concern themselves overmuch about politics, believing as they do that things will mostly take care of themselves; the country's habit of muddling through, after all, requires us to exert ourselves less than we might otherwise have to do, and leaves us more time to go to Homebase for that double dimmer-switch with the nifty gold trim we always fancied.

We can afford to think this way because for most of us, things do take care of themselves. Imperfectly, maybe – but given the A–Z of available alternatives, compared to Albania or Zimbabwe, this country works. It works because so many people in it go about their unsung but essential business – in schools and hospitals, in local authorities, in the police and the fire brigade – for less money than they deserve, with less help than they need, while the rest of us take them for granted (when we're not complaining about them). For me, if anyone really stands for the English, it's those people in public service, and all the other people who volunteer to do this thing or that without reward or recognition – like the guy who ran the Lepton Highlanders' under-10 side for eight years, and who, on the frozen February morning when he told his team that he had to pack it in, left the changing-room in tears.

How this patient and often charitable decency can sit side by side with that ugly strain of racism and violence is the baffling conundrum – but then, maybe bafflement itself is a hallmark trait of Englishness just now. As soon as you start looking into our assorted island identities, after all, it's easy to get very confused, very quickly. In essence, the Welsh are originally British, the Scottish are originally Irish – with the exception of the odd Pict who may still be lurking around Inverness – and the English are originally German or Danish, with an overlay of Norse-French. So you could, for example, look at the Battle of Hastings and view it as a triumph for the French Danish over the English Danish – or something like that.

Mind you, accosting your average hooligan in mid-rampage to tell him that smashing that bar up in the name of St George is a little pointless because really he's Danish – at least on his mother's side – might not go down too well. On the other hand, isn't the whole point that he's smashing the bar up because he doesn't know who he is?

It's a truism that the pathetic need violently to assert oneself is the consequence of a profound insecurity, just as it's easy enough to speculate on where the frustration and self-doubt first arose. After a couple of centuries of pathologically martial and usually victorious history, the rise of hooliganism three decades ago sent every sociologist in sight scurrying for the file marked 'Losing the Peace'. With first empire and then heavy industry headed the way of the dodo, the dispossessed young white urban male with no trade or craft, no sense of self or place, no foreigners to knock about in their own faraway back yard, and no higher idea of pleasure than an excessive consumption of beer, became the usual suspect every time – and, almost certainly, the sociologists were right. The English really don't like change – and some of them started kicking up a mean and nasty affray when change went against them.

If only we could leave it at that – but of course it's not so simple. To categorise the moron minority as 'Them' is to cast the problem out, and pretend thereby that it's not part of 'Us', when it very much is – because all of us who aren't directly culpable are still complicit in the culture that produces these people.

It's an atomised culture, presided over by an imbecilic media, and driven by a demented consumerism; a culture where having a mobile phone seems more important than having anything worthwhile to say on it. It's a culture where stopping and thinking comes so far behind rushing out and buying, that sometimes you wonder if a whole swathe of people haven't given up on really thinking altogether. The acme of this mindset is the tabloids – boorish, mendacious, full of grubby lust and misdirected self-importance – and as long as millions of people continue to read their brainless drivellings every day, who can be surprised that England produces hooligans?

Certainly, in a climate constantly desperate for the short-term high, for the next quick fix of noise and gossip and hollow excitement, our football's been corrupted out of all recognition; if it ever was the people's game, it surely isn't any more. It's the sponsors' game now, the plaything of the executive boxholders and the schedulers at Sky; it's a marketing tool for lager and crisps and computer games and away shirts, ruthlessly designed to filch every penny from every pocket in a huge audience of addicts. To keep the plot good and racy, the players have become protagonists in a weird, two-dimensional soap opera, flitting with their *FHM* covergirls from one splashed affair to another, their drinking habits and their designer labels as important to the storyline as their ability to trap and pass a ball.

As a result, nothing that really matters gets reported – or at least, gets reported properly – while things that don't matter at all become the subject of hysterical and wholly vacuous debate. Wars rage, millions starve, giant corporations bestride the planet belching pollution and cooking up mutant foodstuffs, and all we get to hear about in the muck-rags is the latest overpaid lout to cheat on his girlfriend. You tell me, how many people even knew where Kosovo was before we started dropping bombs on it? And in a climate of ignorance like that – part wilful, part helpless – no wonder some people aren't confident in who they are, or where they stand, or what England is. How can you be confident when you haven't got a clue what's going on? When no one's telling you, and you've forgotten how to ask?

And yet, and yet – whenever I get to feeling this way, it only takes a walk round the block, a chat in my local, or another carshare job ferrying assorted peoples' children to one of their multifarious activities to remind me that things aren't really so bad. Unfussed and unreported, the real England carries on in all the small details of people's lives, regardless of the gibbering clamour that purports to represent us – but which in truth has no more relevance to our lives than a tawdry circus act passing through from some other realm altogether.

The real England, in my life, is the guest beers rotating through the cellar in the White Horse in Emley, and a smile and a natter at the bar. Sue will be worrying about the patients with arthritis that she's nursing just now, and Paul might have a double-glazed window going spare in his shed if I want it for nowt, and Mike's got a hellacious target for those websites he's got to sell. Still, never mind that – we can all agree that David O'Leary's doing a good job at Leeds, even those of us who think Leeds is spelt L**ds.

Then there's Man Utd v. Milan coming up, eh? 'That Ronaldo,' sighs Julie the barmaid contentedly, 'he's got thighs like a heifer's neck.' And whether he plays or not, I don't mind if football's got entirely above itself when a game like that one's looming, do I? Besides, while I'll no doubt enjoy it, it doesn't matter as much as my son turning out for his school team on their puddle-streaked slope of a pitch against Thurstonland on the Monday afternoon before.

Joe's school is pretty small, and they haven't many kids to pick 11 from; as a result, unfortunately, they don't often win. You get used to it; you always say that it isn't the point – because it really isn't – and they seem to wear it well enough. So I stand there with the other parents, and Thurstonland turn up with Godzilla for a captain, and we lose 6-0 because that lad's so good he could beat 11 of ours on his own. Tim's Dad grins and tells Joe if he scores, I'll give him a fiver. I will? Well, I guess in the circumstances I would, too – but he doesn't score anyway, and instead comes off muttering darkly that that Godzilla, 'He legged me up.'

We'd have done better, we tell ourselves, if Chris and Laura hadn't been off skiing in Austria. Laura's the best player in the school, see, and her brother's a tough nut too. Better luck next week, eh? So you stroll home past the church with the scattered winter sunlight sparkling in the stained glass windows, and the Unibond League ground where Emley continue to do remarkably well for such a small village club, even if we do keep mysteriously selling all our best players to Ayr United. Then you tell Joe to wash his grubby knees, you turn some tea round, and you head off to take him to Cubs where, every Monday night, more good people that you never hear about do their unpaid bit to try and help bring a dozen boys up right.

That's the real England. It's the collection box for cancer research on the bartop in the local. It's the Parent-Teachers' Association buying a new printer for the village school's computer corner, and it's race nights at the Sports & Social raising money for the Millennium Green bid. It's the parents' meeting where the condescending twerps from Ofsted were left in no doubt whatsoever that they better not come in our school and criticise our teachers, right? Or it's sharing out the driving duty on a Wednesday night with the other dads, getting four boys to football training with the Highlanders under the floodlights at Storthes Hall – and that's a sight I love, cresting the ridge on the tops in the dark, looking down across Kirkburton in the valley, and seeing that blaze of white light on the far hillside.

With our gripes and distractions – and God knows, I've plenty of both – there are two things we too often forget about England. We forget that it's beautiful, and we forget that it's rich. Have you ever walked along Striding Edge on Helvellyn, and seen the razor's edge of the black ridge cutting away before you through the mist, and felt that you've been elevated to some place as grand as the moon? Have you ever wandered along Hadrian's Wall, and felt all our rich history creep seeping through your bones? From Lindisfarne to St Michael's Mount, from the Downs to the Dales, from Offa's Dyke to the dome of St Paul's, England is a spectacular country – a country truly and lavishly graced.

As for being rich, sure, most of us don't have as much money as we'd like, or enough hours in the week – but I'll take the odd dose of stress and fretful hurry over living on the breadline in Russia or Rwanda. I write this fresh from a month in Honduras, and I can assure you that living with crime so bad that your local supermarket needs a guard on the door with a shotgun does tend to cast the Wakefield Sainsbury's in a pretty favourable light. Or getting shovelled up against a wall by three teenage soldiers toting semi-automatics – that can make you think fairly fondly of England. Or the earthquake one night, when my bed started wandering round the room – we don't have to put up with much of that, do we? The poor sods don't even have a decent football team – and when they do win, there's more often than not some luckless soul who'll lose his life to a stray celebratory bullet tumbling down from the sky.

By comparison, most of the things that get us vexed here are the niggling aches of living, if anything, too well; how bad is it really that you can't find a parking space, or that you don't fancy the look of your electricity bill? At least you've got a car; at least you've got electricity. Even the obsession with trivia, all the tedious, grotty nonsense about airhead models and soap actresses, Posh and Becks – what is it all but froth on the head of a well-poured lifestyle?

So there may be many things that make me angry, and many things I'd like to change – but I reckon England in its heart is basically OK, and that slowly, sometimes unwittingly, we take more steps forward than we do back. When there are nearly fifty million of us, let's face it, you're going to bump into your fair share of idiots – but I'm optimistic that in the end, there are more people wising up than there are dumbing down. It's not simply that you could live in a lot of worse places, after all; the real point is, when you stop and think about it, how many better places are there?

All Aboard! The Trans-Global Football Excess

John Williams

> I do not want to venture into giving my opinions about Great Britain. It strikes me as being a strange country. Five hundred years after the discovery of America we now have to discover England.
>
> Jean Baudrillard

> It was not possible to arrest the English simply because they had shaven heads and were drinking cans of beer.
>
> Claude Journès, on England fans in
> Marseilles, 1998

It is official then. We can forget those stylised line-drawings in dull, 'academic' texts, of orientals kicking rather dubious looking spheroids about; or of medieval Italians delicately practising early *calcio*; or even of wild-eyed, raw-boned English villagers sloshing through mud, and God knows what else, in search of a sodden ball and, very likely, an opportunity to clog or hack a near neighbour on the shins, and much worse. In these millennial times, when advertising is *the* dominant cultural language, it finally becomes clear where the real origins of the new strain of the 'people's game' lie. Today's football has become increasingly difficult to track back, organically, to rustic English village fêtes, or to the best intentions of Victorian muscular Christians, or even to tales of early Chinese decapitations. Why? Because it was instead, of course, invented by – a sponsor!

The TV adverts, in which English peasants from the Dark Ages collectively stumble on a 'whole new ball game' via the wrong end of a Carling lager can, are not really so very far from one important version of the truth. 'New' football in England is so intimately associated with sponsorships of various kinds – especially, of course, from satellite TV – and so different is the current variant of the sport and its packaging from that which was left behind in the Neolithic and hooligan-driven 1980s, that we may as well agree that we have seen nothing quite like English football in the 1990s. 'Invented' by, and for, TV and oiled by lager; watched by global millions. 'New' football in England, the national game, is the playground for politicians and theatre folk alike. It is also a place both for 'big' Ron Atkinson's merry abuse of language and aesthetics, as players are frustratingly 'out-strengthed' whilst trying valiantly to 'put it in the mixer', and for classical composer Michael Nyman's musical paeans to the sport's lost fragile poets. What times are these!

Writing in *The Observer* the influential Marxist cultural critic of these 'New Times', Martin Jacques, described the 1990s as the 'Age of Sport', with football as the predominant sporting metaphor of the time. Sports personalities, especially top footballers, have become truly international cultural icons, sought after by sponsors and advertisers alike. And, where the sport was once distinctly lowbrow now it is the stuff of serious literature and of apparently furious debate among the so-called 'chattering classes'. Once, local rich men invested in football clubs for sentiment rather than financial gain; now city institutions and media conglomerates have been queuing up to take the plunge – though Murdoch's recent rebuttal over Man Utd by the Monopolies and Mergers Commission may, temporarily, put the brakes on some would-be football carpetbaggers and speculators. According to the weekly newspaper, *The European*, in August 1997:

> More than US films, or British rock music, football has become the common currency of popular European culture, the star players as iconic as movie stars – and they are pan-European. Newspapers and TV stations in Europe long ago gave up covering only their national leagues. In the new united states of European football, the players are from everywhere, the teams play from all over, and fans travel and tune in from all points to see them . . . In a continent where industrial innovation is otherwise hedged with trade barriers, restrictive practices, too-rigid labour markets and under-performance, football's free-booting capitalism and resolutely post-industrial digital focus have made it a great European success story. What about a European superleague before a European currency?

There is, of course, a generous dose of hype here in *The European*'s eagerness to praise – and promote – 'free-booting capitalism' in sports Europe. National leagues in Holland, Denmark, Norway and France, ransacked for their best players, may cheer on this particular form of football federalism rather less loudly than the way it is voiced here; although all these countries have also had strong national teams recently. To argue that, either culturally or commercially, sport might rival, for example, rock music in its global influence and commercial power is, certainly, contestable. Still, Ronaldo is at least as recognisable almost anywhere these days as Michael Jackson or Madonna. Certainly, Michael Jordan fits the bill. Martin Jacques is quite correct to argue that the boom in sport and in its increasing cultural centrality is connected to the changing physical and mental rhythms of post-industrial life, and particularly to the associated late-modern rise in concern with 'the body' in leisure time.

But he also points out that the rise in sports' spectatorship is strongly linked in Britain to the perceived 'meritocracy' of late-modern sport, in contrast to its Victorian forebears, and also to the crucial role of television in disseminating, transforming and especially in globalising sporting practice and sports fandom in the 1990s for a swelling international armchair audience. An aggregate of more than 37 billion – six times the world's population – watched on TV the 1998 World Cup finals in France. The Olympic Games, a mere dialect to football's universal language, can manage barely half this global audience. Nothing else comes even close.

Notwithstanding the obvious worldwide popularity of football, it is particularly English football which seems a central focus for at least some of the wider cultural and commercial shifts identified by Martin Jacques. The English game is widely perceived to have 'solved' its hooligan crises of the 1970s and 1980s – though some fans of the England national team would beg to differ – and to have metamorphosed into a mature and dynamic sport which is the leading-edge commercially successful European sports model for the new millennium. A recent economic survey of football clubs put Man Utd as the most commercially successful football club in the world, with an annual turnover some 50 per cent larger than its nearest rival. In fact, United, revered and despised in almost equal measure in England both for its wealth and success, may just about be the most valuable sports club in the world.

The origins of modern sport expressed the largely masculine articulation of ideals around traditional notions of warfare, territory and national values. The new, TV-promoted, worlds of sport and the patterns of consumption they generate and shape are less gendered than they were and they now promise to transcend ethnic and national boundaries.

On the issue, specifically, of gender shift, women are regularly identified these days as the largest growth area for English football crowds. Women are also much more involved these days in the institutions of British football as journalists, administrators and even, modestly, as players – if not yet strongly as club owners and policy makers. Notions of the sport's 'family audience' are now strongly in play in almost all football marketing in Britain, and elsewhere. France's own shamelessly commercial post-World Cup attempt to establish a new national Supporters Club for *Les Bleus* also has women as a key target.

In England, in an age when the rhetoric of 'business' is a key feature of the football landscape, the powerful 'new' marketing of football towards women is simply read by some non-believers as a further signal of the sport's inexorable trajectory up the social scale in search of a more affluent, a more consumption-rich and less 'traditional', following. Seemingly by way of confirmation, broadsheet newspapers in Britain now routinely seek to bolster their weekend and Monday circulations with football-driven sports supplements, which carry thinly 'anthropological' accounts, written by apparently prized women correspondents, of the latter's explorations into the tribes and tropes which make up post-Hillsborough English football culture. Meanwhile, at Newcastle United, two of the club's directors, Douglas Hall and Freddie Shepherd, confided to undercover tabloid journalists in March 1998 that Geordie females were, plainly, 'dogs' and that the club's fans were simply 'stupid' for buying overpriced Newcastle merchandise. Forced to resign over the issue, the pair were, nevertheless, quietly and lucratively back in charge by December of the same year. So much, critics argued, for 'feminised' football.

In this more marketised and diversified era, sporting brands are also among the new international currencies and metaphors of trade. Most of the major English football clubs now offer their name to products and services, ranging from school shirts to 'naughty' nighties, from Nintendo games to even life assurance policies. Man Utd, inevitably leading figures here as in almost all things, recently simultaneously announced the launch of new 'club' brands of tomato ketchup and mineral water, as if consciously making a statement about the current, all-enveloping, scope of that club's extraordinary, and more than slightly chilling, appeal.

Many of the major clubs in England, as well as the FA Premier League itself, are assiduously attempting to plug their brand names into global markets. In November 1997, 'The Superbrands Council', itself a transparent product of '90s' media 'spin', had United as a brand as important as Nike, Coca Cola and BMW thanks to its 'profitability, performance and profile'. In the same year, United appointed the investment banking arm of HSBC Midland to help the club capitalise, via exposure and merchandise sales in Asia, on research which shows the Manchester club to be the single European football brand most recognised by an Asian audience. This fact is confirmed by the burgeoning sales of the official United club magazine in Thailand – in Thai – and the club's plans to open up 'Theatre of Dreams' retail outlets throughout south-east Asia. Tottenham Hotspur have also been exploring the purchase of football clubs in the Far East to help promote the Spurs 'brand' worldwide. With the post-Fordist rise of global flows in players, as well as in fans and capital, and with the relative decline of nation states as effective economic managers, top football clubs can also now increasingly denote the international importance of major European cities and regions. Note Newcastle United's role in promoting the North East of England for international business contacts during the club's recent, if brief, European Champions League appearances.

The increasing 'vertical integration' between football and business in Europe may soon be followed by more integration horizontally between major clubs worldwide as, in the words of Leeds University economist, Bill Gerrard, 'All the leading leagues – Dutch, Spanish, German and Italian – are considering transnational economies of scale.' Arsenal have already looked at establishing nursery-club links with the French club, Cannes. Man Utd were recently linked with Antwerp FC as a possible staging post for the recruitment of young African players who could quickly acquire EU citizenship status in Belgium before making the shift to Old Trafford. Further afield, as player migration patterns extend, Ajax of Amsterdam has recently invested £1 million in the merger of two South African Premier League clubs to produce a new club/player farm renamed Ajax Cape Town. West Ham has a newly capitalised football nursery in Australia aimed at developing the same product – young and cheap raw football talent. Tottenham Chairman, Alan Sugar, mused recently about the attractions to Spurs – and the pitfalls – of multiple football club ownership in Europe: 'The concept sounds simple, but there are problems', he accepted. 'At the moment UEFA does not allow nursery clubs. Also, how would your team in France, for example, react if you took away their best players to put into another team. They would not be happy.' *C'est vrai.* But expect more pressure for 'multi-national' football clubs in search of economies of scale as the European football superstructure creaks under commercial pressures from the so-called G14 top clubs.

The recent media spotlight on the activities of some European football agents, who are central figures in the trafficking of young players from Africa to Europe, also highlights the new commodity status of these young men and the extraordinary human misery of a trade which offers a near unimaginable standard of living to a tiny, chosen few, but penury and alienation to the vast majority who are transported to inhospitable European cities, often with no accommodation and little money. Nor is this cross-national traffic in athletic young males confined to this new version of some very old practices involving Africa and the West. Arsenal recently flew in a 13-year-old South African youth for a week's playing trial, signed 15-year-old Jeremie Aladieve from the French Academy and, on a reported £150,000 salary, Moritz Volz, a 16-year-old German youth international from Schalke 04. Such trends – and press reports that Italian clubs may have paid up to £50,000 to parents for access to *ten year old* prospects – eventually forced FIFA to set up a working party in February 1999 to investigate the international football market in children. It also had UEFA president, Lennart Johansson, describing the trades in young players as having, 'an unpleasant whiff of child labour about them.'

Almost at the same time as this new market in player and club trading has grown, the exploitative underpinnings of the highly racialised, global divisions of labour, which sustain the manufacturing domestic and export boom in English football and elsewhere, have been exposed by Christian Aid. Their 1997 report on *Stitching Footballs* confirmed that 30,000 Indian children were home-working for a few rupees in the sports goods industry, producing goods for sale in European football markets – at massive mark ups – for 'hollowed out' distribution and marketing companies such as Nike, Adidas, Mitre and Puma. The *Wall Street Journal* reported during the World Cup Finals in France in 1998 that political dissidents imprisoned in China had recently been put to work on football products aimed for expanding European sports markets.

In these new globalised economies of 'signs and space', which are dominated by the three stripes of Adidas and the swoosh of Nike, sporting heroes are also increasingly promoted and experienced as the emerging role models for the young. Here, authority and respect is no longer, simply, 'read off' from some established and ethnically exclusive scale of hierarchy. Instead, images of 'whiteness' and 'otherness' take on particular historical and cultural textures and inflections in the search for market exposure and segmentation. The promotion of the 'ironic' blackness of super-rich sports stars such as Michael Jordan and Tiger Woods is clearly central to Nike's global sports sales strategy, as well as to its more localised sales and product placement strategies. Arsenal is one of Nike's most important football clients in England, not least because the club has a good record, in British terms, for attracting black support, and has also featured local black players, including importantly among the latter the iconic, London-born, and hazardous England international forward, Ian Wright.

Indeed Wright's self-consciously inner city 'ragga' persona is now frequently set, for example, against that of the England captain, Alan Shearer's, 'straight' Anglo and timeless sporting hero image, at least in terms of their respective commercial 'branding'. Wright, currently, has his own cultish late night TV chat show in Britain which both celebrates and undercuts the celebrity status of top players. He has also appeared on British TV advertising the virtues of a fantasy mobile telephone conversation, a 'One-to-One', with US civil rights campaigner, Martin Luther King (though significantly Wright's real political hero is actually reported to be the rather more 'radical' American black activist, Malcolm X). The mobile phone, of course, has a particular and specific iconic resonance in Britain, and elsewhere, in relation to popular representations of young 'black' male identities suggesting, as it does, both a stylistic irreverence and de-domesticated mobility and an instrument for illicit street trade, especially in the key currency of the late-modern inner city street, drugs.

Alan Shearer, by way of contrast is, in another recent British TV advert, catapulted back to a 'traditional', blanched, north of England of the 1950s, where he is being 'coached' in a council house back garden in a poor white neighbourhood by an old white mentor. This is, clearly, the domain of a 'trainer' rather than a coaching technocrat. The England captain is being exhaustively instructed to strike a single, battered leather football against a patterned and worn carpet which has been hung on a council house clothes line for cleaning. The trainer's docile, but impatient, wife stands idly by. It is a routine which, in fact, recalls many of the informal, 'industrial' training routines for football of pre-war English footballers of the 1920s and 1930s.

We are taken to this 'place', ostensibly, in order to promote an historically resonant – though, interestingly, one with its own recent nightclub/black/drugs associations – sparkling sports energy drink, Lucozade. This strongly northern locale is certainly depicted as an organic place which self-consciously pre-dates both the recent rise of the European football technocrats in England – Wenger, Gullit, Houllier and the rest – and also the social and economic dislocations associated with the lifting of the maximum players' wage back in 1961. It also pre-dates, of course, any talk or popular experience of the social and economic ruptures – crime, family breakdown, drugs – still routinely associated in Britain with racist discourses about the 'problem' of the British black population.

These images of Wright and Shearer can also be read, perhaps, as signs of aspects of a 'new' England and 'old' England set, head to head, via the ultimate late-modern discourse of commercial advertising. Wright, an ex-plasterer, builder and chemical factory worker has plenty of the energy and edginess of city youth, and he also expresses well the exotic and racialised 'otherness' of street cultures of late-modern inner city England in the late 1990s. His 'dangerousness' and vulnerability – he was jailed as a teenager for motoring offences – but also the sense he imparts that, in an age of inflated football salaries and egos, he actually cares about his team and its fans, goes a long way in establishing an affectionate base for him in English football cities. He is immensely popular with young black and white kids from poorer urban areas, especially in the south, as well as with fly young arriviste executives. Wright was even used, daringly, by the Football Association for a while as part of a major media advertising campaign designed to change the public profile of the FA. For this, the FA was roundly, and predictably, criticised in the popular national media in Britain; Wright, inevitably, has had 'disciplinary' problems with the FA, and with other players and officials, and he hardly represents the footballing establishment in England. Of course, no senior official in the FA is black; nor are any of the policy-making members of the FA Council.

By way of contrast, Alan Shearer, here at least, stands, instead, for the timeless and unreflective 'virtues' of an earlier age; for a 'rootedness' and a pre-commercialised vision of white working-class sport in England – though his main national constituency now is arguably Ford Galaxy and Nissan families drawn largely from the more affluent white suburbs. It is Shearer's yeoman English qualities as well as his businesslike 'sensibleness' and 'ordinariness' – another Shearer TV advert has him, implausibly, buying food from a local fast food chain – which is what is probably most forcefully in play here.

The contestation around ideas of representations of 'England' and 'English' or British football identities suggested by the different ways for the promotion and interpretation of both Wright and Shearer as cultural and commodified products of the 1990s remind us, in the words of Garry Whannel, that, 'neither Blackness nor Britishness is a fixed, stable element and sport and its representations are one site on which the way these elements are articulated is in the process of transformation.' It also reinforces the sociologist, Stuart Hall's, point that in late modernity we should think of identity as a 'production' which is never complete, always in process and always constituted within, not outside, representation: that cultural identity 'belongs to the future as much as to the past. It is not something which already exists, transcending place, time, history and culture.' 'Official' texts on sport, by way of contrast, seem rather more fixed, immutable and exclusionary. Certainly, recent advertising images of Alan Shearer seem much more connectable than those of Ian Wright, for example, to the public and commercial campaigns launched by the English FA to secure the hosting of the 1996 European Football Championships.

In fact, the FA's 'official' video image of 'the island', which was used to launch the Euro 96 bid – its 'imagined community' of timeless, sporting Englishness and one designed to appeal to, and be recognised by, our continental counterparts – was one of an Arcadian England of Rupert Brooke: of the white cliffs and of market towns; of John Major's own publicly expressed preferred vision of England, where 'old maids are cycling to Holy Communion', and where warm beer is being keenly quaffed at village cricket. There are certainly few black British faces here. Nor were there any real signs of a multi-racial England in the various popular symbols and messages around the tournament about football 'coming home', harking back as they did to the World Cup glories of 1966 and to football before, and the 'thirty years of hurt' since. Indeed, Black Grape's 'underground' 1996 Euro anthem, 'England's Irie' and more so, perhaps, the self-consciously anarchic and transgressive 1998 World Cup pop single success, 'Vin-da-loo', from comedian/actor Keith Allen and his crazed urban clan, are arguably much closer to evoking a popular and inclusive sense of city neighbourhoods in England today than any of those football anthems aimed at recalling the England of Stanley Matthews and, later, of the Charlton brothers, Stiles and Bobby Moore. The latter's early death, of course, offered yet more opportunities for the British popular press to lament the passing of a 'Golden Age' in English football – and in English culture and public morality.

Such images and discourses also underpin and confirm tensions around the potential *markets* for top professional football in late-modern England: as football ticket prices continue to climb, so access to top football stadia becomes more and more restricted to a relatively affluent and acquiescent 'family' audience. At the same time, the game sets firm, in poster campaigns and in official statements, its public face against racism and racist exclusion and, indeed, against almost any other obvious social 'ill' – swearing, standing in stadia, collective crowd excitement – which might otherwise scar the sport's new, highly commercialised, ambitions for extended market share. Meanwhile, many of the kids of the poorer black and Asian neighbours who now live near Premier League football stadia – a product of the times (1960s–1980s) when property near hooligan-plagued English grounds was largely unwanted by white families – await their compensatory 'community' visit from the club's junior coaching staff. Work done by clubs 'in the community', it should be noted, is often used by English football clubs these days almost as a shorthand for work with poorer local people from black or Asian households. Certainly, any inquiries to football clubs about 'race' are instantly despatched to the club's community department. Many top English football clubs are also now sited in residential areas which have large black or Asian populations but, as in the USA, most top clubs now draw their active support from areas some way beyond these 'inner city' locales, out in the largely 'white' suburbs. Harpal Singh, at Leeds United, is one of only a handful of recent British Asian recruits to football club *playing* staffs. The international flood of young players to England may limit space for more young recruits who are marked by his particular 'otherness'.

Ben Carrington has argued strongly that, far from fulfilling its 'official' message of social inclusion, the imagery and language of Euro '96 – in the popular media, on TV, in popular culture – effectively *excluded* black and Asian

England followers and also alienated many potential female supporters of England. He lays particular emphasis here on the overtly laddish and allegedly 'racially abusive' work of Skinner and Baddiel in their pastiche *Fantasy Football* TV show, and also on the football/Britpop project as part of: 'An attempt to promote a fixed, closed and racially homogenous sense of national cultural identity that actively excluded black representation from the national imagery.'

On the issue, specifically, of European popular press coverage of the 1996 Euro tournament, Neil Blain and Hugh O'Donnell contend, importantly, that not only is the tabloid press of the sort which exists in Britain missing elsewhere in Europe, but that its equivalent *readership* is also missing, since the breadth and rigidity of British class distinctions is unique:

> In particular, the existence of very large culturally and politically disenfranchised working classes or underclasses is not replicated in the EC formation: nor elsewhere in the rest of Europe. Therefore, to understand the language of *The Sun*, we require to understand the socio-historical conditions of possibility for *The Sun* and also their national specificity.

On this basis, the authors suggest that the kind of relationship which exists between sport and society across Europe, as mediated by the popular press, is closely linked to the degree of political *modernity* of the countries in question. This produces, they argue, three distinctive kinds of 'readings' of sport in different sorts of societies. In societies where a modernising project has been attempted – Spain and Italy, for example – sport has developed as simply one of many symbolic signs of the society in question; it is regarded as just one way of being part of the nation. In this, essentially, *symbolic* relationship between sport and society, a poor playing performance by the national football team, for example, can be read as its failure to live up to society; in other words, national team defeat is experienced here as a painful *footballing* failure, one which is clearly limited to sport.

In the case of countries which have not 'modernised' – England and Portugal are suggested here – football is much more likely to be mediated and interpreted by the popular press as an *extension* of the society. This indexical relationship, which is the product of a post-imperial hangover, is reflected most strikingly in an almost total failure in societies of this kind to disassociate football and history. Thus, in England, especially, for the popular press, football *is* society, and the failure of the national team – and its manager – is read as being synonymous with the failure of the society itself. Hence, the media-orchestrated national hand wringing and ritual self-disgust in England, which spreads way beyond the confines of sport, when the national team succumbs on the football field to so-called 'lesser nations'.

In the third sort of relationship, that of *simulacrum*, the national football team is presented, at least partly, as referring only to itself; it has no real referent beyond that. This is identified as being characteristic of recent press – and fans' – treatment of performances by so-called 'submerged nations', such as Scotland.

Here, win or lose, Scottish 'post-fans' are determined, reflexively, to enjoy themselves anyway, and the popular press, for its part, resorts, increasingly, to self-mockery or parody, or else to celebration in the case of Scotland of its own national tolerance in contrast to the violence and xenophobia expressed abroad by the subordinator English.

The extraordinary role of the British, especially the English, in the global spread of sport, including, of course, football both reflects and reinforces the connections made above. As the historian, Peter Beck, has recently shown, pressure was growing on the British Government throughout the 1920s and 1930s consciously to utilise sport – especially *English* football – as a means of making overt political propaganda in a world in which the 'natural order' of world affairs, with the British effortlessly at its head, was increasingly challenged by emerging and aggressive nationalisms, especially in Germany and in Italy. The dogged independence and arrogance of the patrician FA in England – a 'semi-detached' and occasional member of FIFA up until 1946, and proudly uninvolved in the World Cup until 1950 – and the determination of the British, throughout this period, to maintain a public 'separation' of politics from sport, a feature of the amateur traditions which continued to underpin the governance of sport in Britain – and of the nation itself – meant that England's decline in international pre-eminence in football actually began in the mid-1930s. This decline was merely confirmed, two decades later, by the crushing 1953 Wembley defeat at the hands of Hungary.

Blain and O'Donnell conclude their work on press coverage of Euro '96 by identifying what they argue to be 'contradictory' signs in Britain's attitude towards Europe in the late 1990s. But from their analysis of tabloid coverage in Britain of 'European' issues they argue that the evidence is that small signs of 'Europeanisation' in some quarters of British life may still be offset by chauvinistic and xenophobic tendencies elsewhere. However, Les Back and his Goldsmiths' College colleagues seem rather more optimistic, than either Carrington or Blain and O'Donnell, about the impact and symbolism of Euro '96 and its treatment by the press – at least as far as racism and the issue of racial exclusion is concerned. They have argued that even the *Mirror*'s now infamous attempts to whip up tabloid jingoism in the run up to the semi-final match against Germany was, generally, out of step with the mood of English fans and the nation as a whole. They also offer an account of the experience of black England fans during the tournament which suggests that complex negotiations might have taken place among fans following England, which at least produced partial or temporary disruption of the forms of racially exclusive nationalism which were a common feature of England football support throughout the 1970s and 1980s. During Euro '96, black England fans – though British Asians may lack the characteristics of a preferred masculinity and shared cultural attributes required here – were conditionally 'incorporated', for example, in opposition to the immediate 'other' offered by the historic national and football rivalry with the Scots.

At the same time as these tensions around racialised and hybridised identities and ideas about England and 'Englishness' continue to be played out in football culture and its representations, in general terms it would be difficult to maintain that the English game and its institutions remain as 'closed' to 'new' influences today as has been the case for most of the Post-War period. For all its entrenched iconography and its public appeal to local chauvinisms, Euro '96 *was* a relatively trouble-free tournament and it *did* probably help to extend the cultural space opened up in the 1990s to football support drawn from among women and, more marginally, from Britain's ethnic minorities. My own research during World Cup 1998 also shows that many fans of England are now deeply suspicious of overly-nationalistic press reporting and of 'patriotic' TV coverage of sport, especially of the sub-tabloid variety more usually provided by the commercial channels.

Hooligan incidents involving England fans at the 1998 World Cup in Marseilles might be optimistically read, in this context, as signs of the last death throes of a particular kind of national supporter base which is, itself, already in deep transformation. 'Corporate' England fans, older supporters, and those, including women, who are bent on exploring the more peaceful 'carnivalesque' supporter styles at international tournaments, now at least vie with English hooligans for air time in defining exactly what travelling with the England national team now 'means'. Certainly, 'alternative' accounts of events in Marseilles did emerge in the media and elsewhere, many of them from identifiably 'new' travelling England fans.

In pointing to the importance of the symbolism of the national flag in stimulating disturbances in Marseilles, French academic, Claude Journes, commented recently that: 'At a time when the creation of Europe raises the issue of national sovereignty, football remains one of the pillars of national identity.' This remains true, of course, but there were signs, too, in World Cup '98 of English football fans actually 'adopting' *other* national teams from the continent, as well as England, on the basis of player and club affiliation. Indeed, should we be at all surprised these days that at the moment Chelsea fans also now 'care for' Italy? Or that Arsenal fans have a soft spot for the Dutch and for the French? Of course, strong localisms, other ethnicities, and political and economic isolation have all, historically, conditioned support for England in northern cities such as Liverpool. Today, however, as well as traditional Irish affiliations, many Man Utd and Liverpool supporters now also have selective *Scandinavian* leanings at national level.

All this, plus, in the wake of TV de-regulation and the relative decline of the role of the BBC in ritually articulating links through national coverage of sporting events, between empire, nation, the monarchy and the family, and the sheer scale and pace of 'sports flows' at the end of the century, promises to change important aspects of the 'meaning' of national sport in Britain. We also have upon us the new influences of devolution and new national and, possibly, regional assemblies. Such shifts might even eventually challenge Eric Hobsbawm's now famous modernist dictum about the capacity of sport, especially football, to act as a uniquely effective medium for inculcating, even among the least political or public individuals, a strong identification with the nation. That, 'the imagined community of millions seems more real as a team of eleven named people. The individual, even the one who cheers, becomes a symbol of the nation himself.'

As international football continues to carry heavy symbolic baggage especially for 'emerging' nations – Croatia's 'emotional' World Cup successes in France, for example – Man Utd fans actually began the 1998–99 league season in England by chanting 'Argentina!' to counter rival fans' abuse of midfielder David Beckham, who had been sent off in France against the South Americans, thus scuppering England's hopes of ultimate success. Such chants are also a useful way of cohering United's own, notoriously nationally drawn, fan support. At England international matches at Wembley before and following the Finals the largely southern-based home crowds had amused themselves by singing what is an emerging 'alternative' national football anthem, 'Stand up if you hate Man Utd'. In fact, as Tony King has pointed out, in their new, preferred, guise as supporters of a 'post-national', a regional but fully *European* club, United followers *from* Manchester had already begun to particularise English football nationalism to the south and to other smaller football clubs in England. As a letter to the Man Utd fanzine, *United We Stand*, put it in January 1998:

> The national team is there to give supporters of small time crap little clubs – West Ham, Millwall, Leeds, [Manchester] City, etc. – the chance to lord it abroad watching a team that at least has a chance of winning, unlike their own tinpot lowly outfit. This is a view of the majority of United fans and, indeed, supporters of other big clubs, usually in the North (Liverpool or Everton).

For fans like these, United no longer, revealingly, 'go into' Europe; they seem, increasingly, to be symbolically and materially situated there. By the end of the 1998–99 season an estimated 60,000 United fans – many more, incidentally, even than those who had travelled, disconcertingly for FIFA, to watch England play in France – set up in the Nou Camp in Barcelona to see a multi-national United team, containing only four Englishmen, win the European Cup for the first time for 31 years. Throughout the media build-up to the Final, United were promoted by the English press and radio mediums, not unproblematically given the strength of club loyalties in England and football antipathy towards United, as the country's 'representatives' in Barcelona. A *Daily Telegraph* poll found 86 per cent of the population – though not, one suspects, of football fans – claiming to be 'supporting' United in Spain. Interesting tensions are, clearly, raised here between the status of United as a 'national' club on the one hand, and the strongly regionally affiliation and identification adopted by some United fans against national associations and affiliations with the club on the other.

Tensions, at the formal level, between the interests of club and country are almost bound to intensify as powerful clubs become yet more 'internationalised' and commercially more dominant. Arsene Wenger recently questioned, for example, whether football fans in England were actually *that* interested in World Cup qualifying matches which matched top nations against international minnows. Wouldn't north London football fans really rather be watching multi-national Arsenal or even Spurs, he asked, than losing yet another weekend of top Premier League action simply to watch a poor England stumble against a 'little' Moldova or Georgia? There was little in the way of strident criticism as a reply. In the early 1990s, Silvio Berlusconi, the owner of the then all-conquering AC Milan, a team based on outstanding Dutch players, had claimed that national team football would, simply, die in popularity as the top European clubs became ever stronger, and football followers became seduced by the quality of club football and less tied in a federal Europe by attachments of national belonging and patriotic sentiment to their more limited international teams.

Thus far, although the weight of national attachments has shifted, this notion still seems fanciful. The World Cup remains a global attraction and there seems little or no diminution in the mass public interest in it. But FIFA is, clearly, alarmed by the strength of the new European club oligarchy. Indeed, as part of an emerging power play between the clubs, the federations and national team competition, FIFA has recently instituted its own international club competition. Sepp Blatter, the new FIFA President, also warmed strongly to the idea of having the World Cup every two years rather than on the four yearly cycle which has always been favoured. Why not? The finals are profitable and popular. TV and sponsors are waiting for the opportunity to support a two yearly competition. The move would also strengthen FIFA's international position *vis-à-vis* the top European clubs and the top national leagues – which, of course, is precisely the point.

National identities, then, are still a strong and enduring motivator in football. But, no matter how hard FIFA, and the fans, might wish it, the World Cup finals, themselves, are simply no longer – if they ever were – a separate sporting arena which exists, solely or mainly, for the public expression of deeply felt *national* football attachments, articulated through blood or citizenship ties. Commercial and contractual considerations for players, for FIFA and for national teams are also central to the 'meaning' of the finals these days. For all the media talk of distinctive 'national styles' and of 'playing from the heart', the finals offer increasingly familiar and 'Europeanised' fare, and they are now a vital showcase for players, their sponsors and their agents to try to maximise client exposure and to make a case for negotiating new player deals or transfers to wealthy European clubs. Hidetoshi Nakata, the talented Japanese midfielder, made no bones that the 1998 World Cup was, for him, solely about securing his transfer to a Serie A club. He, soon after, left for Italy. The Nike/Ronaldo saga before the final match itself is, bleakly, probably a further sign of the growing influence of the new sports 'nations' – the sponsors – in these acutely fiscal football times. The finals are also, of course, an important public stage for European *leagues* to better promote their international standing to sponsors and others, and their various claims for being *the* élite league in the world game. Leboeuf, Vieira, Desailly and Petit were all World Cup winners in 1998; crucially, and to much public trumpeting, they were all playing in the English Premiership in 1998/99.

English football *has* internationalised to a remarkable extent, even over the past decade. It may be difficult to trace either in the committee structures of the FA, or among the ranks of 'hard core' England travelling support, any real agreement that white Englishness, in its residual form, must, as Kevin Davey put it recently in *English Imaginaries*, 'unlearn its privilege, to adjust to the global flows and circuits of capital and culture.' But, in the corridors of club power, and in the articulation of fans' relationships to club and to country, a new international order is, indeed, slowly beginning to emerge. Foreign team managers, the new European technocrats, are increasingly the norm in England today. Fans at top clubs, though rightly concerned about the fate of English talent, also expect – demand even – that their clubs recruit players from the international, the global, roster. Bosman has meant the sort of player flow into England – few players yet flow the other way – which mark out the game's top stars as following *internationalised* career trajectories rather than pursuing the sorts of longer standing, stable relationships with clubs which were more characteristic of earlier periods. Support for England is, increasingly, conditioned in turn by the complexities of club and regional identities and by new post-national imaginaries: it is, itself, slowly, accommodating to the demands of a new Europe.

Top club player recruits in England today are as likely to come from Salzburg as from Salford, from Bosnia as from Basingstoke: in short, England's football isolationism must be declared to be over. It is against this complex backcloth of new commercial networks and new connections, of the primacy of legal statutes over 'traditional' national ties, and of an era when representation and identification exceed the space, and transcend the superintendence of the nation state, that new relationships and tensions between club and national football support in England will, necessarily, be expressed and negotiated. Change here may yet be slow and painful. In August 1997 *The European*, opined: 'Europe may still have some way to travel before all of its citizens feel themselves members of the ever closer union demanded by the treaty of Rome, but the creation of a closer continent is certainly being promoted by the culture of football.' English *club* football positively shows signs of reflecting recent changes while, perhaps accordingly, the national team still struggles. On 5 June 1999, after another stumbling, overly-aggressive and essentially ideas-free display by England, this time against Sweden, new manager, Kevin Keegan, called, not for more stealth, or for greater thought or finesse from his team, but for a show of 'the real bulldog spirit' in the country's next performance against struggling Bulgaria. 'Paradoxically', as Kevin Davey has argued, 'if it is to endure, England must first become a nation of strangers.' This means, in the football context, matching and reshaping the undoubted deep strength of aspects of what has become the 'English way' in sport with some of the attributes associated with those from whom we have traditionally been most reluctant to learn. Re-making and re-imagining the work of the 'home' of football will be central to any new agenda in England which is properly responsive to recent shifts in the new international sporting order. There is, clearly, much work still to be done.

Labouring for a Vin-da-loo Nation

Steve Redhead

Margaret Thatcher's spinning of any England football success in the 1980s, when Little Englander politics on and off the terraces were so rampant, made me feel deeply embarrassed to identify in any way with Englishness, especially as for most of my lifetime England-representative teams have been regularly outplayed by foreigners big and small in footballing terms. I see myself less as purely English than a born-again Mancunian living in Europe rather than America.

But I also instinctively want things to change: I want to roll back the associations that I am so ambivalent about but which pack themselves around the England national team. The Falklands War in particular symbolised Thatcher's English nationalism and for the rest of the 1980s it was increasingly difficult to enjoy an England football match if you held any left-wing or progressive political opinions. It was easier if England lost then there would be no chance of the right's nauseating basking in the 'glory game'. By Italia '90 though, a cultural change was in the air – 'football with attitude' as I called it at the time. In this late 1980s-early 1990s period wider political shifts were taking place as the New Right of Reagan and Thatcher gradually started to lose its 1970s and 1980s sheen. Twenty years of neo-liberalism was coming to a close – New Right into Old Right within a generation.

The mid-1990s saw a marked shift in the electoral fortunes of the right's regimes, and philosophies, which had originally emerged in the early to mid-1970s. In Canada, elections virtually wiped out the previously dominant Conservatives at a national level in 1994. In the USA Bill Clinton's new Democrats defeated the old Republicans in the 1992 and 1996 presidential elections. On 1 May 1997, the General Election in Britain produced a landslide victory for new Labour, explicitly mimicking President Clinton's twin electoral successes with the Big Idea of the 'new'. A 179-seat parliamentary majority for the Prime Minister Tony Blair finished 18 years of neo-liberal rule under the premiership of first Margaret Thatcher and then John Major. None of this meant an end to Conservative political thought – far from it, right-wing thinking is strong and highly organised in these and many other countries – but the era of New Right dominance was certainly coming to a close by the late 1990s.

What though did this mean for the culture of post-imperial countries like Britain? And especially England, in the context of Scottish and Welsh semi-independence and the emergence of a new peace agreement in Ireland? Did new Labour herald a new culture? Or was Blairism merely an extension of Thatcherism; a Blatcherism to compare with the consensus-driven Butskellism of the 1950s. Enterprise, freedom and individualism had been keywords of the Thatcher and Major years; what would replace them – if anything – in the new era? What 'cultural' revolution had taken place in the rise and fall of the New Right, and what might the New Britain of Tony Blair's 'vision of a young country' look like? Blair has written of his longing for a revival of the 'Stanley Matthews Culture'. Corinthian values in sport were at the heart of this, as well as a distancing from football's commercialism and greed which had so spectacularly taken over from them. Blair's 'young country' in essence though was England, not Britain. His obvious electoral appeal to 'middle England' had made him favourite to succeed Labour leader John Smith rather than his Scottish rival Gordon Brown. It was a 'Young England' – as the nation's Under-23 football team used to be known – that Tony Blair visualised and success at the ballot box was not long in coming. The whole process reminded me of the way television sports presenters, when interviewing Premier League or Nationwide managers or players, automatically assume that the national team they would be interested in is England – even where, as is often the case, the interviewees are Scottish, Irish or Welsh, or for that matter French or Dutch.

Enterprise culture was as much in evidence in the cultural industries as in any other sphere of economic activity in the 1980s and 1990s. Indeed the 'gains' made by the Thatcher and Major regimes were especially pronounced in the business of the arts. When elected, Labour was left with this enduring cultural legacy. For its own part New Labour's resurrection of D-ream's 1995 dance pop hit 'Things Can Only Get Better' as its Election theme tune suggested a continuity rather than a radical and ultimately decisive break with the recent past. It also underlined, in a rather hamfisted way, Labour's newness, keying in several years too late to 1990s clubcultures. According to Charles Leadbeater, in a pamphlet for the think-tank Demos entitled *Civic Spirit: The Big Idea for a New Political Era:* 'clubbing is . . . the most popular pastime amongst a highly individualistic young generation, foreshadowing a more widespread principle of mutuality in club culture (from sports clubs to local history clubs) which might help to renew civic culture.' Recognising the problem of national identity explicitly, another of Leadbeater's Demos colleagues Mark Leonard has put forward the idea of 'rebranding Britain' in *Britain TM: Renewing Our Identity* which the author described as 'a blueprint for a national makeover, detailed proposals for defining Britishness'.

New Labour's connection to popular culture, such as music and football, is a complex story. Tony Blair thinks of himself as a self-consciously 'modern man'. He describes himself as from 'the rock and roll generation, colour TV and the Beatles'. He even played in his own rock band – the Ugly Rumours – in his Oxford University days in the early 1970s. The fact that the first 'out' gay MP in the House of Commons, Chris Smith, was picked by Blair to take over at the Department for Culture, Media and Sport (formerly the Department of National Heritage) once the Election was won, and that his first Minister for Sport was former Greater London Council member and lifelong Chelsea fan Tony Banks, suggested to some that Blair's sense of modernity extended further than mere rhetoric. Football fandom, rather than the more conservative cricket culture which his predecessor John Major so publicly adopted, seems to be a talisman of the modern man of politics though Martin Kettle, a supporter of Blair, suggested to *Guardian* readers after the Election that the new Prime Minister was probably not quite so keen on football in the mid-1980s when the sport was much less politically correct in the wake of the Heysel disaster in Brussels. Writing in *Perfect Pitch* about the 'people's party's game' journalist and Labour Party activist Simon Buckby claims that in 1999 'football has never had so many political supporters as it currently enjoys. And almost all of them are from the Labour Party . . . Football works for Labour now partly because politics has changed.' On his resignation as press officer for the Chancellor, Charlie Whelan wrote a weekly column for *The Observer* on football not politics. Association with football has however been attacked by those, like Helen Wilkinson, who see new Labour as actively promoting elements of new laddism, in the processs invoking Margaret Thatcher as a lasting role model for the New Feminists.

When he left office, John Major lauded a burgeoning British cultural renaissance, particularly in the field of popular culture. For Major the globalisation of 'Britpop' – a spurious label applied to bands as diverse as Oasis, Blur, Pulp and Supergrass – and the foreign fêting of London as a cultural as well as a financial centre foretold a Tory success story. However, despite some of girl power troupe the Spice Girls being quoted as Thatcher's Girls, the majority of cultural entrepreneurs backed New Labour and lambasted Tory philistinism even if many repented at their leisure and spearheaded a backlash led by the *New Musical Express* in 1998. The *NME* headline was: 'Betrayed: The Labour Government's War on You'. Wayne Hemmingway, chairman of the fashion firm Red Or Dead, lectured the Social Market Foundation on state intervention in the culture industries, a talk which was mischievously entitled 'How To Kill Off Cool Britannia – Invite Mick Hucknall to Cocktails at No 10'. *The Observer* had already announced 'Cool Britannia Going Cold On New Labour' after a member of Chumbawumba threw a bucket of water over Deputy Prime Minister John Prescott at the Brit Awards for selling out the Liverpool dockers whose strike had already attracted support from Liverpool-born footballers Steve McManaman and Robbie Fowler. Former *Marxism Today* editor Martin Jacques dubbed this growing disenchantment 'Uncool Britannia' in his own story of the 'backlash'. Perhaps predictably William Rees-Mogg attacked Labour's arts policy in *The Times* and theatre's Sir Peter Hall criticised Labour for producing a dumbed-down American style culture by underfunding the arts. But, overall, the mood among most artists and cultural workers remained pro-Labour. Alan McGee, the young ex-drug-using boss of former indie label

Creation Records whose bands include Oasis, was vociferously pro-New Labour and joined one of the government's policy task forces alongside other luminaries such as Paul Smith, Mick Hucknall and Robbie Earle. Noel Gallagher, songwriter of Oasis, infamously named Tony Blair alongside his band as potential saviours of youth. Writer and broadcaster Melvyn Bragg wrote to *The Times* that new Labour had a unique and real opportunity to achieve something for the arts in the five years of a parliament, explicitly recognising the importance of the culture, sport, youth, film and tourist industries to the economy in his belief that 'culture could be one of the great engines of growth', especially in cities outside London. The connections between new Labour and the cultural sphere seemed to recall the last time a young Labour Prime Minister took office after a long period of Tory misrule: the year was 1964 and the Prime Minister Harold Wilson. In that era the Beatles were, initially, a symbol of the enterprise of Wilson's New Britain. 1964's slogan 'Let's Go With Labour' hinted at the promise of a cultural rebirth which by Wilson's large 1966 General Election victory had already begun to pay political and economic dividends. Harold Wilson's cultural envoy, Jenny Lee as Minister for the Arts, was fondly remembered in the debates about culture in the wake of Tony Blair's own triumph. It was suggested that new Labour needed a new 'Jenny Lee'. Tony Blair himself made a keynote speech during the 1997 campaign outlining arts and cultural industries policy and introducing the idea of a NESTA (National Endowment for Science, Technology and the Arts) talent fund for individuals. The National Trust for Talent and Creativity, proposed in 'The People's Lottery' white paper following the Election, aimed to create an environment fostering talent and innovation including financial support for creative individuals, grants and loans to help develop ideas for products and services, placement schemes for talented individuals and master classes and summer schools. Such a cultural renaissance is, nevertheless, expensive and funding can obviously be from either the central or local state, the market, or all three. What the rhetoric of the Thatcher and Major years contrived to hide was the massive state subsidy of the arts and sport, not only at national level but at regional level too. Free enterprise culture and market individualism were not all that they seemed.

Furthermore the personal freedom championed by 'Thatcher's children' in the 1980s and 1990s soon enough came into conflict with draconian laws imposed by the most free-market of governments. Laws such as the Licensing Act 1988, Football Spectators Act 1989, the Entertainments (Increased Penalties) Act 1990 and – most notoriously – the Criminal Justice and Public Order Act 1994 flew in the face of the individualism otherwise espoused by the Conservative Party led by Margaret Thatcher and John Major, most in evidence in the naked greed and conspicuous consumption of the financial services sector, especially in the City of London. Thatcher's children in fact forged a different kind of individualism to what the New Right was used to, one which was needed simply to survive in a savage, mercilessly deregulated economic and social environment. It was this new individualism which, manifested in youth culture, was damned legislatively by the Tories and allowed new Labour to claim a popular mandate at the 1997 Election. In Gordon Brown's first budget as Chancellor of the Exchequer – the first by Labour since Denis Healey's finale in March 1979 – it was precisely the cultural industries which underpin this youth culture that New Labour promoted. Brown argued that: 'Britain is increasingly leading the world in those industries which most obviously depend on the skills and talents of their workers – communications, design, architecture, fashion, music and film'. He was recognising that these are the industries most attractive to youth and most likely to have potential for future expansion of employment and mobility. Add sport to this list and the new Labour idea for renaming the Department of National Heritage, created by the Tories in 1992, the Department for Culture, Media and Sport makes sense. Sport is spearheading new Labour's cultural policy around Young England. The bid for the 2006 World Cup is a classic example; just as in 1966 (and Euro '96) the venues will – if the FA is successful – be English, not Scottish, Irish or Welsh. A British football team concept is as far away as ever. Indeed New Football is the area where the problems and possibilities of new Labour's English cultural revolution stand out most clearly.

Hunter Davies, author of *The Glory Game*, the early 1970s classic on a year in the life of Tottenham Hotspur, writing in the late 1990s in the *New Statesman* suggests that:

> New Football is a bit like new Labour. You chuck out the old order, attract new people from the middle classes, bring in more women, spend more money, work hard on polish and presentation, especially presentation. New Football has been here a bit longer than new Labour, almost a decade since the changes began, and several elements combined to bring about the revolution: the Taylor report, the Bosman ruling, Sky's millions, clubs going public, vast transfer fees, vast wages. Out have gone the old stadiums with old fashioned terraces and old-fashioned directors, the butchers and bakers known only in the community. In have come all-seater stadiums, foreign stars and super-rich chairmen who are national figures . . . It's been mostly for the better, I think, with increased comfort and safety, for those who can afford tickets. It costs a fortune now to follow football, yet attendances are up. Lucky old football. Even more fashionable than new Labour.

Hunter Davies sums up a widespread feeling amongst fans that on balance things have got better. However, the story of New Football culture is not quite such a straightforward one. Rupert Murdoch's Sky takeover of Man Utd failed partly because of Independent Supporters Association protests which led to a reference of the bid to a further investigation by the Monopolies and Mergers Commission. Modernisation of the game continues like that of new Labour but in uneven, often contradictory ways.

Modernisation plays out differentially too in popular music's link with football fandom. Labour has in some ways become too closely identified with the Baddiel and Skinner 'Football's Coming Home' brand of uncritical new laddism – Tony Blair was interviewed for example by David Baddiel for Channel 4 prior to the Election and 'Labour's Coming Home' explicitly echoed 'Three Lions'. However, prior to France '98, the usual host of more or less 'trashy' songs were released into the pop/football marketplace. Since Italia '90 and England/New Order's classy 'World In Motion', the genre has become more respectable but it remains firmly part of a trash aesthetic including classics such as Black Grape's 'England's Irie' released at the time of Euro '96. One of summer 1998's releases, ostensibly even more low culture than the rest, involved comedian Keith Allen (co-writer of 'World in Motion', walk on part in 'England's Irie'), controversial artist Damien Hirst and pop band Blur bassist Alex James. Masquerading as 'Fat Les' they put out 'Vin-da-loo', lifting the tune from a South Yorkshire football 'terrace' band. *Awaydays* author Kevin Sampson writing in *The Observer* prior to the record's release lauded it, rightly, as a new representation of England's potential as a multi-cultural society with different kinds of identities for its citizens and not just a catchy singalong. 'Vin-der-loo' rather than 'Ing-er-land' as the chant would run. Kevin Sampson, himself a Liverpool supporter, is ambivalent about the way that New Football has come to represent some of these cultural changes. In *Extra Time,* his diary of the 1997–8 season following his team home and away he notes: 'We have to ask ourselves whether we want to carry on mourning, moaning and dragging our heels or whether we can embrace the new face of New Football. Can we just accept that we've been part of something fantastic, but now it's time to put the memories in the scrapbook and get on with the new reality? Can we sit next to guys and gals in football shirts with radios stuck to their ears, all part of one big, happy, football family?' Old Football has certainly made itself felt in recent novels. Following in the footsteps of *Trainspotting* author Irvine Welsh, whose focus on Scottish football casuals is pervasive, another 'new fiction' writer, John King, has explored English issues through his loose trilogy of what is undoubtedly a cult genre of 'football fiction' – *The Football Factory, Headhunters* and *England Away* and 'The Beasts of Marseille' short story published in the travel fiction anthology *Fortune Hotel.* John King has described to me in an original interview his own fan biography as a Chelsea supporter, an experience which is refracted through his stories:

> Yeah I think it's changed. I think, you know, like in the eighties the aggro was all played up, by Thatcher and the press. I think it was all played up too much. I mean, OK, there was a big young population going around and there was a lot of trouble but if you're at a riot like Chelsea versus Sunderland in 1985 – OK, there was trouble there but not as much as they made out. For me it was interesting the way the media behaves – why is football-related violence such a big thing? And it's to do with the media. Things were going on in the twenties and thirties that were far worse than happens now. One of my Dad's mates' father-in-law – he's dead now – lived up in Poplar. I can remember in the eighties one Christmas he's sitting there you know 'youngsters today – they're nothing special' and he started going into this big

thing about how they used to go with West Ham down to Millwall – they were called the Ironworkers, this is the twenties and thirties, and he was big in the unions. And he said they'd go down in the mornings, said there'd be running battles all day, said that all the street lamps would be smashed, that there'd be stabbings and that, inside the ground, bottle fights, and it would go on till late at night.

The inexorable forward march of New Football means fandom has changed for King as a Chelsea fan:

They say Chelsea has got all these new people coming but you don't really see them. If you go in the East Stand in the £40 seats you'll see them but I don't go there. In the pubs I go in, it's just blokes who have gone for a long time or younger lads who are the same as you. I don't go away much now to be honest with you. I mean in the eighties we used to go from Slough. We used to take one one or two coaches between fifty and a hundred blokes. It was a lot easier. I think people stopped going because of the expense. You can't get tickets unless you're a season ticket holder. Plus clubs give you an allocation of between eighteen hundred and two thousand tickets. So you haven't got that same freedom you used to have. When we were in the Second Division we would take between six and ten thousand to away games. Because you could get the tickets easily or turn up on the day more people went.

'England Away' is something John King himself did plenty of.

I used to go to England games. Yeah I went away. I think England travelling away is very lively, more so than domestic games. You get some great characters, real fun loving people. They were some great occasions. Quite a few people used to go on their own as well because their mates didn't want to travel. I tend to look at the English culture, British culture, and it is very lively. And it's probably not as violent as a lot of the other cultures. You think what is the media all about. I've had that when I've gone to Italy or France – 'English fans are all Nazis'. That's not true; the National Front gets 30 per cent of the vote in France. We don't get any elected, they don't even get their deposit back if they stand. You've got the right on law and order and you've got the trendy left who will never say it hates the working class but it does, so it has to find a nice way of saying it, so it says they must all be right-wing, so you've got those two sides. It's always the outsider. In The Football Factory I try to show that the character isn't an outsider, that the things that are important to him are things that are in the culture. The main difference is that his language is more up front and he takes the violence to a logical conclusion.

John King's commercially successful fiction paints an uncomfortable picture of a certain kind of English identity and football fandom which is acutely at odds with new Labour's portrayal of Young England. Much of John King's subject matter is more representative of attitudes, beliefs and practices pervasive in the 1980s – when Margaret Thatcher and the New Right ruled Britannia, and its waves – whilst the 1990s have seen an increasing marginalisation of Little Englander nationalism and an embracing – in certain quarters at least – of a New Europe. But although the anti-European, pro-free-market Conservative Party of William Hague languishes in the opinion polls, Old Britannia still maintains an irrestible hold for many young – and not so young – men who follow England home and abroad. It is precisely the cusp of this complex and contradictory combination of deep-rooted Englishness going back several centuries and the new, modern identity of the enterprise culture, of 'Creative Britain', of 'Young England', of the new individualism which John King captures in his trilogy of end-of-the-century novels. It is also the possibility of a different vision of this combination that Keith Allen encapsulates in the 'Fat Les' track 'Vin-da-loo'. However briefly and precariously 'Fat Les' offers a snippet of a popular cultural future, sung in pubs and clubs around England as Hoddle's nearly-men went out valiantly to Argentina in France '98. It seems a long way from 1982 and the Falklands War of Margaret Thatcher and the villification of Ossie Ardiles and Ricky Villa because they were Argentinians playing for Spurs in England. However, the old Britain and the new England are interlocked; they are not simply resolvable into past and future. The present is a cultural battleground where English nationalism, and its manifestation in support for the national football team, might – just might – be rehabilitated, and survive its mauling by the right over the last two decades.

The interview with John King is taken from Steve Redhead's *Repetitive Beat Generation*, published by Rebel Inc., Edinburgh, 2000

We've Got the Whole World in our Fans

Kevin Miles and Alison Pilling

The Football Supporters Association (FSA) is a national direct membership organisation for supporters of all clubs. Although it campaigns around domestic issues, it has also had a prominent role in campaigning and support for fans travelling abroad for matches. At Italia '90, it first established the idea of a Fans' Embassy – an information and advice point run by fans for fans. The Embassy idea was repeated at Euro '92. And at Euro '96, with England being the host nation, Embassies were established in the eight host cities for fans of all nations.

During France '98, the FSA again ran a Fans Embassy, funded, in the absence of support from public authorities, by MasterCard, one of the tournament sponsors.

Kevin Miles co-ordinated the FSA France '98 Embassy and is now a National Committee member of the FSA. Alison Pilling was at that time the FSA International Officer and is now National Chair. They met for the first time a month before the tournament, worked together on the Embassy and have been arguing about England and just about everything else ever since!

Alison Pilling: I know we spent a lot of time getting the practical stuff in place, having the right information; getting phones and a vehicle to travel around France in; but was the Fans Embassy as you expected? Did you really spend most of your time giving out information and advice? Because my impression is that we spent loads of time just talking to the media. Perhaps what England fans need is not information but someone to tell it like it is. The way we're policed, how locals react to us. Aren't we just misunderstood?

Kevin Miles: The Fans' Embassy was pretty much how I'd expected it would be. The bulk of the FSA team's time was spent on the advice and information side, but it's certainly true that we ended up doing a lot of media work. I like to think that what we said to the media was useful to most England fans too, in that we tried to give a more balanced representation of what England fans were like. Contrary to the tabloid media coverage – and in fact it wasn't just the tabloids that were guilty – most England fans in France weren't violent racist thugs spoiling for a fight. Most were genuine football fans on the holiday of a lifetime, and perfectly capable of entering into the spirit of the tournament. I was struck by the proportion of them who were making a real effort, reflected in little things like ordering beer in French, things like that.

The bulk of the people there were football fans with club allegiances at home, out in France supporting their second favourite team, Team England. And as far as that goes, I'd be quite happy to be described as a supporter of Team England. Yet I don't consider myself to be in the slightest nationalist. If I'm a Team England supporter, then it's firmly my second team, as I'm a Newcastle United fan first and foremost. Regardless of who Team England are playing against, and in what stage of what tournament, my prime concern is that Shearer, or any other Newcastle player the Team England manager has been wise enough to pick, comes through without an injury, so that their place in the Newcastle side for the infinitely more important Worthington Cup Fourth Round match is not in jeopardy. Given that assurance, then my next biggest concern is that the Newcastle players involved do well. Only after that does any concern for how the team do as a whole emerge.

Ali: I'm not sure how typical that is though – fans of most teams in the League don't have players from their club sides to look out for – the two are quite separate.

Kev: Actually, I'd have to admit that I was more of a Team England fan in France last summer than I was before. Not least among the factors that put me off in the past was the image of supporting England. It seemed to be pretty much Cockneys and Nazis who identified with and followed England abroad. (Not that I have anything against Cockneys, but I've always felt that if I wanted to support the same team as loads of Cockneys, I'd just follow Man. Utd Nazis I do have a problem with.) Of course that's a massive generalisation, but they were the ones who stamped their image on the bigger group, perhaps because at least they had an image. In France, they were completely swamped by a far greater number of normal proper fans. People like me, that I could identify with, that were just like the crowd at any league match.

But I can't help fearing that France '98 was a bit of a one-off as far as England's travelling support is concerned. A much-hyped World Cup, as close to home as foreign can be, in the summer, at the height of football's popularity, hard on the heels of the success of the Euro '96 tournament? Of course it was going to attract a lot of normal fans. But they were Team England fans for three weeks; I'm not sure that it's enough to change the face of England's following indefinitely. Personally, I got caught up in the World Cup stuff, and I felt quite comfortable defending England's following to the world's media, because I knew from my own experience they were getting a rough deal, blamed for the crimes of a tiny minority. But I'm all better now. I'm back home, and I've got my beloved Newcastle to worry about. Although Keegan being in charge has changed once more my attitude to Team England.

God, I'm so fickle. But that's part of the point, isn't it? I'm never fickle about the Toon, I just love Newcastle United, and my loyalty never wavers. But I don't feel the same way about England, and I don't think many people do. It's a part-time relationship for most people. They're a second-favourite team. Sometimes.

When Keegan was in charge at Newcastle, we became – you see, it's 'we' for Newcastle, 'they' for England – everybody's second-favourite team, and only partly because we had the best chance of stopping the Mancs winning the league. In the past, people might have preferred Leeds, Blackburn and Arsenal to win it, but that was an anti-Man. Utd thing. It was a much more positive thing with Newcastle, and there was a clear reason: because it was such attractive football. That's all gone now – not just the attractive football, but the second-favourite team thing.

Ali: Funnily enough, in Leeds, Newcastle United were everyone's second-least-favourite team – even when you were in second place to Man. Utd. What people disliked was the media drivelling on and on about Keegan and the flowing attractive football. To paraphrase the great Kev himself, we love it, just love it, when Geordies think they're going to win something and then don't. That doesn't add to the debate about England by the way, but I feel better for having said it.

Kev: I won't rise to your bait about enjoying Newcastle losing out to Man Utd. Suffice it to say that it's a fact that the Toon were the second-favourite club of most fans that season. I think you've just proved too why Geordies think all Yorkshire folk are twisty and miserable.

Anyway, you have to have a reason for supporting a second team, and one that appeals. And I don't usually get that from Team England. Keegan's as good a reason as I've come across. Temporarily in France, being part of a big mass of fans enjoying the spirit of a truly international tournament, in the sunshine, was something similar. But if all that's on offer is nationalism of the worst kind, that bloody awful Sheffield Wednesday band and an injury that keeps Robert Lee sidelined for a month, well it's going to take more than that to get me to cheer for a team with Paul Scholes in it.

I don't think it's impossible to create a Team England that I could get enthusiastic about. But it'll be the Team bit that's crucial, and almost despite the England bit. There are teams other than Newcastle that I like, and there's usually a reason. They play open attacking football. Or they have a friendly, sporting image. Or I had a really good night out there once. And it's things like that that would win me over to being a bit more faithful to Team England. A joy to watch would be a good first step, and Keegan's as likely as anyone to provide that. A sporting, friendly open image too and Keegan's bound to help with that as well.

But no number of lions on shirts will ever appeal to me. I'm not interested in conquering other nations. I'm not convinced the crusades were a great idea hundreds of years ago, and St George is not a concept that's got better with time.

Most of the best things about England are multi-cultural, so English culture, whatever that is, holds no great appeal. In fact my average good night out involves goals by a Peruvian, Danish or German lager, Indian food and a ride home in a Japanese-made taxi.

So come on then. Convince me why I should follow England.

Ali: The difference about supporting England or any national team is that you don't choose it, you just are a part of it. If you're going to decide to support a team because you like the look of the football, you may as well make the big break and become a Nike-wearing mercenary plastic Brazilian fan. There were enough of them walking round France – Japanese–Brazilians, American–Brazilians, Brazilian children of all nationalities – who just loved watching the football and loved wearing the shoes – or was it the other way round? The point being that you and me are English, attractive football or not, and hence the England team is ours. That's why I don't think we should accept the 'Cockneys and Nazis' image. When my team, Leeds United, were hard to follow in the '80s because the unattractiveness of the football on the pitch was surpassed only by the ugliness of the racists in the crowd we did something about it. That was true at Newcastle as well. I don't think the argument about not liking the current image of England is a strong one, because if you were committed to England, you'd do something about it.

Kev: What do you mean by not choosing England, just being England? Funny from someone who was brought up in Lancashire and goes to the match at Leeds with a Bristol-born lad of Welsh parents. How come you're not just Burnley, or Preston, or Oldham or whatever? At some stage you chose Leeds, although granted it was unlikely to be because of the football.

Ali: Actually, I was born in Leeds and they were a good side to watch then too, but I take your point that people don't necessarily fall in love with a team because they live in its catchment area.

Kev: I don't feel like I'm just English and therefore obliged to support England, in the same way that I'll always be Newcastle. My problem with the plastic Brazilians was not that they'd just picked the best team, it was that they'd picked the most hyped, commercialised team. They weren't that good, but the fans they attracted wouldn't know either way, they didn't generally know much about football. I don't feel in the slightest that the England team is mine, and that I'm obliged to support them. There'd have to be more than that for me, a real reason. Not just a question of image, but that's part of it. I don't currently feel that committed to England, but I am prepared to do something about it. In the same way that I'd be prepared to do something about, say, racism at Sunderland, or hooliganism at Chelsea, or corruption at any club.

Ali: There's another reason why I have trouble with what you're saying, which is a view increasingly put forward by fans of Premier League clubs, namely – 'why should we support England when we've got a good club to support already?' Hence Man. Utd fans chanting 'Argentina'. It makes me angry, not because I get upset that England didn't beat Argentina, but that it's one more example of the Premier League looking out for itself rather than the good of football. One of the major reasons the Premier League took off was because of the support generated for football as a whole by England's performance at Italia '90. We're seeing more and more that national football is getting pushed aside by club football – and that's about money. Why should fans of most clubs get excited by the likes of Man. Utd and Arsenal in Europe? It's not their team in the way that England is or could be.

Kev: In my experience, the idea of 'club before country', or even 'club rather than country', is far from being limited to fans of Premier League clubs. And I don't buy this rather patronising notion that fans of clubs in lower divisions are more likely to support the national side because they don't get to see top-class football at home very often, bless them.

Ali: It's not about top-class football, it's about supporting your own team on the international stage. No one could call all England performances 'top class'.

Kev: I also think it's very important to distinguish clearly between the Premier League and fans of clubs who happen to be currently in the Premier League. Of course the Premier League is more concerned with money than the 'good of football', but I think most fans of Premier League clubs recognise that. It's stretching the imagination a bit to conceive of supporting England as some sort of anti-capitalist protest. The FA are hardly entirely innocent of any charges of commercialisation and profiteering, are they?

It's generally true that clubs are in the ascendancy over national sides, at least in Europe, but it's not a one-way process, and it's not all about money. After all, Man Utd's rivals for the title of most commercially prostituted team in the world are, more than anyone else, the Brazilian national side. A real danger is that because of money football becomes more and more monopolised by a handful of big clubs, only one or two in each country playing in international tournaments, rendering national teams completely redundant. But the answer to that has more to do with wealth redistribution than bolstering national sides. Generally speaking I'd defend club football against international football as it's much more accessible as a live sport.

By the way, I'm not sure that Italia '90 was a significant factor in the launch of the Premier League. It was much more to do with television money. The Premier League was launched for the 1992–93 season, when England were conspicuously failing to qualify for USA '94. Any positive effects of England's performance in Italy had already been erased by the Sweden '92 fiasco – remember the Turnip?

Ali: I suppose, England to me is a bit like family. You don't always like what they do but you're stuck with them, for better for worse. I agree that we can argue about what England means to us though. I've always had trouble with John Major's idea of warm beer and old ladies cycling to church. You don't get many pedalling round inner-city Leeds, and it's the lager that's warm unfortunately. When I was in Rome for the France '98 qualifier, I spent much of my time arguing with a Sunderland 'fan', who thought that England meant Orange Lodges, the red hand of Ulster and shouting 'Fenian Bastard' at Italians – and at me too by the end of the match. Like you say, England is multi-cultural and I'm not going to have anyone say you can't be English and a Catholic for example, whether that's at a football match or on the street or whatever. Support for the England team needs to be as broad as the range of people who choose to live here. The only difficulty is how we get from what we've got now to that position where everyone feels welcome.

Kev: England aren't my family, Newcastle are. Now I don't like everything Newcastle do, and I've tended to get involved in the family rows when things happen I don't like. But Newcastle as a city has never been associated with so many things that repulse me, like aggressive nationalism and prejudice, in the way England has. If it was, I might look again at my Newcastle allegiance. Probably not, though.

I'd be happy to endorse any attempts to improve England's image though – I don't just care about my own family. To me though that goes along with creating a new image as Team England, rebuilding it as a celebration of England as it really is, multi-cultural and not all-conquering, on or off the pitch. Not just for those who live here either, or 'choose to live here', as you so sweetly put it. (Given that half of the people born here would rather live somewhere warmer, and half of those who choose to come here from elsewhere get locked up then deported.)

I personally wouldn't mind if half the football fans in the world turned up to international tournaments in England shirts, if it was based not on advertising and commerce, but on appreciation of the football or the outgoing friendly nature of the fans.

So we need a radically different image for England fans, but I'm not sure it can be imposed. Half the attempts I've seen are pretty crappy efforts to jollify the current prejudices. People dressed up as Crusades knights. Or playing 'The Great Escape', badly.

'Vin-da-loo' was as good an attempt as I've seen or heard, not least because it was not self-consciously worthy. I think most of the England fans in France were basically sound. They just need the confidence to go with their instincts about what supporting a team means. So we need to end the situation where to support England means singing songs connected with nationalism. I mean, 'Rule Britannia'! I'd never sing that, or 'God Save the Queen', even if Shearer got a hat-trick in a World Cup final.

And I wouldn't be averse to a big clampdown on some of the thugs who besmirch the name of Team England with their violence, racism and xenophobia. My objection to many of the measures used in France was that they punished the innocent, while not effectively dealing with the guilty. Winning at least the passive support of the majority is step one, closely followed by turning their passive support into active support.

And if there's to be a serious attempt to change things, then count me in. Because it needs changing. Chances are that in the process of campaigning to change things, I might even develop a commitment to the team. Especially with Keegan as manager. But still second to Newcastle.

Ali: The crux of it is that the image of England needs changing and yet it can't be imposed. That's what's so frustrating about the media coverage we get. When something is spontaneously great about the England following, you get no media coverage, so it's difficult to build on it. Take, for instance, the match in the middle of the Place du Capitole in Toulouse: 50 people-a-side, no goals, no rules, very good-humoured and therefore not a news story. Yet when half a dozen halfwits burn a Tunisian flag, the image of racists and hooligans is reinforced.

I think most people who've been around England for the last ten years would acknowledge that though it isn't radical, change has happened. There's many more people doing the impromptu football matches stuff and there's many fewer doing the flag-burning. It needs a direction without, as you said, being imposed as the politically correct answer to England's image problem.

The difficulty is coming up with an image that most people could embrace. I thought there was the beginnings of something funny and popular with *The Sun*'s Bus in Marseilles, with the impressive Melinda Messenger throwing plastic bowler hats to English, French and Tunisian fans alike. We knew that they helped, temporarily, to defuse the tension, but one message coming out was that they had helped to kick off the trouble. *The Guardian* in particular had a field day in its editorial. I mean what are we to make of this?

'The start of the trouble coincided on Sunday with the arrival of a double decker bus, sponsored by *The Sun*, playing the national anthem and giving out bowler hats. Symbolically in *Clockwork Orange*, Stanley Kubrick's examination of the right to use violence as a form of self-expression, the working-class lads wore bowlers. This is not to suggest that the bowlers caused the trouble but . . . '

I laughed about it for days – I'm still not convinced it wasn't done for a bet, but I'm worried they actually meant it. I've got this image of well-ordered platoons of bowler-hat-wearing yobs wearing football shirts with bottles at the ready – the ultimate *Guardian*-readers' nightmare!

I keep thinking too of that phrase going the rounds in France about the French who 'stole our tickets, killed Diana and if it wasn't for us they'd be Krauts'. The worst form of racism or a bunch of English fans with an ironic sense of humour?

Anyway the point is that what might be popular with us fans might not be with the broadsheets and that's no bad thing. I'm tired of being told how to enjoy football – sit down, don't chant, don't swear and half-time entertainment is an anorak from the local radio station jollying the troops to a backdrop of blaring music for a bloody car advert on the giant screen.

In that context, crowds humming *The Great Escape* is almost a breath of fresh air – at least no one told us that's what we're supposed to sing.

One of the reasons people, including the media, seem to love the Scottish fans is that their image is unthreatening – I mean how scary can a man in a skirt with a blue face and a curly orange wig be? Yet their image also involves being loud, drinking to excess, and leaving a trail of empty cans, bottles and smears of face-paint in their wake. This is not a feature the Scottish FA would necessarily have chosen, but the fans have managed to combine being both rowdy and lovable.

Kev: The Scots have undergone quite a transformation; let's not forget that they too had quite a reputation as hooligans at one stage, when Glasgow Rangers fans were the scourge of European football. So what changed? A typically self-deprecating Scottish friend of mine gives the credit to Ally McLeod; he reckons that he talked up Scotland's World Cup chances so much, people even started to believe they could win it. When the inevitable disappointment happened, there was a national realisation that they were crap, and since then, so the theory goes, no one including the Scots, has taken Scottish football particularly seriously. It's good for a laugh, but not worth fighting over.

There may be something in that, but I reckon there's also something very different about the nationalism of the Scots. Theirs is the liberating nationalism of the oppressed, they do not have a long history as an oppressor nation. So there doesn't seem to be the same deep-seated urge to go round the world conquering foreign lands, they just want to be friends with everybody. There are a lot of English fans who feel the same way, but they don't set the tone.

Ali: So whatever image is developed in relation to Team England doesn't necessarily have to be about 'popular' images of England – it could be something quite different. Can't we take some of the nationalist imagery and make it amusing?

The cards on seats thing at Wembley for people to hold up behind the goals looks impressive, but I'd feel happier with something more irreverent too. My favourite song at Leeds is still 'Let's Go Fucking Mental', because football is about going mental, innit? You can't imagine choruses of 'Let's All Throw Our Bowlers in the Air' catching on quite the same.

We're probably saying the same thing. We like 'Vin-da-loo' and having a laugh, but we don't want anyone else telling us how to enjoy ourselves. So what we need is policies that allow us to get on and enjoy ourselves, because repressive stuff just ends up reinforcing the siege mentality of the thugs.

The alcohol ban in Lens was stupid for lots of reasons but mostly because it alienated decent people. It was almost impossible to do anything positive in Lens because no alcohol meant no bars or cafés open, which meant no TVs to watch the match or places to meet up. In fact the lucky five hundred or so of us who got to see the match in the local cinema had as good a time as anyone, short of actually being in the stadium.

So what do we want for Euro 2000 or World Cup 2002, which frankly scares me to death at the moment, because I've already spoken to at least three Japanese TV channels who keep asking what to do about 'you English hooligans'. Do you think the FSA should be trying to do anything different? What would your shopping list for change be?

Kev: The $64,000 question. I'm not sure I've got any easy answers. And I'd be a bit wary of asking or expecting football to put things right for the whole of society, as it is just a sport, and inevitably reflects the rest of society. And strangely those most prominent denouncing violence on the streets of Marseilles seemed to have no qualms about raining missiles down on Serbia, not to mention bits of Bulgaria, the Chinese Embassy and buses carrying refugees.

But there are some principles. First of all, get fans onside, don't try to impose solutions on us, whether they are 'law and order' repressive measures or patronising themes for us to 'adopt'.

By all means isolate the idiots, take them out. But key to this is putting as much distance as possible between genuine fans and the others. Don't alienate real fans, and drive them towards the mindless minority. Treat fans like animals, and they'll be more likely to behave that way.

At the risk of sounding like a social worker, what about developing some more positive role models? I like a pint or six as much as the next man, but there's got to be more to a football trip to exotic climes than sitting drinking warm English beer in a mock 'London Pub'. But half the time it seems that's all the squad can get up to, so what chance have we got?

What about some investment in initiatives and events to bring fans of different nationalities together? Five-a-side tournaments? Making interpreters available to facilitate communication between different nationalities?

Creating a higher level of expectation among host populations couldn't do any harm. Keegan training with Hungarian schoolkids can't have created a bad impression. Preparing host authorities, especially police forces, for English football culture might help. I'm sure most foreign riot police personnel are a lot braver than me, but they seem to get jittery among a crowd of people chanting exuberantly when I don't, and I can only assume it's because I'm used to it and know what to expect.

Then there's preparing and developing a different culture. There's been some excellent educational work done around racism in football, and progress made, but more could be done. Use the high profile of the England squad to marginalise the racists. From the players' point of view, they would surely more than welcome an end to the team being followed by that minority of racists – why don't we give them a chance to express that forcefully and publicly? What about tackling head-on some of the anti-Irish crap that goes on? It seems that the small minority of people in the world, wholly untouched by the Irish peace process, have found their niche supporting England. What about getting some of the England players with Irish connections – such as Martin Keown, for example – to make statements on the subject with some of the rather more numerous top Irish players with English connections? In some of these battles, the players can be the greatest weapon, they should be engaged.

Use Keegan more. Some fools may criticise him for his alleged 'tactical naivety', but no one I know doubts his effectiveness as a communicator and enthuser. He manifests a 'patriotism' without a trace of chauvinism or racism, and always with a sense of fun – so why not try to spread that culture to the whole Team England set-up?

Ultimately, I have confidence that most football fans are lovely people, quite capable of using the friendly rivalry between us as a means of enjoying the game more rather than as an excuse for a fight. Encourage us, motivate us, excite us and entertain us.

A great first step would be to develop a good, positive, attacking entertaining team that wins things, thereby attracting even more people like me to become diehard Team England fans. It's not essential though – ask the Scots.

The Ingerland Factor Address List : Calling Cards

The England Members Club

The national team's official supporters association, run by the FA with a regional, and national, network of fan-representative consultative groups. The club welcomes new members who support the good behaviour England should expect of all its fans. Only members of the EMC can secure official England tickets to European Championships and World Cups, though, not surprisingly, demand often vastly exceeds supply. For further information and a membership form write to England Members Club, The Football Association, 16 Lancaster Gate, London W2 3LW.

Football Supporters Association

Membership-based organisation that campaigns for the fans' voice to be heard, and responded to, at every level of the game. Produces the magazine, *The Football Supporter*, that is free to members, holds an annual end of-season conference, and represents supporters on a range of official bodies. The FSA has organised 'Fans' Embassies' at European Championships and World Cups since Italia '90. For further information and a membership form write to The Football Supporters Association, PO Box 11, Liverpool L26 1XP.

Kick It Out

The organisation that runs the 'Let's Kick Racism Out of Football' campaign. Works with league clubs, players, fans and community groups to develop anti-racist initiatives, publicise racist incidents and practices, promote positive multi-cultural images of football. For further information contact Kick It Out, Business Design Centre, 52 Upper Street, London N1 OQH.

Philosophy Football

Self-styled 'Sporting Outfitters of Intellectual Distinction'. Produce T-shirts that are decidedly jingo-free, more like a right-on fanzine on your back. Quotes from playful philosophers, and philosophical players, emblazoned across the chest, name and squad number on the reverse. Confused? Well, the proceeds have helped fund the hugely original Euro '96 Europe United and France '98 United Nations of Football festivals of fan culture. So it's all in a good cause. For a free T-shirt catalogue and details of future Philosophy Football fan festivals write to Philosophy Football, PO Box 10684, London N15 6XA. Tel: 0181 802 3499

Index